A PLOD ROUND BRUM

A Plod Round Brum

by

RALPH PETTITT

The Memoir Club

© Ralph Pettitt 2001

First published in 2001 by
The Memoir Club
Whitworth Hall
Spennymoor
County Durham

All rights reserved.
Unauthorised duplication
contravenes existing laws.

British Library Cataloguing in
Publication Data.
A catalogue record for this book
is available from the
British Library.

ISBN: 1 84104 034-7

Typeset by George Wishart & Associates, Whitley Bay.
Printed by Bookcraft (Bath) Ltd.

Dedication

THIS BOOK IS DEDICATED to the men and women who made the story possible. Those who are part of the cast and those in the background. Those who were there because they wanted to be, and especially to those who were there when I wanted you or needed you.

I must also say a thank-you to those who are no longer with us, for whatever reason, and particularly those who lost their lives whilst serving their public, whether by accident or at the hands of others.

Without you all, many things would have been very different.

There is a monument in Washington DC dedicated to Law Enforcement Officers of the USA who have lost their lives in serving others.

One passage on there says, 'It is not how these officers died that is important. What is important is how they lived!'

Contents

List of Illustrations		ix
Introduction		xi
Chapter 1	A Personal Profile	1
Chapter 2	Cadetship	7
Chapter 3	Early Months	18
Chapter 4	The Best of Bridge Street West	38
Chapter 5	Claudine	56
Chapter 6	After Probation	69
Chapter 7	Aberfan and Beyond	81
Chapter 8	The New Approach	96
Chapter 9	Troubled Times	112
Chapter 10	Traffic Patrols	132
Chapter 11	Amalgamation	160
Chapter 12	Policewomen	181
Chapter 13	Digbeth	187
Chapter 14	Bradford Street	224
Chapter 15	Great Changes	248
Chapter 16	The Last Five Years	264

List of Illustrations

Police Cadet Training Course, Liverpool, October 1960 8

Warwickshire Police Cadets, 1961 10

Warwickshire Senior Police Cadets, 1962 14

Youngest Area Car Driver, 1966 78

June's Initial Training Course, Ryton on Dunsmore, 1966 89

HMI Inspection 1968, Cannon Hill Park, Birmingham 110

Diving 128

Diving 129

The tar boiler hit June's car 130

June's promotion to Sergeant 149

The husbands catch up 163

Sergeant Ralph Pettitt astride Norton 750cc Commando Interpol,
  June 1974 167

Visit to school media studies project 175

Regional Specialist Course for Policewomen, Tally Ho!, 1967 183

Christmas traffic, 1976 195

Instructor Training Course, Pannel Ash, 1978 214

Christmas traffic squad, 1983 227

Standard Bearer at the Chichester March, 1986 257

Presentation day for June's Long Service and Good Conduct Medal,
  1988 269

Certificate 278

Introduction

THE RESPONSIBILITY FOR THE enforcement of the criminal law in England & Wales rests, in most cases, with the Police Service. A notable exception is, of course, HM Customs & Excise who in recent years have achieved international success against the gangs and cartels who traffic in drugs of death and misery.

The Police Service consists of men and women, both paid and unpaid, who volunteer to undertake the necessary training and discipline required to be effective in the fight against offenders. These officers are initially recruited locally, but have Crown authority throughout England & Wales. They are ideally selected from all walks of life, from all backgrounds, from mixed religions and ethnic origins. Idealism is not, however, always possible and the Service to date has failed to attract a good percentage of ethnic groups. Neither do recruits abound from the poorer native residents, or to use a phrase I abhor, the 'under-privileged' classes.

The unpaid members of the Service are known as the Special Constabulary Reserve, or the 'Specials'. These men and women are usually employed in full-time work and seek to offer a proportion of their leisure time to assist their full-time and paid colleagues. There is a statutory requirement that Chief Constables maintain a Special Constabulary and as such unpaid Police Officers are common-place, especially in the County areas.

The paid members of the Service are prohibited from having any other employment and many restrictions are placed on the private lives of these individuals, by way of legislation known as Police Regulations.

The task facing the Police today is indeed a daunting one, and is greater every year. Thirty years ago the job was probably less stressful, but no less demanding of ingenuity or common-sense.

I proudly served as a member of the British Police between September 1960 and February 1992 as a Cadet, a Constable and a Sergeant. The majority of my service was spent in Inner City Birmingham.

These stories are about the men and women who made up a small part of the Service between 1960 and 1992. The events are true, but in some cases I have altered names and places to avoid causing embarrassment to persons who would otherwise risk identification.

January 1993

CHAPTER 1

A Personal Profile

THE QUESTION PROBABLY ASKED of me more than any other during my career was, 'Why did you become a policeman?' The answers varied according to a number of factors, not least being the time available to formulate the reply. Sometimes the enquirer was unworthy of a reply and occasionally I sometimes wondered myself. In fairness the question was asked in a similar form when I sought to join the Service. The reasons given then held good for many years, a secure and rewarding job.

I was born in war-torn Britain in 1943, of modest parents. Prior to the war my father had spent all his life in East Anglia, much of it working on farms. He also earned a living as a carpenter and a painter and decorator. At the start of the war he was a happily married man with two teen-aged children at home. Within weeks he was a widower and his children had been evacuated to the safety of rural Gloucestershire. He married his sister-in-law and at the end of the war he was a happily married man with two late teen-aged children and a baby son. After the war we settled as a family in Handsworth, Birmingham, where I grew up.

My brother, John, greatly influenced my early childhood. He was very skilled in building model aircraft, in particular those that flew, and he had a profound knowledge of aviation. He did his National Service within the RAF and I recall proudly having my photograph taken alongside him in his uniform. For many years after that it was my ambition to follow him into the RAF, hopefully to fly. Aviation remains a hobby to this day. My sister had very little impact on me.

John had inherited our father's skills in handicraft, but I was to benefit from Dad's vast knowledge of the ways of nature. He knew which animal had left what track, which bird had laid which egg, which seed or flower came from which plant and which leaf or bark was from a particular tree. I took a special interest in ornithology. My father also enjoyed long walks and I am convinced that those, combined with the knowledge of the country I absorbed during them, steered my interests towards maps and geography, which in turn manifested itself in my love of travel.

It is often argued that what a child does in their first few years will dictate the future path for adulthood. I cannot agree with that statement fully, but in my case many events of childhood still dominate my thinking. My father hated holidays, and he viewed them as a waste of money. The first time he and my mother went on holiday together was when I took them away when well into my twenties. To me, in adult life, a holiday was a necessity, not a luxury. I also loathe DIY probably because that is how my father spent so much of his spare time. I attended Rookery Road School in Handsworth and did fairly well in most subjects, normally being placed in the top five in the mixed classes of the junior school. My stay there was almost totally free of bullying. There was one nasty incident on one sunny summer afternoon when I was about nine.

I usually walked to school but if playing sport after school I was allowed to cycle. I can't quite remember why I was alone when I went to the bike shed but when I got there I realised that someone had been through my saddlebag and moved things about. I fastened my cricket bat to the cross bar and then unlocked the bike from the fence. Suddenly the school bully from the senior school ran from the playground toilets and barged me over. He got on my bike, but at thirteen or so, he was a lot bigger than me and the bike was too small for him. I grabbed the bike and the cricket bat came away but Brian kept pedalling. Somehow I managed to catch him up and I hit him across the back with the bat, and he fell off and broke his wrist.

He shouldn't really have been in mainstream school and had been to a special school a couple of times but always came back to Rookery Road. The school catered for both sexes from five to eleven and boys only after eleven. It was apparently difficult to place him after twelve. This particular afternoon he had simply not bothered to go back to class after lunch.

Geography and English always were my best results. By the age of eight I was a competent cyclist, a keen stamp collector and a member of the Cubs. By eleven I had gone up into the Scouts, and failed the 11 plus. The secondary school had a greater catchment area than the lower schools and I was pleased to retain, in the lower years at least, my place in the soccer and cricket teams. By thirteen I had successfully passed an examination to Handsworth Technical School. I had, however, now become old enough to have a paper round and the money from that dictated to me that I could no longer play school sport outside school hours and I reluctantly ceased to play any competitive sport for the school.

One Saturday morning whilst out cycling I engaged in conversation with a farmer named Bert Edwards. Bert farmed the Manwoods, a rented farm owned by Birmingham Corporation within the City green belt between Handsworth and West Bromwich. That farm, together with its neighbour, is now part of a golf course. Bert was looking for a lad to work part-time for

A PERSONAL PROFILE

him on Saturday mornings, and there was also a possibility of holiday work. Bert ran an arable farm and therefore did not have any significant number of animals to tend. Most of the work was weeding and thinning vegetables, although there would be hay and corn to harvest. I was sent home to discuss with my father the offer I had been given, and to my amazement Dad gave his approval for me to work for Bert.

What I did not realise was that Bert rented out a field and some buildings to a lady who ran a livery stable and riding school. I became involved with horses and learned the basics of riding during the Sundays. The farm gave me access to vast unspoilt areas of woods and hedgerows and I was also able to continue my bird watching. I also made some close friends; one was Bob Cottrell who worked full time for Bert, and the other was a girl named Janet Ward. We had been to school together until eleven, but in different classes. Bob was due to do his National Service, but had been deferred because he worked in agriculture. He later became a Special Constable, and our paths crossed time and again into the future. We still remain friends. Janet and I remained close until she moved away from the area when her father took a new job.

The summer of 1957 was wonderful and sunny but despite having a good harvest of corn we were unable to move the stooks from the field, owing to many days of very heavy rain, late in the summer, leaving fields and stooks water logged, and the majority of it was lost. Bert then made a decision, which presented me with the saddest news I had ever had. He was selling up and would leave the farm in the following March, on quarter day. I had learned a lot from Bert and Bob. I had been taught to drive on tractors and a truck, and I knew quite a bit about agricultural machinery. Bob left the farm later that year and was later still called up into the Army.

As Janet and I grew up we spent a lot more of our free time together. We also became curious of how our bodies were developing and one Saturday afternoon, having cycled to the farm to help with the horses, we experimented with each other sexually, and whilst neither of us knew fully what we were doing at the time, we played with each other's 'parts privy' then had what was obviously full sex. The secret of those afternoons remained for many years. Even our friends didn't know about our 'rude lessons' as we called them. I can honestly say that we were very lucky that a child never followed, because on many occasions during the next two years we often had unprotected sex.

At one stage Dad obviously had an idea that something was afoot because I changed my barber after he told Dad I was buying condoms. Dad mentioned it and I said I was getting them for someone else. A bit later on he casually met Janet's dad and that meeting seemed to put him back on track. Janet's dad had once seen us kissing and he wasn't sure that everything was above board, and mentioned it to my dad.

Dad was rather shy and certainly didn't like to talk about such things. Eventually he said something about 'be careful' but that wasn't exactly birds and bees advice.

I look back in horror at what we did because we were both only fourteen when we started. I suppose that liaison probably did neither of us any long term harm. We were both experienced sexually by the time I was sixteen and for that reason I didn't spend an awful lot of my youth chasing other sexual partners, and I'm sure neither did Janet.

Years later, and often, I heard the comment, 'The kids are growing up quicker today.' Or 'They weren't like that in my day.' Those comments were made by people from my generation who are today grandparents. The kids probably aren't a lot different today. It's the presentation which has changed. Except at the swimming baths I always saw Janet in a school uniform, a jumper and skirt or jodhpurs and boots. She also had a dress for best. She didn't wear a bra until past fifteen, her mother believed in 'natural muscle development' and in hindsight it had done her no harm! Even at sixteen Janet wore ankle socks. This was nothing to do with fashion. The modern fabrics were not available and there was no social need to look sophisticated. Neither did she use any cosmetics. They were quite expensive and probably a luxury. At fourteen we were young adults, we lacked a little height and weight, but everything else was in place and the mechanical bits were up and running.

Nowadays the parents seem to be in competition with each other. As soon as a ten year old girl shows signs of mammary growth, mum clips a bra round her, puts her in high heeled shoes, paints her face and presents her as 'my little lady, hasn't she grown up!' At fourteen she won't be a lot different physically from the girl of 1957, she will just look older and probably pretend to behave older.

Bert's decision to leave farming diverted my attention back towards aviation and I left the Scouts and enrolled in the Air Training Corps. I remained in the ATC until I was twenty-one.

The Air Training Corps was funded solely by the Government at that time and annually all cadets had the opportunity to fly and shoot and spent a week's camp at an RAF station. A wonderful opportunity for any youth, and one I enjoyed immensely. A week at camp cost ten shillings, the equivalent of fifty pence today, so it was affordable to all. We always had at least twenty minutes in a Chipmunk or similar and were allowed to take the controls to

A PERSONAL PROFILE 5

get the 'feel' of flying. At most camps we also got a second flip in something bigger, like a Beverley or a Hastings. Now they probably do it in a Hercules. At Thorney Island a few of us were lucky enough to also get a trip in a Whirlwind Air-Sea Rescue helicopter, by way of the winch. That was unforgettable.

I became a marksman, both with small-bore and full-bore rifle and represented the Squadron locally and nationally, at Bisley. Here, in 1961 I was awarded a 'Cadet 100', a cloth badge awarded to the top 100 shots over the two-day event. It is very cherished award, and one that's rare in the Air Cadets. Most went to the Army Cadet Force. I also collected a couple of shooting medals. At sixteen I became a glider pilot. I went to RAF Kirton Lindsey in Lincolnshire. I came back with my 'wings'.

During the rounds, I became an NCO. I also took a Duke of Edinburgh Silver Award.

School, however, was not as successful as I hoped and it became very clear that 'A' level mathematics was not going to be within my grasp, however hard I worked. That subject was vital if I was to make flying a career. The Officers at the ATC were able to furnish some references to potential RAF recruits but without the basic academic qualifications they could do little. In conjunction with them and the school careers master I was steered towards the Police Service, as an alternative career, should I decide against joining the Royal Air Force.

In many ways both careers offered similar packages. Both were sound careers with a good pension on completion of service. The future was secure (then) and with very good conditions of service and employment. In the event I applied to both the RAF and the Police for positions and I was accepted for both. Warwickshire Constabulary would accept me as a Cadet and the RAF offered a ground trade Commission subject to satisfactory examination results. I was due to leave school at Christmas 1959 and neither would accept me until September 1960. That meant that I would at least need a short-term job on leaving school. Not easy. Not many employers then wanted youngsters for short periods.

I got employment with Birmingham Corporation working as an assistant groundsman on school playing fields. I worked with my old pal from the farm, Bob. He had joined the playing fields after he left the farm, prior to National Service. By law his job had to be left open for him when he was demobbed. He was waiting for a driving job and was filling in time until then. The summer weather was kind and I enjoyed that interlude. I decided to accept the Police Cadet post and in September 1960 I was posted to Sutton Coldfield. I had not dismissed the RAF though and went to night school to improve my chances of acceptance. I ended up with 'O' level GCEs in English Language, Geography, Mechanical Science with Physics and Geometrical and Engineering Drawing.

By now I had invested in a motorcycle and had passed my Driving Test on that whilst still well under seventeen. My brother had been a motorcyclist since 1952 and I had never considered not owning one. Twenty-six years later I still rode one. Surely today many parents would have been against such a venture, despite better training.

CHAPTER 2

Cadetship

THAT MONDAY MORNING WHEN I reported for duty at Sutton Coldfield has remained a vivid memory in my mind ever since. I had travelled by 'bus and arrived in good time, clean-shaven and with a short, but not silly, haircut. I introduced myself at the public counter and to my surprise I was expected. I was taken to see the Admin. Inspector, to whom I would be directly accountable. He was a pleasant man, his left breast full of medal ribbons from the war. He was approaching sixty and was obviously nearing the end of his career. I warmed to him.

He had organised transport which was to take me to Leek Wooton, just outside Warwick, to the Force Headquarters. I had to collect my uniform. I had already been measured for it but I could not be given it until I had actually joined. As no other formalities were necessary at HQ, I cannot understand why the uniform had not been sent to Sutton by way of the daily despatch run. Anyway, it was a nice drive out, and my first ride in a police car.

My duties as a cadet were limited by law and I had none of the powers of a constable. The whole object of a cadetship was to prepare one to be a Police Officer when old enough and my contract effectively said that I would ultimately be expected to join the Police Force. There were at that time three other cadets at Sutton and we spent much of our time answering the station switchboard, sending and distributing teleprinter messages and learning to use the typewriter. We also did a series of training courses based on the Initial Training Course undertaken at the various District Training Centres around the country.

The first course I had was about six weeks after I joined and together with police cadets from all over the country I attended the Liverpool City Police School at Mather Avenue. This was probably the single most useful course available to cadets and was designed to suit the needs of the smaller forces without the facilities to run such a course. In those days some of the smaller, and now obsolete, forces had as few as six cadets. Self-defence, lifesaving and first aid were all featured subjects, considered vital. We also did foot drill, something I had learned with the Air Cadets. The course lasted a month and was the first time that some of the cadets had ever been away from home.

Police Cadet Training Course, Liverpool, October 1960.

They couldn't wait to get back. To me it represented an opportunity to explore the Lake District by motorcycle at weekends, going home after two and four weeks only.

With that course behind me I started to enjoy my work more. I was now seventeen and was allowed to patrol, with a senior constable, the town centre and Sutton Park, the latter on a pedal cycle. How pleasant to be able to be paid for such an enjoyable task. The first course at HQ was in reality a copy of the first weeks of the constables' course and gave us an insight of what awaited us later in our careers. I was well pleased with my 3rd place mark.

The old police station in Station Street closed and business was moved to a new, purpose-built complex, complete with Magistrates Court, on Lichfield Road, just outside the town centre. The fire station was later built on adjoining land.

Here I was to learn the first of the stark realities of life. One morning I had been allowed to ride in a traffic patrol car as observer/radio operator. The regular crew of this vehicle had both served in the RAF during the war and they were both very interesting men to talk to. Brian LeTellier had been a pilot and had the most amazing eyesight of any man. He could identify a car by its shape at anything up to a mile away. The other officer was John Goddard who had been an air-gunner with Bomber Command. I enjoyed that morning out immensely. The next day I came to work to find that John Goddard was dead. He had been found in his car at home. He had apparently committed suicide. I never knew the background of why.

A few days later I was called to see the Superintendent. I was shown the petrol issue register and asked to verify my signature. Although not a driver I had been asked to refuel a vehicle at the petrol pump just before I went home on a Saturday morning. The crew were having their break but needed an urgent refuel. I confirmed my signature and I asked whether I was not supposed to issue fuel. I was assured that my action had been correct. The reason for the question was simply that the next entry was false, in that the fuel had not been put into a police car but the officer's own. PC Bill Gibbs, with twenty-three years service, had stolen petrol. On conviction a few days later he was dismissed the service. He lived in a police house and he and his family would soon be homeless. They were two shocks indeed to my system.

One morning in 1961 I received a personal call at work. It was my classmate from school, David Holmes. He gave me the sad news that his father had died in a car crash the previous evening. He had apparently fallen asleep at the wheel and run into a traffic island, and had died at the scene. I knew the spot well. It was barely 200 yards inside Birmingham from the Sutton Coldfield boundary.

Warwickshire Police Cadets, 1961.

Very simply, Dave's request was for some background information before it hit the papers, and for me to get time off to spend some time with him. To practical purposes we were both lone children, and been best pals since we were eight. Dave's dad was also a friend. He had treated me as his own whenever Dave and I went out with him, and had also been a referee when I joined the cadets. He was a former Army Officer, and a company director. He had given me a splendid reference, of which I was very proud.

The Admin. Inspector was most sympathetic to my cause. He contacted the Birmingham police and they telexed him a copy of what they had given the press. By its very nature it was not confidential, so Dave could see that. He also gave me two days compassionate leave. On my way home I stopped at the scene of the tragedy.

There wasn't much to see. There were no skid marks, but a huge impression of the car on the brickwork. Apart from a few bits of shattered safety glass there was nothing. I went to David's home, did what I could for him and gave him the press release.

The funeral was one of the first held at the new West Bromwich Crematorium. There were more cars than the car park could hold and more mourners than could be seated. Such was the measure of this very highly respected gentleman. His kindness and enthusiasm had touched many.

The housing policy of the Warwickshire Force at this time began to puzzle me. Single constables, both male and female, were allowed to lodge with approved families in the towns where they were posted. The married ones were allocated police houses locally, except for those with something over twenty years service who were allowed to buy their own. It was not unreasonable to suppose that many of the single men would within a few years marry local women, as indeed they did. It seemed to me to be totally illogical then to transfer the newly married man to another part of the county to occupy a police house, when there were many empty police houses in the town.

This policy caused many young couples much heartache. Quite often the wife had a job, and prior to marriage had lived with her parents. If she worked for a bank or similar nationally based company she was probably able to transfer to a branch nearer to her new home, but if not she would start married life out of work and in a strange town. It did not come as any surprise that so many young officers left the Force in disgust or transferred to other areas. More seriously, their marriages broke down. The Police Service has a high divorce rate anyway and it is this sort of policy which has fuelled many, and unnecessarily so. The official reason at that time was to preserve the impartiality of the officer. Marriages between officers were rare then, but common now. I wonder how that housing system would work in those circumstances.

My first motorcycle was beginning to show signs of the heavy use I had given it. In eighteen months it had done 20,000 miles all over the UK. John and I looked about and managed to buy the first, and only, new motorbike I was to own. It was a 350cc Triumph twin. It was a super machine, of which I was indeed very proud. Amazingly the repayments on it were no more than they had been for the first one. They were just spread over a longer period.

I had one special moment of good fortune while delivering some papers to a solicitor one morning. I had been given some urgent reports for a firm of solicitors who were acting as prosecutor and as I left their office to cycle back to the station I caught a glimpse of a girl who had been a very good friend some years before. She had previously lived in Handsworth but her parents had moved to Sutton and I had lost her address, and in consequence had not seen her for many years. I called after her but she did not hear me and cycled away. I couldn't catch her either but I was about to embark on my first piece of detective work.

I really had no idea how to trace someone, other than by using a telephone directory, but I set about tracing Sue Styles with great vigour. Firstly, I went to Birmingham Reference library (in my own time) and checked the Electoral Register for her old address. That gave me her father's Christian name. I then went back to the telephone directory, but no number was listed. I was told to try a *Kelly's Directory*, but there is not one for Sutton, and then Sutton was not part of Birmingham, but a separate borough. Sutton library was able to supply a full list of all householders within the Borough and sure enough there was a Mr Styles of the correct initials shown. I wrote to Sue and received a reply by return. I was very pleased with my efforts.

Sue is fifteen months younger than me and we first met when she was nearly nine. She lived a few doors away from a school friend, and close to West Bromwich Albion and England footballer, Bobby Robson. He would later become manager of England. History also gives an insight of the wages paid to soccer stars of that era. Bobby drove a modest Morris Minor and lived in a semi-detached house owned by the club.

Sue and I got on well. She disliked playing with girls and much preferred the company of lads. At ten I wasn't that keen on girls but Sue's tomboy approach to life was wonderfully refreshing and we spent many happy hours together. I had seen less of her after she went to King Edward's because of the amount of work she undertook to do at home.

We arranged to meet within a few days, and did so in Sutton Park. Sue was still at school and taking her 'A' levels with the intention of taking a place at Oxford. She was captain of the hockey team, Deputy Head Girl and a prefect. Our friendship was renewed and we spent many more happy hours together in the coming years. We have never lost contact again and still remain firm friends. We were never lovers and I always looked upon Sue as the younger sister I never had. That meeting greatly increased the number of miles I travelled by motorcycle because on most days during the summer at least I collected Sue from school in Birmingham and took her home.

My progress through the cadets seemed to be going quite well. I obtained good results on the training courses and passed them in second place out of about twenty. I now knew what the Initial Course was all about. With the help of the Air Cadets and sponsorship from the police I was able to pass the Duke of Edinburgh's award. I had hoped to get the gold award, but the age limit then prevented me from having a full year between silver and gold. There was a Cadet of the Year award every year and I missed it by 2 points; a gold D of E would have clinched it. I, however, was becoming disillusioned with the system.

The contract which had attracted me to Warwickshire stated that senior cadets would be taught to drive cars, prior to joining the regular service. The reason for this was in fact financial. It was cheaper to put a cadet on a course than a constable. Simply, cadets were paid less and any allowances were less. I applied for my driving course and was carpeted for insolence. Did I expect to be taught to drive whilst there were still constables who could not? What contract? How dare I. That same contract also stated that senior cadets would be sent to an Outward Bound school. For some reason I was found to be medically unfit to undertake mine.

The official medical report from the Force Surgeon, a GP in Warwick, was that I needed a tooth to be filled. My dentist did not agree! I did not have the pleasure of Outward Bound.

I was learning, fast, that if my career was within the Police Service, then it certainly was not within Warwickshire Constabulary. I could not accept that the housing policy was in anyone's favour and I had already had two written promises broken by Senior Officers.

I re-applied to the RAF, using my membership of the Air Cadets to the full. I could still be accepted, subject to a reference from my present employer, for training as an Air Traffic Controller. I could get a Commission, but there were no current vacancies at the time of the application. I made no decision. I was given a form to apply for appointment as constable. The form was a Home Office form as supplied to all Police Forces. Where it asked 'choice of Force' the word 'Warwickshire' had been typed in. I completed the form, crossed out 'Warwickshire', inserted 'Birmingham City' and

Warwickshire Senior Police Cadets, 1962. Left of front row is Cadet Muir Ball with Cadet of the Year Baton.

submitted it to Leek Wooton. Two days later that form was on the desk of the Superintendent in Sutton and I was in front of the same desk. He was sitting behind it and was not a happy man! 'Pettitt, lad. This is not the way to get on,' he growled at me.

I said, 'Sir, for reasons of which you are fully aware I do not consider that my future rests in this Force. I have therefore applied to join Birmingham.'

'Your agreement states that you will join Warwickshire.'

'My agreement states that I will join the Police. It does not specify a Force.'

'A lot of money has been spent on training you.'

'Sir, my agreement says that a lot more should have been spent. I have not been given a driving course, and I have not been to Outward Bound. In those circumstances I have decided to apply to Birmingham.'

The Super. reached into a drawer, took out my personal file and flicked through it. 'When you had your interview you were asked why you had chosen this Force in preference to your local one and you replied that you wanted to work in a rural environment. There is no rural environment in Birmingham.'

'Since I have been here I have seen many things which I feel I would find unacceptable in the future. For example, the housing policy, of "move on marriage". In Birmingham that would not happen. Not that I am in any hurry to marry, but I will one day. My father's health is also giving some cause for concern and I would be allowed to live at home if necessary. Here I wouldn't.'

'You will have to resign from here if Birmingham accept you. You cannot transfer.'

'I know.'

'Doesn't that bother you?'

'No. If Birmingham don't accept me I will have to resign anyway.'

'Very well. I will send this through, but I am not happy about it. In fact I am very annoyed. You have let us down.'

I left the office a little confused. Clearly, the Boss was peeved about the affair, but I honestly felt that I had been cheated. Conned. My reasons for going to Warwickshire in the first place were quite simply that I had been offered a better overall package there than from anywhere else. The object of a cadetship was to prepare one for the real thing. I had been offered a better prospect as an inducement, but in reality better was on offer elsewhere, because promises had been broken. With that in my mind I would never be at ease in Warwickshire so if my future was to be in the Police it had better start away from there.

My colleagues were no great comfort to me. The general opinion was that I had blown my future. I would be branded as a troublemaker and that title would precede me.

The application form was duly transferred to Birmingham and I was seen at home, by a local Inspector. I knew him well. I had been at school with one of his sons and had once had a crush on his daughter. His visit was to assess my home environment and verify that I was who I said I was. He made an appointment for me to sit the entrance examination at Thornhill Road later in the week. I passed with comparative ease and attended the Recruiting Office for interview and medical a few days later. Chief Inspector Pickard was in charge. He was a tall, upright, ex-military man with a brusque attitude. He was quite amused as to how my application had been received at his office.

Some comments accompanied it and they had not been too favourable. In the years following, I was to encounter Ron Pickard many times, and I now understand why he was amused. He did not suffer fools gladly and whilst diplomatic enough not to say so at the time he obviously had very little time for his county counterparts. With the formalities completed I was told that I had been accepted for appointment and given a joining date. That date was a Saturday two days before my nineteenth birthday. I would go to the Training Centre at Ryton on Dunsmore three weeks ahead of Dave Jephcott who was also a cadet at Sutton and one day younger than me. I was quite chuffed. The system had in fact worked in my favour and in the short term I got an extra three weeks wages at PC's rate.

On return to Sutton I resigned my cadetship. I left a week earlier than necessary and had a week's holiday. Some of it was spent motorcycling with Sue. That week was the only week I was ever out of work between school and retirement.

I left Sutton with mixed feelings. I was to be a policeman. Not an airman. My cadetship had prepared me for the job to some degree at least, but would I settle? Would I cope? Would I succeed? How do I define success? What could the Police Service and I do for each other? That had to be a double-edged sword. If I had a good living, and a good life, then I would work to the best of my ability. Only time would tell.

One factor above all others pleased me. I had been posted to the City's 'A' Division. In the main that was the City Centre but with a section station based in Newtown. Many considered the 'A' to be the premier division because it was the City Centre, the first policemen visitors to the City saw. For that reason, very few of the men posted there were less than six feet tall. We were good ambassadors, 'A' stood for ambassadorial! I had also been allocated a room in Single Quarters at Steelhouse with a proviso that in time I might get moved out to live at home if the accommodation was required for someone else.

The concept of quarters for single male officers dated back at least into the 30s because Steelhouse Lane was built in 1933 and that had rooms for forty-eight men on two floors. Creature comforts were not great: there was a bed, a wardrobe, a chest of drawers and room for a desk and chair. The floors were parquet with a rug. Some had radiators, others huge pipes running through.

There was a communal lounge, a dining room/kitchen and the usual toilet and laundry facilities. If you had a TV in your room you bought the licence. There was a communal TV, usually a rented one, to ensure that we always had the latest available.

Quite a bit of thought had gone into the rules because there were cooks preparing a main lunchtime meal and that was compulsory if you were on duty that day. That at least meant you had one balanced meal a day. There were a few other simple rules surrounding cleanliness, personal hygiene, occupancy of rooms and a rule that men on early turn or First Day Watch were in quarters by midnight. That was in place to ensure we had adequate sleep. There was no rule about going to bed and card schools often lasted way into the small hours. If we intended to be absent from quarters it was expected that we could be found in case of emergency. Given that home telephones were rare in the early 60s that wasn't a bad idea.

Before I retired these rooms had all been allocated as office accommodation.

CHAPTER 3

Early Months

THE WINTER OF 1962/63 still ranks as one the coldest and longest on record. Snow fell in December and was still on the ground into March. The temperature barely went above freezing. It was indeed very cold.

The Training Centre at Ryton-on-Dunsmore, near Coventry, had only been open a few months for initial training, having formerly been the Police College. Before that it had seen service as a displaced persons camp for wartime refugees. It was a stark place. The billet blocks were single storey army huts with cold individual rooms. These blocks were placed around the outside edges of the complex and the teaching blocks, of similar design, were located nearer to the main building which housed the admin, canteen and social facilities. The gymnasium was stuck on the front of the main block as a sort of afterthought. The drill square dominated the roadside edge. If ever a place could deter people from staying there, then this was that place. The only good feature was that Ryton was only one of two centres in the country which accepted female students.

The male students were from the Midlands, the female students and staff came from Forces all over the country.

Everything on the course was geared to giving us a framework of knowledge and skills around which to build. Like all training courses, this one could only provide a basis for experience. That could only be learned in the workplace, in our case, on the streets. I was quite pleased with my overall results. From the three stage exams, I had come 9th, 5th and 5th out of 42, giving me overall 3rd place on the course: the highest marks for the City and ahead of a former Warwickshire cadet. I had also updated my first aid certificate and upgraded my lifesaving qualifications to Bronze Cross.

The passing-out parade was conducted on the drill square around which were banks of dirty snow. These we had shovelled there much earlier in the course. My parents attended that parade, the only real involvement they ever had in my career.

On my last night at the centre I was pleased to find the gymnasium unlocked. Rozzy, a student from the Hampshire Force, had arrived at the centre on a later course and was a little sad that I was leaving. We had got on very well socially and we felt we had to say good-bye in the warm. We were

18

both very embarrassed later, when, with some of our clothes removed, we were disturbed by the drill instructor, Jim Suthers.

It was much to his credit that the matter was dealt with there and then. Careers could have been cut very short indeed had it been taken further. I worked with Jim for some years when he returned to the City and we often reminded each other of that evening. Jim sadly died whilst working for the police as a 'civilian' driving instructor.

There was a system of Continuation Training at District Training Centres and I undertook mine at Bridgend. Rozzy returned to Ryton for hers and we renewed our acquaintance on her middle weekend there. She stayed with my parents, and shopped in the City Centre.

Once back with our Force we all went to our respective divisions for three weeks to await the return of the course three weeks behind us. That gave me a chance to see Chief Superintendent Young, his deputy Superintendent Bob Wanklin, and get to know my way round the offices. Then we all attended a local training course together, mastering By-Laws, Standing Orders and local procedures. This course also included visits to various specialist departments to see how they functioned, and how we could help each other into the future. Information Room, Lock-up and CID Clerks were all 'musts'.

So was the mortuary, and a Post-Mortem conducted by Professor Webster, a Home Office Pathologist. This was a hands-on piece of training: a PM where we openly discussed the corpse and probably what had caused him to be there in the first place. There was the opportunity to handle various organs. One girl fainted, one lad threw up! Our particular man had been a life long smoker and that is what had caused his death. Instead of being clean his lungs looked like the bottom of a dirty engine sump. He got like that for pleasure.

We were the last course to undergo local training at the Digbeth School. All further courses were held at a new and purpose-designed centre at Tally Ho! on the Pershore Road near to Edgbaston, the Warwickshire Cricket Ground.

That local course, and the monthly training days which followed throughout our probationary period, cemented us together as a team and as friends. We were all more than just colleagues to each other for the rest of our service. There were twenty men and two women at that time. When I retired I left just ten men.

The first time I walked out of Steelhouse Lane police station as a uniformed Police Officer filled me with immense pride. I was accompanied by PC Ted Schuck. Ted was a very experienced policeman, and I learnt much from him. He was later promoted to Sergeant and awarded the British Empire Medal for services to community policing. He was that sort of man, a true ambassador of his profession. His son followed in his footsteps.

I described earlier that most of the 'A' division were over 6 feet tall but that statement does not emphasise that not only were they tall but they were big as well. I was by far the smallest man in the room on the first morning I paraded with my shift. The average height of 6'3" seemed almost a norm. Many of them must also have weighed more than 17 stones. Bill Duncombe was huge. He stood around 6'5" and weighed some 21 stones. He wasn't fat and he was amazingly fit. Not only was I one of the smallest men (at 6') I was also very obviously the youngest. Even men with not a lot more service than myself were older by two or three years, with few exceptions. Virtually all had seen military life by way of National Service and most of the older men had been through the war as well. Most had at least one row of medals, some two.

I was surprised that I had been posted to the 'A' division but I was told that all men from other Forces were posted there, thus, having been in Warwickshire, the recruiting department had posted me there. I also learned that the division was often used as a punishment posting to accommodate officers who had been the subject of discipline hearings. I can honestly say that I enjoyed the company of this mixed bag of individuals. I was taken under their collective wing and given all the help I could have wished.

The first six weeks of my beat service was spent in the company of another officer. This was a normal process and covered a full duty cycle. That consisted of 24 hours cover, 8 hours each shift, and 14 days of each shift with the odd day off thrown in, a little randomly it seemed, around them.

One or two postings were left solely for older officers and by the very nature of these tasks it was obvious why. One man carried the dubious title of 'Reserve Man'. He was just a reserve. At that time the main 'Chief Office' door to HQ was in Newtown Street. On days the posting was split between two men set aside for the purpose but on nights it was manned until 11 pm. From 10 till 11 it was the responsibility of the reserve man. It must be remembered that the Information Room and CID Clerks Index Office were also in this building and providing a twenty-four hour service. He had other functions: the city mortuary was not manned at night and keys for that were with the reserve man. He was also security man for the Courts, which were accessed from the same building. Finally, and more importantly for us, he was the night duty cook.

During my first few nights I worked with Bill Duncombe. We went all over the place. I was shown short cuts, back alleys, fire escapes which interconnected giving access to flat roofs and all manner of other useful places. I also learned which flats the caretakers lived in. They were a great source of tea and biscuits, and some single men had regular Sunday lunches with the families. A great deal of the city centre could be seen from these vantage points. I was also shown where the known trouble spots were.

It should also be remembered that personal radios had not even been invented, so the location of telephone kiosks and police pillar phones had to be memorised. These were blue posts with a telephone handset contained in a cupboard at the top and a small locked flap to write on. The base contained a locked vault where the cape or raincoat could be stored in case of unsettled weather. The key also fitted the traffic signal control boxes. It was always carried on the whistle chain.

One night Bill and I were sent to a pub called the Castle. It stood in Lancaster Place on the site of what was later the casualty department of the General Hospital. (This is now the Children's Hospital.) It was an old building. The bars were downstairs and there was a lounge-cum-dance floor upstairs. The lounge often had a jazz band and it was a popular spot with American servicemen and women. On this particular night five American airmen were entertaining a small group of prostitutes and they had taken exception to demands from the licensee to leave the pub at closing time. They were sitting tight. Bill's instruction to me was, 'Watch, listen and say nothing.'

We went up the stairs with the licensee. He told the party to leave. They refused. Bill explained, in simple English, what would happen if they didn't.

One of the women was known to Bill and he said to her, 'Edna, go to the toilet and take these girls with you.' One by one the women went out of the room. The licensee started to collect up their glasses and then Bill said to the men, 'The girls have gone and so have their drinks so leave or get locked up.'

One replied, 'The copper who can put me outa here ain't bin made.'

'You've just met him,' said Bill.

'Bullshit,' he replied and lunged at Bill.

Bill cast him aside and he half fell, half staggered to the top of the stairs and disappeared.

Just as a second man went for Bill the first reappeared up the stairs, very angry. He hurled himself at Bill and was stopped abruptly with a beautiful right jab on the chin. Bill then hurled the second man towards the top of the stairs. Bill was certainly making his point.

The other men then up-ended the table and we were all ankle deep in broken glasses and beer. Still they kept coming. All three of the remainder came at us as one. Bill pushed two past him and I shoved the third through the door. The one who had been punched then jumped on Bill's back. To my surprise Bill walked towards the door and his passenger didn't see the lintel and didn't duck as Bill walked under it. He looked so peaceful in sleep. In the chaos which followed, one fell headlong down the stairs and the rest collected each other and left the pub. The doors were bolted. The women had long gone.

Bill asked, 'You OK?'

I said, 'Yes, does that happen often?'

'Most Saturdays,' was the reply. 'Want a pint?'

It is an offence to offer alcohol to a police officer on duty and an offence for a police officer to drink on duty. I was unsure what to say when two pints of mild appeared on the counter.

Bill said, 'One's yours or I'll have them both.'

I rarely drank then but that beer tasted like nectar after that scrap.

As we left the pub the man who had fallen down the stairs was just getting to his feet. There was no sign of any of his mates. He swore at us and was arrested.

A very useful agreement existed then and during the night he was collected by the US military police and dealt with by them. This arrangement was not a local thing but had been devised nationally to ensure a consistent manner in which to deal with minor offences committed by foreign servicemen. There was, thus, no paperwork or Court appearances as a result of this incident. I discussed Bill's strategy with him and he said he had sent the women away for two reasons: firstly to prevent them getting involved in any fighting and secondly to remove any reason for the men to remain at the pub. Women fighting, I was told, was best avoided at all cost. The rest of that night was fairly uneventful.

On the personal side, a major priority was to get the car driving licence sorted out. I had had loads of practice on private land and I could drive reasonably well but I needed to pass the test. I took out a Provisional Licence for 1 April 1963 and had a test date for 10 April. I arranged eight lessons between those dates and did not trouble the Testing Centre again. I had been recommended an instructor known as Cockney Bill. He was a former Army driving instructor and had been a traffic policeman in the Met. On retirement he became an instructor with East Yorkshire School of Motoring. He was absolutely brilliant and packed in a lot of 'the system' into my lessons.

Three months on I made a rash decision. The Triumph would have to go and I would buy a cheap hack for getting to work on and get a small car. Dad's health was poor. He had smoked since he left school at thirteen and forty-eight years on he was still using huge amounts of tobacco. He was horrified that someone of nineteen should even consider having a car, but he never failed to enjoy going out in it! I bought a scruffy but very reliable BSA Bantam off an old school friend and ran it to work for years.

Incidents which remain in one's mind over a period of years are really few and far between and in the main these are not the major events of life but the trivial, unimportant, almost routine, and probably unrecorded ones. There were many of these in those early days.

One of the new lads was terrified of being out in the dark at Bridge. He wasn't too bad in bright lights in town, but flickering gas lamps and wrinkly tin roof sheets flapping in the wind were not for him. One night a group of us played a joke on him. Someone got hold of a white traffic mac, a sort of white oilskin bell tent that you wore on point duty. We then fastened it to a wire coat hanger with staples and tied the whole thing on a piece of rope. From a vantage point reached from the fire escapes above the offices in Colmore Row it was lowered down the front of a building until this lad walked round the corner. When he did, it was shaken about, accompanied by ghost-like noises. Our new boy did not like that and ran like hell. It is to his credit that he remained in the job but I do have to say that he worked hard to keep off the streets and at the back of some quiet office for most of the rest of his service.

The city centre had, at this time, around five low-grade hostels for men. Some were run by the Salvation Army, and some by other charities. The SA ones were graded and they were selective as far as possible as to who they accommodated but the others really did cater for the true down and outs. The very nature of the establishments and the kind of men who used them meant that some police attention was necessary during most days.

There was a large hostel in Ryder Street, literally 100 yards from the police station, and it was not unusual for a call for help to be received from there for the most trivial matter. One evening I was sent round to investigate an alleged theft. After a few questions I found that one dirty individual who was staying there had left some rotting food in his haversack. This had attracted rats and one had died in the haversack adding to the rotting. Somebody had complained about the smell and upon investigation the staff had discovered the problem and resolved it by way of the dustbin. The owner was protesting and demanding the return of the haversack. He refused my offer to permit him to search the dustbin if he wished, and the matter ended there.

Because the hostels made a charge, and also because the demand on them was great, many potential customers chose to sleep rough around the city centre and in the void houses of the Newtown Area, which at this time was undergoing a slum clearance programme. In most circumstances sleeping rough was prohibited and even if it could not be prevented the authorities did like a degree of monitoring done. The men were known collectively as the 'dossers' and many were well known to the police. Some had quite serious criminal records, others countless numbers of convictions for drunkenness and others were just unfortunates who had fallen on hard times. Early in the week and probably during the small hours it was common for us to make a thorough check of all likely places and check which dossers we had on the area.

Some chose to sleep in the public toilets and they were always moved on after they had been woken up. Waking them up was the clever bit. Obviously they were very street-wise and used various ruses to avoid discovery. One used a sort of hammock so that by looking under the door we did not see him. He forgot he snored! One always left a turd in the cubicle either side to prevent us reaching over the top and flushing the toilet under him. He said it also stopped any others sleeping in the adjoining cubicles. He always had some housework to do before being moved on. In the summer a great many slept under the stars on benches in the churchyards and the grounds of the Civic Centre. The real hardy ones, or those too drunk to do otherwise, also slept out in the winter. I often wondered how many of those we kept alive by waking them up and moving them on before they froze to the woodwork. I know we were too late with some.

I found one dead in an old house, right up in the attic. He was so awkward to move down the steep stairs that the coffin was lowered out of the house by way of the window and a long piece of rope fastened to the floor joist. I cheated with one I found and left him for someone else. At 5.20 am I did not fancy dealing with a dosser out of a canal. He was well dead, and there was nothing I could do for him so I turned a blind eye to him and went home. He came out two days later, in daylight.

There was sometimes a danger in waking up the tramps. They often reacted unusually. I remember Bill Martin waking one up in an old shop only to have him drop dead at his feet as he tried to stand up. It was a long time before Bill got over that.

Very occasionally there would be large commercial properties awaiting demolition and these attracted dossers in big numbers. They were also dangerous places to search so if one was available we occasionally had the services of a police dog and handler. An officer named Jess Brown was with me one night whilst we checked through an old office block. The dog had been sent upstairs and I was following Jess up them when all hell broke loose. The dog barked and started to run along the landing. Suddenly Jess stumbled backwards, cursing loudly. He then threw something onto the stairs. Before I could see what it was the police dog had come between us and nearly knocked us both over. Jess bellowed at the dog and peace returned. We found our torches and sorted ourselves out. Jess said, 'Bloody cats.'

I said, 'Is that what it was?'

'Yes. The poor little sod landed on my mac and hung on.'

The dog had obviously sniffed out the sleeping cat, which had dashed off in a panic, and the dog had followed for the fun of it. Even highly trained police dogs chase cats. That was enough for that night.

Jess Brown was later promoted and spent many years with the Drug Squad. Just before he retired he was awarded the British Empire Medal for his services to the community in the prevention of drug abuse. Jess and I went back a long time. He had been our local Bobby when I was at Rookery Road School.

Within a few months of being 'let loose' alone, I was walking a partly residential beat in Gosta Green, when I was called into the General Wolfe pub. The building was lovely red brick and timber with the inn sign showing Wolfe at Quebec. The problem was that the licensee couldn't wake one of his customers. That wasn't really surprising, as he appeared to be dead. A quick ride to the hospital in the ambulance confirmed that, and I lodged him in the mortuary. I then went back to the pub to sort out details with the licensee.

The man was in his late seventies and a regular customer, who lived locally. He'd gone in at about 7.30, sat at his usual table, near the fire, had a pint and a couple of Woodbines and apparently died where he sat. I mused that having just enough money on the table for another pint, a cigarette to smoke and a mouthful of beer left in his glass, he probably couldn't have gone off in a nicer way. His wife had only been dead a few months, and he could now join her.

Premises with burglar alarms fitted were scarce in the early 1960s and consequently there were far fewer false calls. By their very nature they required a quick response and well organised cover by officers at the scene. It was also possible that you would find yourself at premises with which you were not familiar. Because we did not have personal radios, communication was slower. However, the area cars were radio assisted and quite often they would collect one or two beat officers on the way to calls. As the area cars could be sent off the division you sometimes finished up on strange ground.

The first time was at night and I was in Broad Street when the Land

Rover stopped and I was told 'get in'. We had a call to just off the division on the Ladywood patch. A metal yard, backing onto the canal towpath, had a 'precious metal' i.e. brass or copper, store in the middle and this was alarmed. A call here was normally successful. We made a silent and lights off approach and I got out, followed by the observer. The Rover was then backed against the gate and we got into the yard by the simple expediency of stepping onto the bumper, bonnet and roof and dropping about six feet in the yard. Sure enough the store had been done. We followed where bags of metal had been dragged to the canal wall. I looked over and saw a youth below moving, and dropping sacks into the canal.

I put my finger to my lips and pointed over the wall. I guessed the drop to be about seven feet. I went over, and it was a bit more than that. I landed beside the lad and brought him down. He was so surprised that he just sat on the towpath. The crew then dropped me down a pair of handcuffs. We then had a problem of how to get this kid back over a ten foot wall. I opted to walk him off the towpath, but wiser men suggested that he might not be alone. There was a safer option. The Land Rovers all carried a sectional ladder and as we now had two Rovers at the event we could make up a decent ladder. Young son went up first. When the owner arrived we left him to recover all his metal from the canal and used his strength to bring one sack back up for evidence.

Luck was with us, and Ladywood Bobbies later got the two who came back for the metal.

Over the years I witnessed or was involved in many excellent arrests from alarm calls. I also saw some super cock-ups.

In the early hours of one summer morning I was whisked away to an alarm call at a large house in Edgbaston. The house was in its own grounds and obviously everywhere was pitch dark. Three cars attended, making about seven officers in all. There wasn't a dog handy so we did our best without it. Someone blew a whistle then shouted for a man to stop. Whoever he was, he didn't, and was chased through the grounds by a policeman. Another whistle blew and a second shout to stop followed. I saw a man running towards me and I tackled him to the ground. From where the first chase had gone I heard the smashing of glass and some shouting but I could see nothing. Another policeman came to help me with the man I had arrested but as he did so a third burglar came out of the house chased by another officer. I stayed with my prisoner and he went off in pursuit of the third man. Seconds later there were two splashes.

When everything was assessed, we had, between us, three prisoners. Mine was straightforward. He was safe and dry. The first one had vaulted over the garden wall and landed through the greenhouse roof next-door. He had cuts to his legs and arms. The officer cut himself when he jumped down to make the arrest. The third had fallen into the fish pool and one of the two officers chasing him had followed.

All three arresting officers were strangers to the area. It brought home to me just how important local knowledge can be, especially in the dark. It also proved how important quick response was in those circumstances.

Very early in my service we had a reverse scenario. At about 6.15 on a sunny Sunday morning the alarm went off at H Samuel, almost opposite C&A in Corporation Street. This was a silent to the police and then five minutes before the bells went system. This one was known as a good alarm and the previous two calls here had brought scalps. We swarmed out of the station in big numbers. Sunday was a late parade because of night service bus times. Another Area Car was sent to help ours. (They changed over one hour later than us.) We got the place surrounded just as the bells went off. There was an entry at the back in Cannon Street, which gave access to the fire escapes. Two of us went down there and found two men. Whistles! Oops, these might not be our 'burglars'. Two men committing an act of gross indecency with each other won't have much interest in other things. There were more whistles and one was locked up on the roof. Samuels had been done. They'd tried the safe.

Three into the Lane. Our two must be the most unfortunate two men ever to have been locked up for what they were doing. The odds on them being found there, in normal circumstances and at that time of the day, were about the same as finding two pots of gold under consecutive rainbows.

If you mentioned safecracking to a senior detective in those days he would have immediate apoplexy. This was major organised crime, and most unwelcome. Headless chickens were called from their beds. Certainly what we had was serious stuff. An attempt had been made on a safe at a major jeweller. The one off the roof was the watchman. He'd seen our miscreants as he'd looked at the fire escape. No doubt had he known why they were there he'd have made a run for it. He thought they were police so he had kept his head down.

The headless chickens brought with them panic. Search the City, find their vehicle, they must be up from London. Within the hour a Bobby on Digbeth had found a Bedford van with tools and welding bits in it. That's it. Bring it in and fingerprint it. Inside the next hour British Transport Police are on the phone. One of their contractors from New Street Station has had his van moved. He thinks we've got it. Oops again.

There is a craze now called 'ram raiding' involving smashing into premises with vehicles and stealing goods, usually electrical items. In 1963 we called it 'smash 'n' grab'. Modern premises have large plate glass fronts. Then the windows were smaller and had to be smashed with a brick or sledgehammer. Goods were then stolen and removed by car, usually a stolen one.

One night towards the end of the summer of 1963 I answered the police pillar telephone and was told about a raid at a musical instrument shop. Witnesses had described the car involved as a Jaguar. No other description. I was instructed to check my car parks and those on the next beat, as I was nearer. A Jaguar is fairly distinctive so the task was not that demanding. On the first two there were no cars at all. When I went onto a car park at the end of Snow Hill my heart gave a little flutter. There, right in the middle, was a Mk. 5 Jaguar. The driver's window was down and the car looked empty. I went to the car, felt the bonnet. That was cold so I went to the driver's door and opened it. As the door opened, the interior light came on. I saw a man and woman, stark naked, in the back, making love.

They didn't know I was there until I had closed the door. I presumed that this was not the Jaguar I was looking for! The man climbed out dragging his trousers on as he did so. He apologised profusely. I explained to him what had happened, told him I would not bother him further and left him to comfort his lady.

A few days later I received a letter at work. It was signed 'Jaguar driver' and read simply: 'Thanks for your understanding the other night. Have a drink on me.' There was a ten-bob note attached. It left me in a dilemma, but once I had convinced myself it was not a bribe I dispensed it as prescribed.

Another car park which saw a lot of courting couples was the one known as the West End car park. This was inside the area bounded by Easy Row, Broad Street, Bridge Street and Holliday Street. It was dotted about with small triangular huts that had been entrances to wartime air raid shelters and others were service shafts for the railway tunnel underneath. Primarily we checked for stolen vehicles and vehicle thieves. It was a favourite with couples because it was handy for the West End cinema.

An added attraction to this car park was the attendant's hut which had a coke stove in it and was a super place for a warm and a cup of tea on a cold day. Over the years the older blokes had got a system working in the winter, where the man on nights would ensure that the fire was kept in, so that it was cosy when the attendant came on at about 7 am. The key to the hut was on a piece of string inside the letter box. It was not unknown for the man on nights to succumb to the warmth and fall asleep. Two finished up with discipline fines.

I was on there one night when I saw a man behaving furtively, to use a police term. He was flitting from one hut to another. The place had no lights of consequence so I had to move about to keep him in view. He wasn't a car thief: I discovered him peering into an occupied car. He spotted me and ran. I shouted after him, but lost sight of him. Then I heard a scream and a thud. I couldn't see him. The chap in the car had by now come out to see what the commotion was and he lit up the car park by driving round in a big circle. Nothing! Then it all fitted into place. In the lower corner there was a small wall. That gave access to the railway line. My peeping tom had left by this route and dropped about forty feet onto the tracks. I could see him in my torch beam but there was nothing I could do but dash up to a phone box and get him some help. His help duly arrived after the signalman had set signals and he was stretchered away with some very serious injuries, which took a long time to heal. Oh well, God works in strange ways.

As I became better established I was allowed to work from the section station at Bridge Street West. This was a little satellite station, at the junction of Bridge Street West and Summer Lane. It was built in 1939. Its strength was a shift of eight including the sergeant and the station officer. Often there were a lot fewer than that. The entire district, except for the bus routes, was lit by gas lamps. They were subject to the vagaries of the wind and were often victims to stone throwing. The area was mainly factories but had a few areas of high density, back-to-back Victorian houses, which were being demolished and replaced with tower blocks and some maisonettes. I had spent a few days there earlier and had enjoyed the change. I would work alone, on paper, but in order to learn the area quicker I would 'double-up' when it was quiet.

There was also a Single Quarters at Bridge, as it became known, and therefore canteen facilities for most of the day. Len Marsh lived at the station and he also worked from there. He was to be my guide. Len was about thirty, recently divorced, and ready to emigrate to Australia, although that was not common knowledge. He was a shrewd officer and knew the area well. He also socialised around the local pubs.

One afternoon whilst we were walking together he asked, 'Are you married?'

I told him I wasn't.

'Girlfriend?'

'Not as such,' I said. 'The girl I spend some time with is at Oxford but she's more of a pal than a girl friend.'

'If you are interested there is more spare skirt on this pitch than anywhere else in Brum. Every house has got a couple or three women in it. The Council are building all over the place and anyone wanting a house is getting one down here. If their rent stays good they get moved onto one of the new estates and another moves down here. That will happen until they've knocked them all down. The married ones are best, the younger ones love the copper to call when the old man's out and the kids are at school,' Len told me.

I listened intently as Len explained that as he lived, worked and drank around the area he probably knew more about the private lives of the locals than they did themselves. One thing the local girls missed was a bathroom. They either had a zinc tub in front of the fire or went to the public baths. He reckoned that if you took one out and let her use the bathroom in the nick she would probably want you in the bath with her. There were two big baths in quarters.

I spent a few evenings out with Len when we were both off duty. Sure enough the contacts were made. The next year was bliss, a bachelor's paradise.

One of the men from another shift had recently been banned from working at Bridge because of his indiscretions with a woman. Goldilocks is not a nickname you would normally associate with a 6'4" former Guardsman with jet-black hair. It was derived from his surname but probably adapted to extol the sexual prowess of his genitals! This man didn't smoke, rarely drank and although married, was a 'wow' with women. They apparently flocked around him like pigeons round corn.

I had worked with him on overtime and didn't much like him. He had an annoying habit of trying to wind up any female you were with, with a comment like, 'Who's the new chick, I haven't seen her before,' or 'This is not the same girl you were with the other day'. He wasn't too well liked because of it, but that was only one of his failings. Within weeks of the Bridge ban he got a 'PRB' move (penis rules brain) to Digbeth.

He had a very smart, mid-fifties Vauxhall Cresta, which he only brought to work on nights. This he would regularly use, on duty, to 'bed' any damsel in distress who would allow him to. He was, in reality, the station stallion, anyone at any time and almost anywhere. He got caught by the sergeant and was moved Sub-divisions.

He got his comeuppance at Digbeth. He had obviously fallen out with a colleague with access to the vehicle removal keys because someone got into his car and left a 'gift' there. His wife used the car on days and she found a pair of dirty knickers and two used French letters wrapped in a lady's handkerchief in the glove box. She was beside herself with rage and found him at work. They had a first class domestic brawl out in the yard at Digbeth, witnessed by fully half of his shift and everyone else who was in earshot. That was some barney.

She promptly left him. Apparently she had suspected his infidelity and the 'gift' gave her all the 'proof' she needed. It was generally accepted that the gift was a 'reward' for him winding up another officer's female companion one night. The source of it was probably a deep and dark doorway off a gas-lit avenue used by a courting couple. Indeed such finds were not unusual. If they hadn't got a car a doorway would do. Goldilocks left the service within weeks.

On one of the first nights I worked at Bridge I was out with Mick Hornby. Mick was not much older than me but he was very shrewd chap and missed very little that was going on about him. The area we were on was dotted with piles of rubble that had been houses; and around the edges strategic buildings such as pubs and small factories had been left. On one of these sites we found a Rover car. It was an unusual motor for that district. There was nobody with it. It didn't give any impression of having been stolen so we assumed that the recent occupants were up to no good.

That decision made, we concealed ourselves amongst the debris and sat and waited. It wasn't long before we saw the silhouettes of two men on the roof of a factory. Mick put two and two together and we sat tight. After what seemed like forever there was some movement near the factory and a bloke came over the gate. He was followed by a couple of duffel bags and a second person. This was to be the moment of decision. If they went away from the car we had blown it. If they returned to it they were ours. They came back to the car and got themselves locked up. Mick and I were commended for those arrests. The Chief Superintendent agreed that if we had acted differently we would probably have lost them.

Mick went into the CID shortly after and was later awarded the Queen's Police Medal. I believe it was well deserved and, unusually, awarded to a sergeant.

One of the first mornings I spent at Bridge on my own was in the late summer of 1964. It was a lovely, sunny midweek day and ideal for a chat and a chin wag with the natives. Mid-morning I was wandering about in New John Street when I stopped to speak to a painter who was sprucing up some office windows. He was up the ladder and we exchanged pleasantries before I walked away to meet the chap on the next beat at his tea spot. After that I'd meet the sergeant.

I'd only got about a hundred yards when I heard a person scream, then some sort of heavy thud, followed by what was obviously a car crash. I was dashing back up the road from whence I came when I saw a horse, dragging something behind it, galloping off into the day. There weren't many horses about then, but a couple of rag-and-bone men still kept some. I guessed that this was one of those.

When I got to my painter he was in a heap on the footpath, with a broken leg, surrounded by wet paint. His ladder was shattered. A rag-and-bone cart was upside down nearby, minus its shafts. That's obviously what had been behind the horse. Two or three parked cars had got damaged and Charlie Chance, the rag-and-bone-man, was going through his bad language vocabulary, nursing a split head and a broken arm. Somebody had already dialled the nines and the ambulance was soon with us. The area car also came, but they went off in search of the horse, last seen going towards Aston.

We got the injured away and then took stock of the situation. A couple of old women had seen everything. Charlie had set off from his yard at the top of the hill when suddenly the horse decided to bolt. He apparently tried to stop the beast, but couldn't, possibly because of the hill. On the way down the hill the cart hit a parked car. Charlie got thrown off and the horse ran down the pavement and took the painter's ladder away. By this time the animal was in blind panic and took off between two parked cars. Unfortunately there wasn't room for the cart, which got dragged over the bonnet of one car before it broke free from the shafts and fell off the car. The horse then made a successful bid for freedom.

The area car crew found the horse outside Aston Hippodrome and collected another tatter to bring it back. Charlie's mate brought the horse back on a lead rope and the shafts had been left somewhere handy for collection later. The animal seemed none the worse for its ordeal. When everything was done and dusted I found Charlie at the General Hospital.

He was then nearly seventy and had worked horses all his life. The horse was new to Charlie. It had spent most of its working life as a carriage horse, hauling tourists around Lincoln, or some such place, and was now owned by a friend who used it for weddings. It was staying with Charlie to get exercise.

From its history it had probably only pulled carriages with rubber tyred wheels. Charlie's cart had iron-hoop wheels and the road was full cobbles, and thus quite noisy. Best guess is that the noise startled the horse, which then decided to get away from it. The horse went back to the wedding stable.

This incident attracted the news hounds and it made all the papers. It was probably the last recorded horse and cart accident in the city. A silly day, but different.

Although this accident was serious to those involved it had a quite light-hearted moment or two. Not all accidents do and a few weeks later there was a very nasty accident on Aston Road near Dartmouth Street (where Dartmouth Circus is now). A perfectly normal fit, able and healthy man literally stepped off the footpath into the path of a number 65 bus. This was a good solid, front-engined Guy or Crossley and it ended the man's life there and then.

The next hour wasn't very straightforward. He was wedged under the bus, between the axles and right under the prop-shaft. I was there in seconds but I could do nothing, except direct traffic. The area car, some more Bobbies, ambulance and fire brigade all arrived. When the bus mechanics from Miller Street got there with some workshop jacks and other kit, things did start to move. Traffic was in chaos so we switched off the traffic lights and directed the traffic by hand. It also became obvious pretty quickly that our man was far from intact. At least a leg had been severed. There was by now also huge amounts of blood about so we needed Public Works and loads of sand. Too many nosey Joe Public gathered and some of them puked so we cleared everyone away and left those with their gruesome task at least some space.

Eventually we all did what we had to do and the Inspector had himself a Coroner's file to prepare. That was my first fatal road accident. They don't come much more gory.

As I started to settle into working at Bridge I was aware of a feeling of unease about the place, not outside but within the station. Len told me that there was a thief in the building, one with legitimate access, especially to the bedrooms. Money was being stolen, nothing else. Money is the easiest thing to dispose of and one of the easiest to make identifiable. Obviously, within reason we were all suspects, but that was qualified in that it had only happened recently. There was no history of the problem.

Covertly, a senior detective was preparing a trap. It transpired that he, in league with Len, had funded a 10/- note to the social fund, which, wrongly, was kept in Len's room. This he had treated with an identity chemical. He had also noted the number of the note. What Len didn't know was that he had also given the number of the note to the licensee of the Cross Guns. It was quite a surprise to learn that the note was taken by a single man and presented at the Cross Guns, within a few days. Carl Lewis, one of our number and a new recruit, had handed it in. He was arrested after a phone call from the pub. Carl was dismissed the service after conviction and there were no more thefts from then on.

There was some satisfaction drawn from the fact that the press were never aware of that particular problem.

The rules at Bridge were simple: get the job done, well. Work in the firm's time and play in your own time. By all means make your contacts whilst on duty, but leave it at tea and biscuits. Boozing and bonking encouraged Inspectors to move you around. Those rules, although unwritten, were sound. They also got broken occasionally.

One of my evenings out with Len was spent at the Cross Keys pub, which was literally a hundred yards from Bridge. He introduced me to Isobel Cox. Izzy, as she was known, was a strapping big girl. She played water polo and was a County standard hockey player. She stood all of 5'9". She was great company and told me about her job as a jewellery setter. She also told me that she thought she had seen me before somewhere. That we resolved later. Her hockey club used the playing fields where I had once worked. I still visited that ground occasionally to see my old pals.

Izzy wore a wedding ring and I asked whether it was for real or merely to keep the vultures away. No secret, she was married, hubby was in the army in Germany and likely to stay there. She was living with her mother locally. She explained that having had a lot of internal problems as a teenager she thought she was unable to have children. She suddenly found herself pregnant and had got married. She then miscarried and hubby had shown very little interest in her since. He had even spent his last leave on a skiing holiday with his mates. He probably wouldn't return as part of her life. She would not be offended if I dated her and we agreed to go out on the following Tuesday.

I collected her on time and we had a nice Chinese meal and a few drinks, in town. Nothing special, even then, just a nice evening out. She was a very intelligent woman and I found her to be excellent company. We agreed to meet again on the Friday evening and on the Saturday I would take her to her hockey match at Leamington in the afternoon and spoil her at the Falcon in Warwick on the way back.

On the Friday I called for her at exactly 7.30. I knocked and she let me in. 'I'm nearly ready, wait on the settee.' I did just that and suddenly she came out of the kitchen without a stitch on and hurled herself at me. This was every man's dream but things like that don't happen to me.

'Trousers off, off,' she shouted. She seemed almost out of control. I was about to be introduced to adultery.

She forced my trousers off and straddled herself across the top of my thighs. Bang, everything was in place in a second. She really was randy. She wriggled, writhed, bucked and pivoted. All the time she was making the most hideous grunting noise and throwing her head from side to side. How many times we both went all unnecessary I have no idea. I was in agony. I hadn't got comfortable, my back was twisted, my tackle was sore, both from the friction and from the weight Izzy had on me. When she had satisfied herself, I had no control of proceedings, she lay forward across my chest and whispered, 'Thank you,' in my ear and gave me a super kiss. She then calmly stood up. I'd just been raped.

I moved to the sitting position and said, 'Jesus Christ, Izzy. That must have been urgent.'

'Sorry, it was, I haven't had a man for months and after Tuesday I wanted you. I've sat on that since then but it had to be done.' She seemed genuine because a tear appeared on her cheek.

I stood up and looked for my trousers. Izzy handed them to me. 'I am sorry, I didn't mean to shock you.'

'You didn't shock me but I had one hell of a surprise. I was hoping I might have got round to something near that tomorrow. Hell, my balls are tender. You are no slip of a girl. And I've never been raped before.' I said that with a smile.

I rearranged my clothes and got myself tidy. Izzy got dressed and we decided to go out for a drive and get some fresh air. We both needed it. We drove out to Barr Beacon and sat in the car just chatting. There seemed little else to do after the experience of earlier.

I asked, really out of curiosity, 'Have you ever attacked a man like that before?'

'Not one I wanted. At the hockey club Christmas party three years ago there was a bloke there shouting his mouth off about who he'd had, where and how, how good he was, and all the rest of it. He was a wimp so I sat on his knees and worked him up. He squirted his manhood before I'd even got comfy, and that was with us both fully clothed, and in front of an audience.' She said this proudly.

'What did he do about that?'

'He pissed off home with everybody killing themselves laughing. Like I said, he was a wimp.'

I took her home and went off to get some sleep. I was sore, and I was knackered. Izzy was one hell of a woman. More importantly she was really good company.

The next day I was still very uncomfortable in the thigh region but Izzy and I kept our appointment. Her team won 3-2 and we had a lovely evening at the Falcon. I was due to start nights so I wouldn't see much of her for the next few days. That was fine by her. We would remain friends and she joked that she would not attack any more men. I saw her many times during the next few months and although we were intimate on many occasions we never again managed the frenzied urgency of that first night.

Despite having been a qualified First-Aider since I was a cadet it was Force policy for all probationer constables to undertake First Aid training under the supervision of a doctor. The man charged with this task was Dr Shilvock, a retired GP. I got off to a very bad start with him. He parked his car in a place reserved for a police vehicle and I advised him so. He then knew that I had not the slightest idea who he was. He had permission to be there. I failed his exam at the end of the course and had to re-take it in my own time. The strange thing about his course was that he advocated very little first aid. His maxim was: 'Get them breathing, stop them bleeding.' Those were the priorities, and anything else was best done by people better qualified. In the City that was the ambulance crews.

After one of these lectures I was sent out to do a pedestrian crossing on Broad Street at Bridge Street. This was our furthest outpost at the time and we shared the duty with Ladywood. We were only covering it because there was a show on at Bingley Hall. The two of us were doing a roaring trade keeping things running when I heard a coming together of metal and glass from a three-timer tail-ender. It was on our side of the crossing and my partner suddenly vanished off the face of the earth. The middle car was the Chief Constable's official car driven by a policeman. Derrick Capper was on board. He was super, made sure everyone was OK, got details of all concerned and left me with the paperwork.

That must have been the first accident report book to leave the division after office hours and be on the Chief's desk by 8 am. Bob Wanklin had taken it there personally.

A few days later I saw the Chief at Tally Ho! He said, 'I am sorry, when we spoke the other night I forgot to ask about your father. How are things there?' It was he who signed the paperwork, whilst Deputy Chief Constable, for me to leave Single Men's and he had remembered. He made no mention of the accident. He later became Sir Derrick. In my opinion he was the best Chief Constable of his generation anywhere and certainly the best I ever served. He was a thorough gentleman and very much a supporter of his staff. More of him later

One thing that the Police Service taught its officers was self-reliance: the ability to cope and get by. Over the years at Bridge we had developed a number of tea spots where we were always sure of a warm and a warm welcome. Some of these were used by everyone, but others were private ones which the individual had cultivated. The rules really had to be that one complied with the requests of the hosts, particularly in relation to times of day and duration of visit.

One place where we were always welcome first thing in the morning was at St Joseph's hostel. The hostel was run by nuns and was home to a number of homeless women and girls. There was always a slice of toast and a cup of tea for the policeman.

Some of the nuns had had no experience of the outside world but others were worldly and had become nuns for reasons only they knew. Certainly some had not been celibate before they were nuns.

One such woman caused a deal of embarrassment one morning when she was caught by the Mother Superior in an embrace with a young policeman in the kitchen. Kissing and cuddling was not allowed and that incident soured the relationship between the hostel and the police for some time. It was ages before tea and toast was again forthcoming.

Before the days when household telephones were commonplace it was not unusual to be asked by a family to make a phone call for them, either from a phone box or from the police station. There was a facility whereby they paid for the call and were given a receipt.

I remember one night I was having my meal at Bridge when a man came into the office and requested the use of the telephone as his wife was in labour. She was in his car and the birth seemed imminent. As a matter of some urgency she was brought into the station and with the help of ambulance crews she gave birth in the cell passage at Bridge to a bonny baby boy. Had that birth been tended only by the police, the Watch Committee would have paid the officers the princely sum of £2.

Another public service which was occasionally asked of us was the laying out of a corpse. Quite a few of the older residents were terminally ill and a lot died in the comfort of their own homes. If we were reasonably sure that there were no suspicious circumstances, and the doctor had certified death, that little service meant so much to the bereaved family. All they asked was that their loved ones looked comfortable in death.

CHAPTER 4

The Best of Bridge Street West

ONE OF THE SADDEST TASKS that can ever fall on the police is that of urgent messages. It is not so prevalent now with the telephone being a part of most homes but thirty-five years ago, much urgent news was conveyed by the police. It was a duty, which was enacted even at the training centres.

My first still remains foremost in my mind. A ward sister at Dudley Road had phoned for us to notify a lady that her husband had passed away and could the lady contact the ward to arrange formalities. I rehearsed with the station officer what I had to do and I set off on my task. Quite nervously I knocked the door and it was opened almost immediately by a very attractive woman, probably not even into her fifties. 'Mrs Smith, June Smith?' I asked.

'Yes, is it about my husband?'

'Yes, it is, I've some bad news for you.'

'The only bad news you can bring me is that the bastard's still alive.' She had no sense of loss in her voice.

'Well, he is dead, I'm sorry, Mrs Smith.'

'Don't be, he's better off dead. He made my life hell. I only stayed with him for the kids.'

'The hospital have asked for you to phone them to sort out undertakers and his property. Can you do that or do you want to use our phone?' My offer was genuine. It was a thing we often did in these situations.

'They've got him, they can bloody well keep him. Sorry, I'm not getting on at you. Yes I'll come up with you and phone.'

We walked back to Bridge together and I did her a cup of tea whilst she made her calls. She still showed no emotion. On the phone she was calm and rational. She made the call, thanked me for her tea, and left.

Whatever had happened during her years of marriage had surely left hatred in her. No death message would ever be so easy to deliver.

The most amazing reception I had to a message concerned a young motorcyclist. This was many years later whilst I was serving as a traffic patrol officer. The lad had gone out on his motor cycle around 5.30 in the evening and whilst travelling towards Drayton Manor Park on a very fast dual carriageway he had fallen victim to a car which was doing a 'U' turn through the reservation. The impact was immense. The front seat passenger had died instantly and the motorcyclist was very seriously injured.

The accident was dealt with by Staffordshire Police and at their request the Birmingham Traffic Patrols had assisted with the ambulance escort to Birmingham Accident Hospital. The lad was dead on arrival there. A Staffordshire officer had travelled in the ambulance and I sorted out with him documents for the bike and the rider from his jacket. We then went to the lad's house to break our news.

When we got to the house 'Coronation Street' was on the television and his mother was sitting transfixed in front of it. I spoke to the father in the kitchen and established that we were talking about the right lad. I asked for the TV to be switched off but the father said not to bother. I explained to dad what had happened and that his son was dead and he said, 'D'ya hear that, mum? Our David's bin killed on his bike.'

Without looking up she said, 'When?'

Father replied, 'Just. The coppers are here now.'

'You deal with it, I'm watching this.'

The dad looked at us and shrugged his shoulders, 'Fucking Coronation Street, the world could stop and still she'd watch that shit.'

We took the lad's father with us to sort out identification and a statement and I left him with the Staffordshire Officer. I didn't envy the task of either of them.

Within weeks of first meeting Izzy I had to tell her that her mother had been knocked down on her way home from Bingo and that she was in hospital. At least she was able to recover but it was not easy telling a friend that her mother had been hit by a bus.

Domestic disputes were really nothing to do with the police but if I had a pound for every one I have attended I would be a wealthy man. Most families have domestic disputes to some degree but they are only a dispute within a family. We used to call them a family barney and often they were treated very lightly.

There could be no hard and fast rules in dealing with one because they were all different. The general rules were, if it wasn't criminal it was beyond our duty and if it was, could we get a satisfactory prosecution from it? In most cases where drink was involved the urge to complain about the conduct of a family member subsided with the drink. Obviously if there was some serious injury action had to be taken.

The first I can recall attending was at a backyard house in Hanley Street and involved two families living side by side. The houses did not have inside toilets, but a block in the yard with a toilet allocated to each house. They were normally kept locked. On this particular occasion, and I went there many times, the grown-up son from one family had used the toilet of the other because his father was in their own. Words had been exchanged and an effort made to drag the son out of the cubicle before he had finished. He got cross and blows were exchanged. He adjourned back into the bog to finish. The family then put the padlock on their toilet, locked the next-door son in, and sent for the police. Dad finished in the family toilet and found his son locked in the neighbour's so he kicked the door down to free his son.

However, the door had been there for about a hundred years and it shattered and did some harm to the occupant who was still sitting on the throne. He didn't realise that it was his father who had kicked the door down so in a rage he set about the father of the other family. When I got there there was a real good scrap in the offing, and all the inhabitants of the yard were cheering on. Everybody got dusted down. Undertakings were made to replace the door and we all parted friends, until next time . . .

Others were more serious though and one such involved a regular Saturday night call. On Saturday nights at Bridge we worked in pairs when possible and we took the pillar call at about 11.20 to go to a house in Tower Street. This particular house stood in a row awaiting demolition and the only difference normally meant that it would have windows in. This night it hadn't; they were on the footpath, together with a table and a TV set. The usual story was that Arthur came home drunk, beat up the wife and smashed some furniture. This looked about par. When we went in Arthur was sitting in the armchair. His wife was trying to tidy up the mess surrounding him and at the same time swearing like a trooper.

I said, 'Best you stop drinking, Arthur.'

I then asked his wife what had occurred. She replied, 'He came home pissed and hit me. I hit him back so he picked up the telly and threw it at me. I ducked and it went out the window. He threw the table at me and that went out as well.'

Arthur said, 'She didn't tell you she stuck a fucking knife in me, did she?'

'Did she?' I asked him.

He moved his left hand away from his side and there was blood everywhere. It was even dripping through the armchair onto the floor. Suddenly this was serious; with that much blood about he could die. I ripped down a curtain and told Arthur to pack it into the wound to stem the flow of blood. I told Dave, my partner, to stay put and keep an eye on everything, including the wife. I ran along to the phone and got an ambulance and some more help and dashed back to the house.

By this time Arthur was starting to lose consciousness but we daren't move him from the chair for fear of causing more damage. Whatever the damage to him was.

The ambulance got to us very quickly and the crew got to work. Arthur was rushed away to hospital and his wife was arrested. So serious was Arthur's wound that he was on the danger list for ten days.

Arthur's wife got twelve months for the stabbing. That was a fair result. She could have killed him. It was also one of the few domestic disputes where a prosecution could succeed.

When a family falls out the resulting venom can often generate an urge for revenge and I remember two such occasions when such revenge caused 'guilty' parties to be arrested.

One notorious family, with many sons, and many generations from them, stole a lorry load of wheels and tyres for Minis from a compound at the Austin factory. They were suspected but there was no proof. The lorry had been found empty and a car owned by the family was found nearby, out of petrol. I had had dealings with the car before, when the owner had lent it out, then reported it stolen, thus getting his mate locked up. I spoke to one of the detectives on the case and he was interested. We went to visit the lad I had dealt with before and spread a bit of scandal. He sought his revenge for his earlier problem and told us where some of the wheels were.

We went to the house and found all the curtains drawn. The house had no back door so we knocked on the front. There was no reply. We knocked again and I heard the upstairs sash window open and a man shout, 'Who's that?'

Bob, the detective, hadn't called there before, but I had. As he shouted, 'Police,' I stepped into the entry just as the contents of the bed pot came out of the window, urine, turds and two French letters. Bob got well splashed.

Bob looked at me and said, 'I hope that bloody kid told the truth.' He stepped back and kicked the front door halfway along the front room.

We need have no more worries about the front door. The room was packed from floor to ceiling with Mini wheels. There were even more in the cellar. Jimmy Dane, who had tipped the pot over Bob, had a lot of explaining to do.

Bob and I were commended for the arrest of Dane and his co-accused.

The second time I saw revenge it was on a more light-hearted scale and the event itself was quite amusing.

I stopped one afternoon to talk to a young mother who was waiting outside Brearley St school for her daughter to come out. She had a real shiner of a black eye. They were not unusual round that area and it was often best not to ask of the origins. In the end my curiosity prevailed and I was told that her brother had done it. The brother had a serious gambling problem and had tapped all known sources of cash dry. He was seriously in debt and when his sister had refused him a loan he had beaten her up. The matter had rested there. She had not reported it to the police and had no wish to do so. Her own husband, to use her words, was bloody useless, and he had done nothing either. Then she smiled and suggested I visit her brother and just look at the inside of the house. She gave me his address and a car number. I had no more to work on than that, but I was content that I was not being set up.

A couple of days later I called on the brother. His car was outside, untaxed, so we had a talking point. The house was another back-to-back but fronted the street. He invited me in and initially I just could not pinpoint what was wrong. Every member of the family was huddled in the front room, so was the bed and loads of clothes. Then it all fitted into place. She said look inside the house. The skirting was missing and there was no architrave round the doors. There was painted wood on the fire, waiting to be lit.

Access to the stairs in these houses is from behind a door in the front room and I guessed from the layout that the left-hand door as I looked at them was the stairs. When we had dealt with the business concerning the car I casually opened the door and found a void. The stairs had gone, so had the bedroom doors. I later found out that all the woodwork from the upper floors had been removed and burned on the fire. The family had been that skint.

I spoke to the housing officer and that family were moved to three old houses before proper re-housing. The sister moved to her new house within weeks.

I generated a domestic one night in Miller Street. I found a drunk in the gutter. Where he was he was in danger of getting run over by a bus from the depot up the road. I stood him up but got no sense out of him. There was nothing in his outside pockets to identify him so for his safety I decided to lock him up. He was heavy and I was grateful when a chap asked me if I wanted a hand with him. The chap then thought he recognised him and knew where he lived. That suited me fine. It was a lot nearer than Bridge.

My helper pointed out the house and I propelled my incontinent cargo towards his front door. At this point he seemed to regain some composure and pleaded with me not to take him there because the 'old cow' would kill him. I knocked on the door and was told to wait. Good, someone at home. After about a minute the 'old cow' came to the door. His description was fair; she was as ugly as sin and the size of an elephant. She snatched the man through the door, hurled abuse at him, and thanked me for my trouble. Her abuse at her husband continued and I beat a hasty retreat.

There have been occasions when I have looked at a person and thought, 'I'm not sure about you,' and this happened to me with a policeman; he was Craig Morgan

Craig did not work on the 'A' division but lived in single quarters at Steelhouse Lane and consequently he tended to socialise with other residents. Although I was by now living at home I spent some spare time with my colleagues, especially when there was something special on. There was a social fund which was used to finance the occasional party, such as at Christmas, and I had opted to continue to contribute to that after I left quarters. Invitations were also forthcoming for special functions at nurses' homes.

On a few occasions I knew that Craig's station had tried to contact him at quarters and he had been found to be absent with no contact address. This was not approved of on days when one was on duty. Most of us knew that he had a girlfriend who lived at Stechford.

She was Christine Jackson, a teacher. It was Christine's house, but she shared it with two cousins, Jean and Dawn. They were sisters and shared the same surname as Christine.

One party invitation resulted in a most bizarre finale. About six single men including Craig and myself went to a Valentine party at Vesey House. The function was greatly over-subscribed by women and we were heavily outnumbered. Craig introduced us to Jean and Dawn. Jean was also a teacher and Dawn was a nurse. After about an hour Craig obviously scored heavily with one of the older nurses and went to her room for the rest of the night. Before he went he left word that we had not seen him that night.

The party became tiring and Jean, Dawn, another couple and I left together to go back to the girls' house for supper and a game of cards. We got some fish 'n' chips on the way. The couple would drop me back in town on their way home. Within an hour the girl of the couple fell ill and was violently sick. They left immediately and left me behind. Christine had the only car and she had been out with some friends and had drunk far too much to drive. I was reluctant to use the night service bus and I was invited to stay the night. Sleeping arrangements would be easily resolved. As Jean and Dawn had a double and a single bed in their room, Christine would go in with them and I would use Christine's room.

That suited fine and I was quite excited when I woke in the morning to find Dawn sitting at the foot of my bed in just her nightie. No action then, but a promise to the future.

Christine and Jean had gone to work and Dawn had got the day off and was going to have look at the shops in town. The plan was to travel to town together after breakfast. The coffee the night before had depleted the milk and Dawn set off to the shop for some. Seconds later I heard a scream and a shout. I dashed to the front door to find Dawn with blood streaming down her face and a woman screaming at her and calling her a 'slut' and a 'whore'.

I intervened but I didn't really know what had happened. I sent Dawn into the house and calmed the attacker down. She explained that she was Craig's wife and had traced him to the address of a Miss Jackson. When she had spoken to Dawn she had asked whether she was Miss Jackson. When Dawn answered that she was she had been butted in the face and punched. I assured Mrs Morgan that Craig was not at the address and had not been there all night.

The story Mrs Morgan related about Craig vindicated my original dislike of the man. He had been a police cadet in Wales a few years previously. He had been called for National Service in the army and had then signed on. He married and there were two children. He had deserted the family. There was a maintenance order which was well in arrears and a warrant for his arrest, from that. She had been unaware that he had left the army until after the warrant had been issued. Her own efforts had traced Craig to Birmingham and then to the Stechford address.

Craig had woven a web of deceit around himself, and his friends and colleagues had become innocent victims. Christine would be furious. She, much more than many, believed in the total sanctity of marriage. She would also have been very unhappy about his actions at the party. We felt that he had let us all down.

Mrs Morgan presented herself at police headquarters and gave her account of events. Things then moved very quickly indeed, although the grapevine was much slower. It transpired that once the details of the warrant had been confirmed Craig had been sent for. He was questioned about his past and his services were dispensed with forthwith. This was allowed for under Police Regulations in the case of probationer constables. The warrant was executed and we never saw Craig again. Dawn did not pursue any assault charges and they all went off policemen. Thank you Craig Morgan!!

It was about this time that I had my first major telling off. Because I was living at home and still actively involved with the Air Cadets, I spent a lot of my social time with mates from there and some school pals. One evening a crowd of us went to the swimming baths, and because it was a nice evening, my pal Colin Rotchell and his sister decided we would then take my dog to Sutton Park for a walk. (Both Colin and Yvonne later joined the police.)

After the walk I dropped them off at home and went home to bed. Next day at 1st Watch breakfast I found that my wallet was missing. That had a few quid and some personal papers in it, but more importantly my Warrant Card lived in there as well. I knew it hadn't been pinched at the baths because I'd bought petrol after then.

Hopefully it was at home in my civvy trousers. It wasn't. I nipped out to Sutton Park on the bike and retraced our walk as best I could. There was no sign of it, so I rode straight back to the Lane and went to see Admin Inspector Pat Dixon. He gave me a mild tatering and sent me in to see Bob Wanklin who gave me a mega bollocking and a lecture on security. Once I mentioned Sutton Park he also added a lecture on bonking and the removal of trousers in public places. I hoped to God I never lost another Warrant Card. I didn't!

As I got settled into the job I never ceased to be amazed how paths crossed. I met the same people time and again in different places and I met in the course of my work people I had known years before. One Sunday morning I was covering the office at Bridge whilst the station officer had his breakfast. I answered a phone call from a colleague at Digbeth. A burglar alarm had gone off at a factory on their pitch, and when they phoned the key-holder his wife had said that he had gone to visit his daughter. She lived on us and was not on the phone; could someone contact him and send him to the factory.

I wrote down the relevant information and saw that the man concerned was Eric Goddard. There had been an Eric Goddard at the Air Cadets as a civilian instructor and I wondered whether he was the same man. When the station officer returned I showed him the message and I would soon find out; he sent me off to do it even though it was not on my beat. There was a degree of urgency about it, so do it.

Sure enough, it was the same man. He would go immediately. If I wanted a cup of coffee his daughter would oblige and if I was still there when he returned we could have a chat. I had seen Lorna some years previously but would not have recognised her, certainly not at the moment and probably not anyway. She sported two black eyes and a broken nose.

'Who hit you?' I asked.

'The bastard I used to live with, unfortunately,' was the short reply.

'Who is he?'

'Keith Dunn.'

'Charming. I take it the police are involved?'

'Yes, that's part of the problem. He stabbed me with a fork.' She showed me a nasty scar on her right hand. 'I went to the police and they locked him up. The bleedin' Magistrate give him bail so he came home and beat me up. "Something to remember me by," he called it. Anyway he got locked up again and he's up on Wednesday.'

'What happens then? Committal or a plea?'

'Remand, I think, and probably on bail. That's one reason Dad came over, we're moving away.' She seemed relieved with that statement.

'We? You aren't going with him, are you?'

'God, no, I've got a little boy, Jack. He's asleep at the moment so I'm leaving him to it.'

'You moving far?'

'Just over to Sheldon. One of Dad's friends has a shop over there. The flat above is empty and I'm having that, but it's been empty for ages and it's like a tip, so there's a lot to do. Dad wants me to go away for a few days while he gets it ready. Then I would move straight there. Trouble is, can't find anywhere to go this time of the year.'

'What sort of thing do you want, cottage? Caravan?'

'Caravan would be fine, but they're all shut now.'

I reassured her. 'I'd better go now but I've got a mate with a caravan. He can't rent it out at the moment but he would probably let me borrow it. He wouldn't have to know that you were there alone. Speak to your dad about it. I'm on till two, tell him.'

I went back to Bridge and phoned my pal. I told him a few minor untruths and the caravan was mine for a few days if I wanted it. It would be a couple of quid, though, to cover the gas, I was told. The keys were at his house if I wanted them.

Eric found me on my beat and I sat in his car. 'That caravan idea is grand. Can you do it?' he asked.

'Done it,' I replied, 'Two pounds, ready any time.'

'That's what I like about you, no messing about. She really needs to be there before Wednesday, where is it?'

'Arley.'

'Arley? How do we get her there this time of the year?'

The place was off the main bus route after the summer. Eric knew that, I didn't. I'd been there regularly on the bike, but not on the bus.

I paused. 'Eric, can she go on Tuesday afternoon? If she can I'll take her across, or I've got Wednesday off but I'm back in at six on Thursday morning.'

'I've got to say yes, she needs to be away from here. I'll go and see her and I'll see you at the nick at two, OK?'

True to his word Eric got back to Bridge just as I was finishing. He was smiling and he looked a lot happier than when I had seen him earlier.

'Tuesday it is then. I've told her you'll see her before then to finalise times and that. It is bloody good of you, you know.'

'No woman deserves a smacking like she's had. Where did she meet Dunn, anyway? He's always been a nasty bugger.'

'Ralph, I don't know. He was all right till they had the baby, then he just flipped. Out on the piss, out shagging, fighting, you name it, every night. Then he started to hit Lorna. What he needs is a damned good hiding.'

'He's had a few over the years, he must be a bit slow learning.'

We shook hands and agreed to keep in touch. I sorted out an early finish on the Tuesday and on the way home I called on Lorna and made the necessary arrangements for Tuesday. I'd come to work in my car, get changed at work and be on the road by twelve. I had done the journey loads of times, so we would have time to ourselves and still get there in daylight.

The drive to Arley was a pleasure. Much more so than nowadays; there was much less traffic. We got there in good time and the caravan had been left nice and clean and we were well established in time for tea. I had bought some steak and that was a special treat for Lorna. Her face looked a lot better though her hand was still sore, but she said she would be OK on her own. I was sure she would be; her parents would be with her by the weekend. After tea I started to get ready to leave and she asked, 'Aren't you staying?'

'I wasn't going to, I was going back, that's why I asked you to bring your food, because I wasn't going to be here to shop tomorrow. I can if you want.'

'Please, just until I get used to the place. I can't ask you to sleep with me because everything's all wrong and my face and all that, it wouldn't be fair.' She seemed close to tears.

'It wasn't part of the plan to stop, so it certainly wasn't part of the plan to get into your knickers.' I put my arm round her shoulders. 'OK, I'll stay for tonight. I'll go and get a couple of bottles of beer.'

The night was uneventful. Jack woke once, Lorna had slept better than for weeks and I always slept well there. I left Lorna a ten shilling note in case she got short of cash, and drove back to Birmingham to resume normal life.

When events had slowed down Lorna wrote me a letter, which she left at Bridge. It said simply:

> Monday,
> Ralph, Thanks for fixing the holiday, it was
> nice of you to stay that night, I enjoyed it.
> Have returned your money and dad sends 10/- for a drink.
> New address is . . . Phone number to follow
> Love Lorna xx

That undated note, totally innocent in itself, caused me a major problem a few years later. I had kept it, with others, in a suitable place, solely to have a note of the address, although I never used it. Eventually it went missing.

Despite promises, I never saw Eric again but the paths of Lorna and me would cross in the future.

Another face from the past was Pat Mills. Pat and I had been at school together until we were eleven. She had been a friend of Janet and was at one time part of the horse scene. One morning I saw her walking along Newtown Row, and, although I hadn't seen her for many years I recognised her immediately. We stopped and spoke. She looked really sad and unwell.

Pat had always been a happy girl, full of life and vitality. Today she looked ten years older and very drawn.

'Are you all right, Pat?'

'Not really,' was her reply.

She volunteered that her life was in ruins. Her brother had died a few weeks before. She had recently got married, only to have her husband arrested from her. He had committed bigamy, and her baby had died suddenly and with no explanation, a cot death. With all that in a few months, no wonder she looked tired.

She lived nearby, just off St Stephens Street, so I walked her home. The house was a tip. Not like Pat at all. 'What happened about hubby, Pat?'

'He's gone, he couldn't face the truth. The wedding is annulled.' She burst into tears and sobbed uncontrollably. What do I do now? I asked myself. Brainwave. 'How do you get on with the neighbours?'

She didn't know them. Try again. 'Any friends nearby?'

No friends at all, everyone shunned her because of what had happened.

'Pat, stand up and come here.' I held out my hands.

Slowly she walked towards me, her arms outstretched, eyes fixed beyond me. She fell into my arms and sobbed onto my tunic. I just stood there and spoke to her, reassuring her. Gradually she pulled herself together. She spoke, 'I bet you think I'm stupid, behaving like this.'

I just shook my head. I didn't know what to say. I hadn't done this at Training Centre. Had she a job? No. No job, no money, no interests.

Second brainwave, 'Tell you what, put some make-up on.' I paused. 'You have got some, haven't you?'

She had and she put a little on. 'Come on then,' I said and walked towards the door. 'Lock it up and come with me.'

'Where are you going?'

'We are going out.'

She trusted me and we walked along the street to the shops. I led her into the hairdresser's and sat her down. I spoke to the girls, told them what had happened and asked them to tidy her hair as she wished. About an hour then. I'll come back then. Pat was dumbfounded.

I phoned Bridge and explained what I was doing. As I was able to suggest that she might commit suicide, I was left alone for the rest of the shift. When I called back at the hairdresser's Pat was nearly finished. She looked a lot better. I paid and walked her back to the house. We discussed the untidy state of the place and the fact that it had just got too much for her.

Everything had happened there. It was where they had set up home, where the baby had been conceived, where they had got married from, where the arrest had happened, where the baby had died. She had no faith left in it as a home. Unfortunately her parents were little help; they still grieved their son.

I had a third good idea that morning, the housing officer. A re-location would probably be possible in these circumstances. I took her some flowers later that day with the news.

It was possible; inside a week she had moved and inside two she had a job. We celebrated her new job and new home in some style. Pat quickly got her act together and was soon hunting down a new man. We said goodbye, with thanks.

Because of demolition Izzy and her mother were by now becoming more isolated and the families from the yard in which they lived were being moved out. They had become concerned about dossers using the void houses, if only because of the fire hazard they presented. There were also instances of prowlers.

At Bridge we kept a big ledger entitled 'Special Attention' and the book was used to record minor incidents which perhaps required to be monitored in case of escalation. It was little more than a community service to keep people at their ease. Their concern was recorded in this ledger.

Apart from the unwritten rules of Bridge which were occasionally broken there is one golden rule in the Police Service which says that if you are somewhere you should not be, have a good reason for being there. I was grateful to have heeded that advice in the small hours of one morning.

Whilst Izzy's mum was in hospital after her accident Izzy was for the most part on her own. She was also convinced that she had heard footsteps in the yard at night. Her mother was involved in a long-term affair with a married ambulance driver from the local station and he had a routine whereby he stayed at the house about two nights a month. For his domestic reasons that routine could not be broken and on a night when he and Izzy had been there alone he had also been aware of something outside.

One night, things were particularly quiet on the beat and I called on Izzy. As usual she was glad of some company and we spent some time talking about prowlers and even sat in the bedroom with lights out and curtains open watching into the yard. Beds and Izzy worked very well together and eventually our minds became distracted and we made use of the facilities. I suppose that in all I was at the house about an hour and a quarter and I left at 12.30 am. As I walked out of the entry I saw the Inspector's car parked a few yards away. I went to him and presented myself. It was Ted Morris.

'Get in the car,' he ordered.

I obeyed the order. I knew what was coming.

'Pettitt, I posted you down here because I thought I could trust you, but damn me, you're at it as well.'

I thought quickly. 'At what, Sir?' I asked.

'Women, you know what I mean,'

I was certain then that he only had a suspicion of the truth so I said, 'There are some women living up there and they have complained about prowlers. It was quiet tonight so I've been up and had a look. It is in the book.'

'I saw you go up the entry. When you hadn't come back after twenty minutes I went up there, and there wasn't a light anywhere,' he said accusingly.

'The lights were off so that we could see out. The prowler only gets up there when it's dark, sir.'

He started the car and said, 'Let's go and look at this book then.'

He drove me round to Bridge and walked stern-faced into the office. He grabbed the book and there was a look of stunned amazement on his face when he saw the entry. It was there, just as I had said, and initialled by other officers who were aware of the complaint.

'Keep up the good work, don't spend too much time on that though.'

That was a close call, as the rule said, bonking had attracted the Inspector, but the event was quickly forgotten and nothing more was said about it.

I have an excellent memory for vehicle and telephone numbers and I was able to accurately date, within a couple of months, all vehicle numbers issued in Birmingham prior to the implementation of the suffix. I had fair success with other local issues. I used this knowledge to good purpose many times. The first was the most memorable.

I was assisting at an accident one afternoon when a youth came past on a Lambretta scooter. There was nothing untoward and I gave him only a passing glance. The number plate certainly pre-dated the machine by about three years. The combination could only be correct if the number had been retained on a fee. It was not apparently special so I guessed that the bike was on false plates and probably stolen.

The necessary enquiries were made and I had the details of the owner. The machine had very recently been re-taxed after many months. The lad lived away from the 'A' division, in Handsworth, and for that reason I commenced the enquiry with an older officer. We went to the house and found in the back garden a number of scooters, in various states of repair and disrepair, including one about the right age for the number plate on the one I had seen earlier.

There was no one at home so we waited patiently in the car for signs of life. Our patience was rewarded inside twenty minutes when the scooter appeared and was driven into the driveway and pushed into the garden. We addressed the lad and identified ourselves (we had coats over our uniforms). He was quite unflustered as he gathered his documentation for us to inspect. The logbook gave the frame number and when he showed us the frame number on the scooter he had ridden home it was not the same. The old scooter was the one to which the logbook referred. He immediately confessed that all the scooters, except his old one, were stolen.

He was arrested and subsequently charged with stealing a number of scooters. Better was to come. He identified four more youths who were dealing in stolen scooters. In all during the next week I arrested those youths and recovered eleven stolen scooters, including one out of a canal. The paperwork was very interesting and the most complex I had dealt with at that stage. I was allowed to prepare the prosecution file myself, a task normally then undertaken by a detective. I was commended for the work and I was well chuffed with my reward.

A brief respite from the beat saw me back at the Training Centre for the Final Continuation Course. This was again at Bridgend. This time instead of going in the police coach I had approval to take my car. The reasons were two-fold. One was that the middle weekend was the Battle of Britain air display at St Athan and the second was that I had got a few days holiday booked immediately after the course, and was taking my tent down to Pembrokeshire. Bridgend was half way there. The course went well, I worked hard at it, and I was top student. Bosses back on the Division were delighted.

I was by now reaching the end of my probation period and had never realised how quickly two years could pass. I would be appointed on time and receive my first pay increase. A nice time all round, except for one incident, which was potentially fatal.

I was walking, alone, on my beat at about 3 am when I decided to re-check my shops. They were old buildings with deep front doors, and display windows on either side of the corridor. As I walked along I was aware that I was standing on broken glass. I shone my torch and was confronted by a man climbing out of a hole he had made in the front door. In his hand he had a shard of glass about a yard long, which he was wielding like a sword. I knew then what fear was. I was terrified. For a split second I froze.

There were only the two of us so desperate measures were necessary. I threw my torch at him and went back a couple of paces to get some more light from the street. I drew my truncheon and as he came at me I smashed the 'sword' with the truncheon and then with the adrenaline flowing I hit him in the face with the truncheon, using all my strength. He dropped like a stone. He stayed unconscious long enough for me to run to the phone box and dial 999 for help. Help came very quickly. The man was whisked off to hospital for twenty-seven stitches in his wound. I was indeed a lucky man. Either of us could have died.

There were many 'characters' about at this time and many were real old rogues in their own way. One such was an old man named Duggie Plumb. He had the record for the number of convictions for drunkenness at Birmingham. When he died in the 70s he had been before the Magistrates something like 350 times. He was a real pest to arrest. If you were the slightest bit rough with him he would hang on to lampposts and school railings and not let go. If you told him to come with you he would, like a lamb. He had to be locked up for his own safety, as most of the time when drunk he directed the traffic like a policeman on point duty.

'The Yank' was another. Patrick Mallon was not an American but a native of Dublin. He called himself 'The Yank' because he said it sounded tough. He didn't need a tough name. He was a hard man, very hard as a younger man. When he got drunk, and he frequently did, he needed more than one to arrest him and even then one had to be careful. He was strong and fit and he knew how to hurt you. His pal was a man called 'Ginger' Young. Ginger was so called because of his bright ginger hair, which he normally wore in a crew cut. That, his tattoos and his hob-nailed kicking boots made him look pretty evil. His face bore the scar of a razor slashing which he collected in his native Glasgow. These two together meant trouble, with a capital 'T'

A chap named Sam kept a pub called the St Mathias on the corner of Bridge St West and Great Russell Street. It was demolished as the district was developed but it had been a great pub for the area and occupied a nice corner spot, with the main doors right at the apex and all other doors off a little hallway. Sam had a very pretty wife and she had two equally pretty sisters. It was rumoured that Sam was seeing to her sisters as well as his wife, and there were occasionally frightful rows between them.

THE BEST OF BRIDGE STREET WEST

I went past there one night with Dave Breeze and found Sam having a problem with Ginger. He wouldn't drink up and eventually we persuaded him to drink his beer and go. Ginger didn't like being tipped out of pubs and the next evening he went back there and threw the big brass cash register out of the pub by way of one of the front windows. It landed in the street outside, well bent. Ginger then left.

When we came on duty for nights we were sent up to the pub to get a statement off Sam in case Ginger was arrested during the night. The window had been boarded up and the till was back in its place. It was still able to collect money! Sam was busy and asked us to call back after closing time, which we did. Whilst we were doing the statement in one bar there was a crash in the other as a brick came in from outside. By the time we had got the bolts off the door there was no one in sight.

Within minutes there were three knocks on the front door. The police. More of us. It was the area car crew. They had just been stopped by a man who thought that they were Inspectors. He made a complaint that there were policemen drinking in the bar. Davy, the driver, had got his name and address.

No doubt he was the same man who had lobbed the brick through the window. That was good. We'd try and lock him up on the way back if the details were right.

The car crew left and we concluded our business with Sam. We then went to the yard where the bloke who had stopped the area car lived. There were no lights downstairs but the bedroom was lit. Dave knocked on the door.

'Who is it?' asked a man from inside.

Quick as a flash Dave replied, 'Police Inspector. About my men in the pub.'

'What about them?' came the voice.

'Can you pick 'em out?'

'Yes.'

If he could identify us then obviously he had seen us in the pub. If he had seen us in there I was satisfied that he was the owner of the brick which had come through the window. He was about to get himself locked up.

'Come out and come down the nick, then.'

As he opened the front door, wearing only his pants and slippers, he realised that he had been tricked. He lurched out into the yard and Dave slammed his front door shut. There was much cursing, swearing and shouting from him as he was walked down the road to Bridge. He was the man who had thrown the brick through Sam's window.

Ginger got himself locked up later in the week at another pub.

A light-hearted incident that remains a good pub story is concerned more with public reaction rather than police action. One Saturday afternoon I was met, on my beat, by the area car crew, Fred Sawyer and Len Whitcombe. Len enjoyed the odd practical joke and told me to go to New Street, near to Woolworth's. He told me to say nothing when he stopped, but to point upwards. A few minutes later, bell ringing and headlights on, Len screeched to a stop beside where I was standing. I pointed up onto the roof of the office block next to Woolworth's. Len and Fred got out of the car and pointed as well. Len shouted, 'Don't do it, don't do it,' and continued to point.

We had, by this time, got an audience and the public, from bus stops and shops, were all looking upwards at where we were pointing. 'I can see him, he's there,' said one. 'Oh yes, by the chimney,' said another. 'Where? Where?' said another.

Len shouted, 'I'll come round the other side, don't do it.' Then he said to me, 'Get in.' I did and we drove off.

'That's brightened their day. Give 'em something to talk about, yes.' Len seemed quite pleased with his success. By now we were all roaring with laughter, and I didn't know what to think. It was funny and not, I understand, unique!

It was the same crew again who played a joke on Ted Morris, the Inspector for many years at the Lane. There was an old, even then, Austin A40 Farina allocated to the Lane for use by the Duty Inspector, at his discretion. It was becoming quite decrepit at the end. Len and Fred found it parked near a pub in Lower Tower Street. Ted liked a drink and they assumed that he was in the pub so they moved the car to the car park in the Lane.

Ted came out of the pub and found it missing. He went back into the pub and phoned in. He sent for the area car. The crew weren't sure if they had been rumbled or not and left Ted to do the talking. They hadn't been sussed out at all. Ted thought that it had been pinched. They got Ted back into the Lane without him finding the car. Word got round to us, on the beat, that the A40 was safe and not to worry ourselves. Ted, in the meantime, had spoken to the Information Room and all area car crews were instructed to phone the Room.

They were then told that the A40 was missing and to look out for it. Ted reckoned that if it was found before he went off duty, it would save a lot of bother.

Ray Parfitt was Ted's relief on earlies and when he came in Ted told him that the A40 was stolen. Ray said, 'Whoever pinched it knew where to park it. It's on the car park now.'

Ted realised that he had been the victim of a prank. He also knew that everybody else knew. He said we were all bastards. Of course we were, there was a saying, 'All coppers are bastards'.

Somewhere around this time I was back up in town for a few days and working mainly New Street and Corporation Street area. We had a police pillar phone on this junction, and shared it with Digbeth. On quiet evenings we could be plagued with young male drivers showing off to all and sundry with some quite nice cars. One favourite was to roar away from one set of traffic lights with great gusto and just slip through the next set before they changed to red trapping those following.

I was at this pillar one evening when a lad came hammering down New Street from Victoria Square and had a clear run at my lights. He would probably have nipped through on amber but he saw me so he locked the front wheels up and slid to a stop against the finger kerb that divided the traffic between Corporation Street and Stephenson Place.

Big mistake. The heavy braking had obviously dipped the nose and he cleared the kerb with the body but the sump caught it. The full inertia of the car stopping abruptly had been taken via the engine mounting. Not a collapsing zone, so the energy transferred to the body shell and buckled both the floor pan and the roof.

Result, one very nice 1961 Singer Gazelle reduced to scrap value. I mused that he probably wouldn't do that again when his insurers saw my statement on the accident file. They were sure to buy a copy before settling his claim.

CHAPTER 5

Claudine

IMMEDIATELY AFTER APPOINTMENT I attended a refresher course and for the Christmas period of 1964 I was posted to the Traffic Squad. This was a legacy of the distant past. Prior to the creation of the Corps of Traffic Wardens and the installation of parking meters, chaos prevailed with city centre parking and traffic flow. This chaos was controlled by experienced police officers from the 'A' division and probationers from the outside divisions. It was thought that the experience gained was of value to all those who worked in the suburbs. Traffic Wardens meant this experience was later lost to outsiders.

Those of us on the division were still posted to control pedestrian crossings at peak times in the week but at Christmas we had the job all day and every day for about a month. It was cold, mundane work, but a source of overtime unknown elsewhere. The operation was really quite slick. We were detached from normal duties and worked under the charge of an Inspector, also detached from normal routine. The squad that year had been running a week when I joined it on the second to last Saturday before Christmas. The events of that cold day were to have a profound bearing on my life, and I can recall that day more clearly than probably any in the past.

I started work at 9 and would finish around 6 pm depending on the volume of people and traffic. I was to work New Street. A team of seven of us would be a self contained unit manning all the pedestrian crossings between us, all day. There would be no meal breaks as such and we would be expected to fend for ourselves. In such circumstances ingenuity prevails and the lads who had already done a week had a system well established. We all had sandwiches which were left at various shops where we knew someone, and tins of coffee had been delivered there as well, and milk came via the milkman, so we could have a supply of hot drinks throughout the day. The co-operation of the traders was much appreciated by us all.

I was taken to a dress shop and introduced to the staff. Our coffee was there, in the staff kitchen. I left my lunch there. No formalities, just common sense: leave the kettle full and the cups and place clean. Madeline and her girls were great. Madeline was in her mid to late twenties, a tall, leggy, busty girl, quite typical of a fashion expert. I went to the shop during the

56

afternoon and Madeline said, 'The boss is out the back, no problems, just so you don't think you are on your own.'

The boss was stunningly attractive. I guessed her to be a year or two older than Madeline. She was barely 5'3", had brown hair and very deep brown eyes. 'Hi,' she offered her hand, 'welcome to chaos city, I'm Claudine.'

I shook hands, 'I'm Ralph, I'm the new boy on the team. Your girls have been letting us have our coffee here, I hope that's OK with you.'

'Gosh, yes, nice to see so many of you about, reassuring.'

She seemed quite pleased that the facility had been provided. I drank my coffee and heated the water for the next man. Just as I was about to leave Claudine asked, 'Will you be back later?'

'Hopefully, yes, if that's OK.'

'It's Madeline's birthday tomorrow so we are going to have a few drinks before we close. You, and the others, will be most welcome.'

I thanked her and left. I dearly hoped to go back, if only to talk to Claudine. Something about her said 'class'; she was more than just attractive, she was special. The day wore on slowly and my turn came round to go for coffee. It was by now approaching 5 pm and the crowds were thinning out. Two of the team had already finished and there was no rush for me to go off. I might even be joined if conditions really slackened. The 'party' was just warming up. Champagne, real champagne was flowing. The shop had had a good day and the bolts were going on at five and everybody would be leaving by six. I allowed myself one glass of bubbly, I was cold, my sandwiches were lonely and I didn't really know that much about champagne anyway. The coffee was far more sensible. The girls chatted amongst themselves and I listened on. Claudine gradually directed her attention towards me, saying that I was quiet and not saying much, I smiled. 'I know better than to interrupt gossip.'

'We don't gossip, we merely exchange news,' she scorned. 'Anyway, I'll talk to you. There is not much news.' Claudine sat contentedly on the edge of her desk, swinging her legs to and fro. I felt I was being chatted up. Did I drive? Did I like my job? Where did I live? Who with? Then she said, 'Am I fit to drive? I feel quite tiddley.' She didn't seem to have drunk much and she looked sober enough to me and I told her so. She then searched for the chink in my armour. Would I, she asked, drive her home?

'I can't. My car is at home; I come to work on a motorbike because of the parking,' I told her with due honesty.

'You can drive mine.'

I could feel myself being driven into a corner, I would love to date her but today was not a good day. I was cold, and I was tired but I didn't really want to refuse either. So I said, 'If I drive you home, how do I get back?'

She soon resolved that one. 'Use my car and bring it back in the morning.'

That suggestion made good sense and as I formulated my reply she said, 'Look, if you drop me home, I'll buy you dinner on the way.'

That offer finally clinched it; I said, 'You win. I'll do it.'

She made a phone call and booked a table. From the conversation it was apparent that she was well known at her chosen venue.

At some stage I had got to go back to the station to sign off and change out of uniform. So I decided that I would sign off by phone from the shop, leave with Claudine and go back to the station in the car. I made my phone call and there were no snags with the arrangements. Madeline's boyfriend called for her and we all left together. I walked with Claudine to the car park in Hinckley Street. On a contract space was a very smart 1961 3.4 Jaguar, a lovely British Racing Green, with wire wheels. I was impressed.

'Nice, very nice,' I said.

Claudine gave me the keys and I let her in. I spent a few seconds to familiarise myself with the car and then started it up and listened to the sweet sounds from the engine. Lovely. I had not driven a Jaguar on the road before and I was totally impressed with the car on the journey to the station. I handed in my armlets, changed and got back to the car inside ten minutes. I tossed my flying jacket onto the back seat. (It was too bulky to go in my locker and I didn't like to leave it lying about.) 'Where to?' I asked.

'Head towards Kidderminster, dinner is at the Gypsy's Tent.'

'Kidderminster? Is that where you live? Strewth, I didn't think you lived all the way out there.'

'Sorry, but you didn't ask,' she said, finishing with a lovely smile. There was nothing I could say to that. The car was in splendid condition and had 48,000 miles on the clock, a fair average for those days. I asked if she had had the car from new.

'Sort of, it was my husband's.'

Warning bells started to ring in my mind: 'was my husband's', I didn't like the sound of that. I asked, 'You divorced, separated?'

'No. I'm a widow.'

I sat in silence for what seemed ages, cursing the casualness of my question. That had wrong-footed me completely. I could only utter, 'Sorry,' before resuming my brief silence. Then I said, 'I am sorry, I shouldn't have asked that.'

Claudine was not perturbed. It was, she assured me, a valid question in the circumstances.

'Can I ask how long?'

'Ask all you wish. It's been three years now so I am quite used to talking about it,' she replied.

I drove out of the City and into the darkness of the Worcestershire roads. The headlights were wonderful after those on my old Volkswagen Beetle. We were soon on the car park of the Gypsy's Tent. It was a large pub with a function room and a good restaurant. The table was ready and we were shown to it immediately. Claudine said, 'Anything you like, it's all on.'

I chose a rump steak and it was perfect. I had eaten there once before but not with such a lovely companion. I was totally captivated with her pretty face. During the meal it came out that she had been married for eleven years. That, I thought, plus three as a widow makes my original estimate of her age way out. She was obviously a very well educated lady. She spoke with what I called a BBC accent. She was immaculate, as was her car. Her attitude suggested wealth, without edge, she was quite unassuming. The meal over, she paid the bill and we left.

After Kidderminster I had to seek directions. Eventually we turned into a lane on the Ombersley side of the town and then onto a pebbled drive to a large and imposing Georgian mansion-style house with a separate, two car garage. I parked outside the front door.

'May I ask you in?' she questioned.

I didn't want to sound too enthusiastic but it looked to be a magnificent place and probably well worth a peep inside. I agreed and locked the car.

The interior was sumptuous, the carpet was the very best quality and the furniture was a mix of old and quite modern, the soft furnishings blending perfectly. I was staggered. I had only dreamed about houses like this. Claudine invited me to sit in the lounge, pointing to a luxurious three-seater settee, and offered me a drink. A bottle of beer was forthcoming from the fridge.

'Put some music on if you wish, I'll just go and change. Work clothes are for work.' Claudine spoke as she disappeared. I browsed through her records; she had a wide selection to suit all tastes and her record player was of the very latest with long play and auto-change facility. It sounds old hat now but then was front row high-tech. I selected a varied assortment of Lonnie Donnigan and Mantovani. Claudine re-appeared wearing a tight pair of designer trousers, a silk blouse and a silly pair of fluffy pink slippers. They looked funny against the fresh primrose colour of her outfit, yet again she looked stunning. She started to play my music, poured herself a large gin and tonic and sat beside me on the settee.

We talked a lot about not a lot. Claudine poured herself another drink and asked if I wanted one. I looked her in the eyes and said, 'I've got twenty-five miles to go home, I've got a very valuable car to take care of so I must say "no thank-you".'

'There are five bedrooms here; they are all ready so you are welcome to stay, you do not have to leave until the morning.'

I had been chatted up, I had been dined, I was being supplied with drinks and now I was being offered a bed. I decided to stay. Yes, please, I would have another drink.

Claudine put the car away and brought back a bottle of champagne from the kitchen. She opened it very skilfully and poured a glass each. Over the next hour I heard her life story: a very interesting story told by a very interesting lady.

She had been born in Jersey in 1925 of Anglo-French parents. Her mother (whom she referred to always as mummy) was French. She was still alive and living in France. Her father was very English, had received a public school education, and was a senior banker in Jersey. He had vanished in the United States, whilst on Government business, in the first months of World War II. The circumstances of his disappearance were never revealed, if indeed they were known. Subsequently her mother had moved back to England and lived just outside Oxford. Claudine and her sister were withdrawn from public school and worked at the Morris factory at Cowley, for the Ministry of Defence. Her mother spoke fluent French, German and reasonable Italian and worked then at the Government listening station at Bletchley Park. Both Claudine and her sister spoke fluent French as all conversations during their childhood had been bi-lingual.

After hostilities ended the three continued to live near Oxford until both girls had settled. Then their mother sold the family home, moved back to France and gave the girls £1000 each (a vast amount then). They bought a house, which they shared. Her sister, Annette, married an American pilot from Brize Norton, and she now lived in the United States. He now worked as a pilot for TWA.

Claudine lived and worked in Oxford, latterly at Smiths Instruments, until she and John married and moved to Kidderminster in 1950. John had been an executive in the carpet industry. He died suddenly, from cancer of the stomach, in June 1961. The house, they had bought in 1957, unfinished, from administrators for a bankrupt building contractor.

Claudine's business had been started as a hobby. She was a very competent dressmaker. Her main source of supply was the Art Colleges of France who sold all their creations. She had only been in Birmingham for five months.

After more champagne Claudine showed me my room. It was a flat within the house. Originally the room had been designed for a snooker table but it had been altered to make a large bedroom with a bathroom and studio/lounge en suite. It was a brilliant concept of design.

'This,' Claudine announced, 'is the guest room. I've put you in here.'

'This is lovely, thank you. Thank you very much.' I was quite humbled. The bed was enormous and the decor was as everywhere, immaculate.

I looked Claudine in the eyes, those lovely, deep brown eyes, and said, 'You say this is the guest room.'

She nodded.

'Am I allowed guests?' I asked her with a grin.

She leaned up and kissed me on the lips and said, 'Only me.'

I took her hand and led her back downstairs.

We sat back on the settee to finish our drinks, Claudine held up her glass and said, 'May the night be long and our bodies be strong.'

I looked at her and asked, 'What did you say?'

'I said, it's time for bed, come on.' She took my hand and led me away to my room. She left me at the door and wandered off along the landing, 'I'll be back in a minute.'

I got undressed and got into bed. Claudine returned a few minutes later in a dressing gown; she removed this to reveal a pair of silk 'baby-doll' pyjamas. They didn't stay on long. We made love for most of the night, snatching some sleep, only to wake up for more. Widowhood had made Claudine very greedy, but it had not harmed her memory. She knew what was supposed to happen and made sure it did.

When I awoke in the morning at about 7.40 Claudine was in the studio wearing a lemon leotard with legs on, a sort of a cat suit under which she wore nothing but herself. She brought me a coffee and sat on the bed. Despite all we had done during the night I sat up in bed and dragged her towards me. She looked beautiful. The sheen of the silk was so sensual. She obviously sensed my arousal because she put her finger to my lips and said, 'Save something for later.'

I hoped later wasn't too long away.

I was amazed when Claudine told me that she had already done her morning exercises and had got the lunch in the oven.

'You will stay for lunch, please, it is beef. I warn you, though, we will not be alone. A girl from the tennis club will be here. She's a widow, also.'

'Provided I can borrow the car to pop home to get some clothes, yes, love to.'

'Help yourself. And if you like a drink at Sunday lunchtime have it whilst you are out. Carol has hit the bottle a bit since she lost Mike so where possible none of her friends encourage alcohol. She also swears terribly if she feels upset, but she means no harm.'

I was invited to remain in bed if I wished or I could get up and have breakfast. I opted for a shower and breakfast. Both made me feel a lot better. Claudine's leotard didn't. My trousers were quite tight.

Claudine looked good in whatever she wore; a chunky sweater and an apron looked cute.

I got the car out and drove home. My dad was in the front room when I arrived and saw the car draw up. His first question was, 'You haven't bought that, have you?'

'No, I've borrowed it from a friend.'

'Bloody wealthy friend. Got a good job, has he?'

'Own business,' I replied truthfully. I didn't let on that the owner was female.

My father was not now enjoying very good health and he was generally a bit offhand about things that my generation found normal. Cars were things which 'people like us' had no use for. My own little car was, to him, opulence. To him, the Jag would be way over the top.

I changed, told Mum not to expect me home until late, and set off back towards Kidderminster. On the way back I collected a bunch of flowers for Claudine.

I arrived back in good time for the meal. There was a Riley Elf on the drive so I presumed that Carol had arrived. There was a house key on the car ring so I let myself in. I gave Claudine her flowers and received a hug in return. 'Lovely, darling, thank you, come and meet Carol.'

We were introduced and it was difficult to see what Claudine and Carol had in common. She was about 5'7", overweight and under-clad. She was wearing clothes which were two sizes too small. Her hair had been bleached blonde and was now showing dark roots. Her make-up was caked on and she looked a mess. She was, however, well spoken and very knowledgeable. I took into account that she was a widow (that was in common with Claudine) and probably rightly assessed that her untidiness manifested from that situation.

Lunch was excellent: beef Wellington, with all the trimmings, beautifully cooked and presented. Claudine was without doubt an excellent cook. Suddenly, during the meal, Carol asked me, 'Ralph, are you married?'

'No,' I replied. It occurred to me that Claudine had not asked that question directly.

'That's nice. Men should not be allowed to marry. They should stay single and then they wouldn't have to fuck whores, get pissed, and kill themselves on the way home.' She said that with venom.

Claudine looked up at me and shrugged her shoulders. She didn't need to say anything. She had warned me.

'Surely not all men do that.'

'Mine did. He found this slut. She used him, and when she'd finished with him she got him pissed and sent him back to me. He didn't make it, he went to sleep, ran off the road, hit a tree and died.'

'I am very sorry for you; it must have been hard to come to terms with,' I offered.

'Not as hard as frigging my fingers at night, alone. Anyway, that's enough about me. Claudine tells me you are a policeman, how exciting.'

'I do enjoy the job but I wouldn't call it exciting,' I replied as honestly as I could.

'You'll be good for each other, best of luck.' Carol smiled and continued with her meal. For the rest of her stay she was good company. She even did all the washing up.

After Carol had left, Claudine and I spent the rest of the afternoon in bed. As we lay there getting our breath back Claudine asked, 'What did you think of Carol?'

'Not sure. How long has she let herself go?'

'About two years.'

'How long has she been alone?'

'Thirteen months.'

'In that case I think she may carry some blame. I wouldn't rush home to cuddle her, especially if I had something like you hidden away in the country.' I answered truthfully and Claudine knew it.

'Actually, you are exactly right. Carol started to become complacent and lost a little interest in the things which matter so much in a marriage. Mike was a very handsome man and he found a very pretty woman at Tewksbury. He stayed with her when he was away overnight, even if it meant a lot of extra driving.' She paused and snuggled lower against me.

'We all knew at the Tennis Club. Carol found out who she was and screamed at her over the phone. She then gave Mike an ultimatum, wife or mistress. Mike, I think, was about to opt for mistress when Carol phoned her house and asked to speak to Mike. She said she had taken an overdose. Mike panicked and insisted on dashing back to her, despite being well drunk. The girl wanted to drive him but he insisted. The rest you know.'

'Had she taken an overdose?'

'Only of gin, about a bottle. Carol was in pieces when she found out Mike was dead. At least she had the news gently. The other girl found out from the papers. They both went to the funeral and Carol caused a disgraceful scene.'

'How old is Carol?' I asked.

'Guess.'

'I'm not very good with ages this weekend,' I joked, 'but probably about the same as you.'

'Twenty-six. You failed again.'

I dragged Claudine under the bedclothes and said, 'Not here.' We made love again.

Claudine took me home later and we agreed to meet on Monday evening, if we didn't meet at the shop. Yes, work called. The holiday (honeymoon?) was over, but it had been a wonderful two days for us both.

Back at work on Monday I was on a high. I had a reasonably peaceful day organising queues of stationary traffic into and out of a car park and realised that most drivers did not know what the word 'FULL' meant when it was written on a board outside a car park. During my mid-afternoon break in the station I had to suffer not a little teasing about Claudine. Apparently the kettle had been in use and Madeline had revealed that I had taken Claudine home. Claudine had arrived at the shop during the morning, very happy and pleased with herself and rumour was rife. Did I take her home? Yes, why deny it, you know anyway. Did I score? If not why not? Neither answer would have pleased so I said nothing more. I saw Claudine briefly and we wished each other well for Christmas.

The last few days before Christmas were always very hectic, the City was really busy. I saw Claudine during the week, but she had previously planned to visit friends in Oxford for Christmas. I arranged to see her on Saturday evening, before Christmas, and this time I would buy the meal.

The Saturday evening out with Claudine was a splendid success. I had been recommended to the Copper Kettle at Bewdley and I had booked a table without ever having seen the place. It was a truly romantic atmosphere, and the meal was, indeed, excellent. We went back to Claudine's house and spent a very similar evening to the one the Saturday before. I was asked to relate my life story to her and she revealed more of her past to me.

The disappearance of her father had been quite traumatic all round and she and Annette had become closer than ever and were almost inseparable for around a year. The uncertainty of how, or why, or when, or even where their father had vanished had been the hardest part. If they had known any one of those things the pain would have been eased. She made it clear that she had never been a promiscuous woman and had always followed the high standards taught by her mother. That was why, she thought, she had coped so well with the loss of John. He had apparently been working very hard just prior to being taken ill and they were having a few days at Bournemouth when the illness manifested itself. He had woken in the night in agony and had been rushed to hospital. The hospital had referred him to his GP and the

GP in turn referred him to a specialist. The specialist carried out an exploratory operation and could do nothing more.

Claudine was told to prepare for widowhood and within twenty-six days from being taken ill at Bournemouth John had been cremated. It had been sudden and devastating. John's company had an excellent pension plan. It was one of the first private schemes to have been set up and it had paid good reward on investment. The mortgage had been paid. She had received a lump sum and was drawing a monthly income. The Jaguar had been John's company car and when everything was finalised ownership was transferred to her, and her company Mini had gone back. She remained a shareholder.

After visiting her sister in the States and taking her mother with her for company, Claudine had concentrated all her efforts on her business. I was the first man, other than her husband, to have made love to her since 1950.

She looked me in the eyes and confided, 'You were well worthy, thank you.'

I felt humbled, and asked, 'Was John your first lover?'

She laughed gently, 'Oh, no. The first was totally frivolous. That happened when I was eighteen. I went out one Sunday afternoon with a friend on our cycles. It was a beautiful hot day and we swam in the Thames with no clothes on. As we lay on the grass drying in the sun things just happened as nature demanded and I ceased as of then to be a virgin. He went off to war a little later. I had a brief romance after the war, but that came to nothing and then I met John.'

She had, she was sure, done nothing of which to be ashamed and I had to agree with her.

As Sunday was not a busy day we went to bed fairly early and got up fairly late. I left after tea on Sunday and we arranged to meet on New Year's Eve.

I worked on Christmas Day, the afternoon shift from Bridge. The policy then was that single men worked on Christmas Day and married men worked Boxing Day. It was a good system but one which fell by the wayside in the future. It was quite a busy day and unfortunately we spent most of it dealing with family disputes of one sort or another. We did, though, find time to eat a splendid meal prepared by big John Seddon. He had just married a policewoman and she was working as well, although well away from him.

The week at work was not to be good, but it was eventful. On the Tuesday I had a man drop dead in front of me as he asked directions to the train and on the Wednesday, the late Ken Blakeman and I were assaulted. We were standing beside the Town Hall when I was punched in the small of my back. At first I thought I had been stabbed. As I spun round to see what had happened Ken was hit in the face with an empty whisky bottle.

Then all hell broke loose. We both grabbed the man responsible but having drunk the contents of the bottle, mixed, we found out later, with meths he was a handful. He was well drunk, but he was fighting mad. He fought and kicked, struggled and screamed and he hurled his abuse with a broad Glaswegian accent. Once he was overpowered we managed to get him into a Land Rover and then into the station.

Whilst in his cell he commenced to chew, yes bite lumps out of, the toilet seat. He was seen by doctors and once sober was transferred to a mental hospital. Ken and I both went to hospital for check-ups, but we were both none the worse for the experience.

Claudine was very upset about the incident, and sobbed down the phone when I told her. 'Are you sure you are all right?'

I had doubted the wisdom of telling her at all but I knew she would be hurt to hear from a third person. She was honest and she respected honesty.

The New Year came in quietly and I saw Claudine only briefly over the following weekend because she was driving to London early on Sunday to fly and see her mother for a few days. We would spend the next weekend together. I would after then be returning to shift work and our social time would be curtailed. It would not be untruthful to say that I missed Claudine whilst she was away and the Saturday evening seemed a long way away.

She cooked a magnificent meal that evening and we ate by candlelight. I again spent a Saturday night with her. During Sunday I explained that I would have to see less of her in the immediate future because I was about to commence a shift of nights back at Bridge. She then dropped her bombshell.

'I think it will be better if we do not see each other again,' she said, with obvious sadness in her voice.

'What have I done wrong?' I asked.

She put her arms round my neck and said, 'You have done nothing wrong. I am the one who has spoilt things.'

'You haven't spoilt anything,' I assured her.

'Ralph, I love you. Without much effort I could go completely head-over-heels about you. I must not allow that to happen.'

She stood in front of me shaking her head; tears were welling up in her eyes. 'I am so sorry. It is so silly of me, I ought to know better.'

We sat down, holding hands. 'Why is it silly?' I asked, probably a little naively.

'You are barely twenty-one, I am nearly forty. With such an age difference a relationship would be doomed. Yes, we could keep each other amused for a few years, but before you were forty, I would be in the queue at the Post

Office drawing my pension. I have spoilt things by falling in love because we had such a wonderful time up to now.'

I knew that what Claudine was saying was true of the future but I hadn't realised how much I meant to her, and that was something I should have found out.

'When did you discover you were in love?' I asked her.

'Oh, I took an instant liking to you. I suppose it grew from then but I knew when I put the phone down after you told me about getting hurt. I felt I had been hurt as well. I missed you terribly whilst I was in France. The drive back from London was hell, I just did not know how to tell you.'

'Well, you have told me. Thank you for being honest with me.' My comment was genuine, but I felt an immense sadness.

'I have written you a letter in case I could not bring myself to tell you to your face. Take it with you when you leave and open it at home, please, and not before.' She buried her face against my chest. 'You have done me so much good and I repay you with this. I feel so horrid.'

I was a little puzzled and asked, 'What "so much good" have I done?'

'You have brought me out into the world again. For years I have not known whether I could love again, whether I could make love again or whether I would even want to again. You have answered all those fears. You have also had three firsts in that you were the first man to take me to bed since John died. The first man ever to have made love to me on a first date and certainly the first I have been afraid to love.' She sat up and said, 'I am lost for words now.'

We sat in silence for probably five minutes before I said, 'I'll do a coffee and then I'll go home. The forecast is for a very cold night so I'll leave in good time.'

I went to the kitchen and prepared two cups of black coffee. We finished our coffee and I collected my flying jacket. The old Beetle was a cold car and the jacket was as useful in that as it was on the motorbike. I put my hand on Claudine's shoulder, bade her farewell and went to my car. I knew I had to go. If I faltered or hesitated there would be tears all round and we would have the pain of parting all over again. I put my letter on the front seat and set off without looking back. I felt awful. I had never knowingly been in love. How I felt suggested that I had just found out how painful love can be.

The journey home was bad. The roads were quite icy, and there was some fog. The heater in the car was crap and the windscreen kept freezing on the inside. I stopped twice to clear it. Each time I fingered Claudine's letter but resisted the temptation to open it. Finally I reached home. I then did two things that were not part of my routine. I let my flatcoat retriever, Raq, back into the main part of the house, for company and I poured a big scotch, which I had neat. I then settled to read my letter.

The envelope contained a beautiful photograph of Claudine, signed 'With Love, Claudine', an eighteen page letter and a £20 book token with instructions that I bought the books necessary for my promotion exams. I read the letter, which was written in almost copperplate style, twice. It contained much of what we had already said but there was one passage which brought home to me the immense concern Claudine had felt.

One of the reasons for her flight to her mother was for advice about me. Her mother could not, I suspect, give her the answer she wanted, but had told her, 'In love you must do as you think right, and only you can know what is right.' I must remember that! Claudine had booked to fly to France again on Monday. It was mainly for business but also to make a clean break from me. I felt that I had caused a lovely lady an awful amount of avoidable heartache. I sent Raq back to his bed and I went to mine, a wiser and more mature man, but a very subdued one.

I was to see Claudine once again in the future. I treasured her letter and photograph dearly. They were later to be stolen together with the letter from Lorna.

It took me some while to get over Claudine and it is ironical that within a few days I was to meet the woman who would be my wife.

CHAPTER 6

After Probation

I STARTED BACK AT BRIDGE on Monday night and got my feet back on the ground by arresting three men breaking into a factory. During the week I also got involved in an incident which was potentially serious but finished on a light-hearted note. I was waiting in Summer Lane, near Tower Street, to make my point (visit with my sergeant) when I heard an old van coming towards me. The exhaust was blowing and there were no lights on. I went into the middle of the road and flashed my torch for the van to stop. The van driver changed down and changed course towards me. Realising that the van was not going to stop, and that the driver was provocative I threw my truncheon through the windscreen and jumped out of the way. There was, to be fair, no great risk to life, the van was only doing about 25 mph.

To my amazement the van veered to the right, bounced up the kerb, rocked and overturned. Shit! It was an old Morris Commercial, ex GPO vintage, with sliding cab doors. The upper-most door opened and a man climbed out and ran away. I gave a token chase, but urgently wanted my peg back. I found it in the cab, wiped it down and put it back in my pocket. I then walked about fifty yards to the pillar phone to report that I had found an abandoned and overturned van. Assistance arrived and the road was cleared. The van had been sold for scrap some months before and an owner for it was never found. Neither was any record of the true circumstances.

One of the most amusing things I ever witnessed involved a policeman from Digbeth named Ken Deaville. Ken was one of the Old School nearing retirement and a little eccentric. He had an old, upright 1947 Ford Anglia, which had broken down because of a failure in the back axle. He had sent out word to locate one and a few days later bought one from a scrap man in Lozells.

Ken had one problem, he had no transport. His car was broken down in Small Heath and the part was probably four miles away. The axle itself was quite heavy and because the vee-shaped stabilising bars were attached, bulky as well. There was no way the two could be united without ingenuity and Ken had plenty of that. He presumably had some sort of approval to be absent from his beat to do what he did, but even then it was nothing short of outrageously amusing.

I heard a rumble along the cobbled street, which got louder as it approached. I stood in the entrance to a 'green man', a gent's street side urinal, and watched in amazement as Ken, in full uniform of flowing cape and helmet, pushed towards me a market trader's barrow laden with this metal monster.

I laughed, but Ken scorned me. 'Give me a hand, this is bloody heavy.'

I helped him to the edge of my beat and wished him well. I stood in silent disbelief as Ken walked off into the night with his barrow. I found out later that he walked it home, unloaded it and returned a very oily barrow from whence it had come before its owner was back at his pitch. But that was Ken, bless him.

Market barrows had for many years been an irritation to the Digbeth men. The barrows were, in the main, owned by the Corporation and were rented on a daily basis and returned to the pound after use. Any deposit was then returned. Sometimes the traders had such a good day that they didn't bother to return them and they were abandoned like supermarket trolleys are now. The police had power to impound the barrows but that was pretty ineffective because it meant that fewer barrows were in circulation the next day.

The cure was to collect them up, stack them together, run a chain through the wheels and park them on the best sales pitches. The old hands soon knew how to find out who hired which barrow last. They then meted out their own justice. Any privately owned barrows were normally left minus wheels, which had to be collected from the police station before they were available for use. Very time consuming. I suspect that Ken's barrow fell into one of those classes.

Handcuffs were not a general issue in these times, but they were always carried on mobile patrols. I arrived one night at a large fight outside two pubs, the Britannia and the Dolphin; they stood diagonally opposite each other on the crossroads of Hospital Street and Geech Street, on the Bridge patch.

Apparently the dispute had started in the Brit. and had been quickly defused by the gaffer pitching the contenders into the street. The commotion had been heard in the Dolphin and the customers from there, together with an ever-increasing audience from the Brit. spilled onto the street to offer support and see fair play. I had not been sent to this brawl so getting involved was ill advised for two good reasons. Nobody knew I was there, and I was seriously out-numbered. I, wisely, I think, waited in the shadows.

I had a grandstand view and was able to identify the main participants. Soon I heard the sound of the bells of the Area Cars converging on the junction. The noisy approach was often useful in dispersing these unscheduled events, and sure enough that happened. Two cars, or rather a Land Rover and a car, pulled up together and suddenly we were six, not one. We arrested seven in total; the first four filled the Rover and one was such a real handful that we could only get him and one other into the car. Bill Duncombe decided to use the handcuffs and we put number seven in the 'cuffs around a street lamp.

Logically, someone should have stayed with him but the one flailing his arms and legs in the car had to be held down for safety and we all needed to help. We unloaded at Bridge, the Rover had gone into the Lane, and we went back for number seven.

He had gone, vanished. He had scaled the lamppost, passed his hands over the top, dropped down and run off. I looked at Bill and he looked at me. 'Bollocks, more paperwork explaining that.'

I knew that number 7 had come from the Dolphin so questions were asked there first. Nobody had seen anything. They had all been in the pub all the time, what fight? The toilet was outside and I checked it, empty. The ladies, nothing. The gaffer was left in no doubt what we thought of him and his punters. No doubt one of them had assisted the escape. Across to the Brit. Try the gents, stinking place, not there. Ladies, 'Sorry love, wrong door.' Speak to the gaffer. Can't help at all, but is writing an address on a beer mat. Goodnight, sorry to trouble you. We used the radio to explain why we were about to patrol the 'D' division.

We left the car a few yards up the road and walked to the house; the lights were on but there were no sounds. We listened at the doorjamb but still nothing. I checked the toilets in the yard, and they were all locked. I checked the brew houses, and there was only one unlocked. I beckoned Bill and nodded to the door. Bill ambled across, glared at the door and knocked it down. A petrified man cowered in the corner as splinters rained around him. Glinting in the torchlight I saw the handcuffs, still locked around his wrists. The ultimatum to him was clear, 'The handcuffs are going back to the car; perhaps you would like to return them.' He did and no more was mentioned about his escape. What we had that night was, on paper, an affray. All were fined £2 the following morning for 'drunk and disorderly', and why not, an affray carried about seven years, and a good, clean, old-fashioned, drunken brawl was worth a couple of quid.

On occasions I would go back and work at the Lane for a few days to cover holidays and the like. One evening, in 1965, I was in St Philip's churchyard when there was an enormous explosion. The city rocked. I heard glass breaking and falling from windows. Alarms were going off all over.

Obviously something serious had happened. The noise had come from somewhere at the end of Corporation Street. I took my helmet off and ran down Cherry Street. When I got into Corporation Street there was panic and pandemonium. People were screaming and running about. Shop and office windows were out all over the road. New Street was even worse. Suddenly, there were police and firemen everywhere.

At the time the City Centre was at the mercy of the demolition vandals, and where Hitler had failed, they had recently reduced the old Midland Bank in Stephenson Place to motorway hardcore. The wood they were burning on the site. Sometimes they left the gates open, sometimes they didn't. Health and Safety laws had not been invented then; everyone was sort of trusted to do what was 'right'. They hadn't made the welding trolley secure and somebody or Mr Nobody had shoved it onto the unattended bonfire. When the cylinders had reached a good high temperature the cylinders exploded with astonishing effect. Glaziers were kept busy for days. June was also in the City that night. As a cadet, she was receiving her Duke of Edinburgh Award at the Council House.

I had to take the promotion examination in two parts. The education paper I had already passed and I had a year to study for the police duty subjects. I bought the books I needed with the book tokens I had been given, and set to work. Claudine had obviously done her homework well; there was just enough change to buy a paperback. I found the study reasonably easy. I had kept abreast of change and also had retained most of the knowledge from the basic training. I went to evening classes, organised by the Force, in my own time and studied around the framework from them.

I had by now met Penny Field, who I would later marry. We got on very well and she must have created a good impression, because she was a smoker, and I very rarely dated girls who smoked. I am a lifelong non-smoker and I found the habit utterly repulsive. Penny knew this and gave it up, quite willingly, and apparently with ease. Our relationship was not as intense as the one with Claudine had been, and the evening classes limited my free time but we got on with the courting and she renewed my interest in horses.

Work wise the year was excellent. I spent about two months as observer/radio operator on the area car and enjoyed it very much. The drivers were older men, all top grade advanced course graduates and very experienced policemen. The vehicle used was either an Austin A60 Cambridge or a Land Rover. It was also a divisional resource, which gave me access to the Digbeth side of the division, of which I had no previous knowledge.

I had witnessed a close-knit team at Bridge but the closeness of the staff at

Digbeth was uncanny. The entire shift were like brothers, but none the less dedicated, honest men as I was to witness early one morning.

The car crew tended to take their meal at 2 am and at about 2.30 the Inspector asked for the keys to our car. He was qualified to use it and he was given the keys, without question. He returned them about thirty minutes later, very solemn and sombre. Two of his shift had been arrested, by a third, for burglary. The poor man was close to tears.

We all felt a sense of anguish. For a policeman to commit a crime is a dreadful insult, not only to his colleagues but, worse, to the public. The division had suffered enormously about four years before when five men from Bridge were arrested for a spate of similar matters. Four were convicted and imprisoned. We had just got over that and now this! It was made worse because all that was taken was a selection of soft porn, 'dirty books'. Jerry, the Inspector, never fully recovered from that tragedy. They spared Jerry the heartbreak of a trial and pleaded guilty; they were jailed.

Jerry left Digbeth and took up residence in the public office at the Lane. He was a big man and he looked formidable behind his big oak desk. He probably felt a need to reflect and there was a good place to do so.

One Sunday morning in the summer shortly after 6 am I had taken him and the office man, Tony Savage, their cups of tea and was just going back into the canteen to enjoy my coffee when I was aware of a commotion in the restroom. A chair had gone over and there was a lot of shouting. As I was about to enter I was almost stampeded by half the shift leaving. 'Don't go in there,' said a voice.

'Why?'

'A scrap. Roger and Tony are having it off at last.'

I understood. They had been blowing hot and cold with each other for weeks and it appeared to have come to a head. The gist of what had happened was that Roger, not an early bird, had come into work on the night service bus, paying night service fare. He had been cursing about that when he had offended Tony who was reading his Bible. Tony had recently been converted to Christianity and often strutted about with the Bible under his arm. He was offended by Roger's language on the Lord's Day and said so. The end product was that Roger had blasphemed and they had come to blows.

In the circumstances it was an incident better not witnessed so all witnesses had left. Jerry obviously knew something was afoot when we were all out of the front door by ten past six. Not heard of on a Sunday.

When the combatants had tidied up Roger complained of a sore cheek. He complained to Jerry who much preferred the company of men to wimps and said, 'I don't care what he's done. That's nothing to what I'll do if it happens again. Now sod off and get some work done.'

One night, within a short time of this I was working in St Philip's churchyard. The night service buses all left from this area and the benches were regularly full of couples having a good night kiss before catching their buses. This was one such night and it was shortly before midnight. As I went past one couple who were getting well warmed up, I heard a rustle in the bushes. Not wanting to disturb them I walked away without changing my stride. I then went into the back of the gardener's compound and I could see what I had heard. Hidden in the bushes was a man, on his knees, watching the couple intently and masturbating himself.

He was now the other side of the fence to me so I had little chance of arresting him so I found a broom, crept up to the fence and placed the broom gently behind the man. Then I thrust it forward. He fell forwards out of the bushes in a heap, disturbing the couple. I got out of the compound, and hurried round towards the couple, and the man. There was quite an argument going on when I got back.

On seeing me the woman said, 'He's been watching us with his "thing" out.'

'Is that right?' I asked. His flies were still open.

I doubted whether she had seen anything before I tipped the bloke out of the bushes so I was on safe ground when I said to him. 'Any more complaints about you and you're nicked. Now clear off and do your buttons up.'

With that resolved I left. About fifteen minutes later Jerry called me on the phone at my point and asked about the incident. The man had complained that I had been rude to him and Jerry wanted some facts. When I told Jerry the story he agreed that the man was drunk and should be arrested. He arranged for the man to be arrested in Steelhouse Lane as he left the station.

The Digbeth area, at this time, was undergoing major reconstruction work, on both buildings and roads, and as a result there was considerable disruption to established routes. The area was host to the wholesale meat, fish and vegetable markets and lorries from all over the country delivered produce. Most of the drivers knew but one way in and one way out. Divert them and lose them seemed to be council policy. Lorries finished up in the strangest of places. For a few weeks most produce lorries were stopped by the police and an area car escorted them to the markets, unless they knew the new route. This was not a police function but one that was greatly appreciated.

Penny and I married in October 1965, with the blessing of her parents, but not, I was to find, with good grace. My friend Sue Styles had met Penny and hinted that I might live to regret my marriage to her. There was never any suggestion that Sue and I would wed so she had no reason to be vindictive. Penny and I had planned to marry in the winter but a combination of events dictated otherwise. Penny had been forced to leave home following a dispute with her mother, and was temporarily lodging with my parents. That was not totally satisfactory. I had wished to save for a deposit on a house, but police accommodation had become available so I accepted it. I had saved well for many years and had sufficient funds to furnish our home.

My future in-laws planned a wedding reception at a hotel. In the event, because, they said, the shorter time scale had reduced their available capital, that would not now happen and we had a reception at their home. We had a brief honeymoon in Pembrokeshire.

The promotion examinations were held shortly after the wedding and I passed them successfully. I was the only City member of my initial course to do so. That result was rewarded with an attachment to the CID for four months 'in-house' training. The experience was considered necessary for any officer in the offing for promotion. A minimum of five years service was a requirement before consideration of advancement, but Chief Superintendent Wanklin was a great advocate of early grooming.

The CID at that time was a headquarters posting. Only uniformed men were divisional strength. I found that this tended to result in an imbalance of commitment. CID officers could be moved readily around the City to suit demand. Thus those working on any division would have almost certainly spent their uniformed service elsewhere. Their local knowledge was limited and in consequence their arrest rate was abysmal. I honestly believed that they had become recorders of crimes and statistics to the detriment of their function to investigate and detect crime. To a man they were superb in the presentation of paper work for forwarding to prosecutors and I took due care to learn much from them. In my four months I dealt with only eight arrested persons, far fewer than would have been the case in uniform.

I was to play a small part in a murder enquiry during the attachment. At least I would have the benefit of seeing how a major crime enquiry, using HQ resources as well, was handled.

Kuverji Gordhan was of Indian origin, born in South Africa. He was the eldest son of a large family and had been sent to Britain by his father to build a business. He was a hard-working man and well thought of in his

Sparkbrook community. He was in dispute with a younger brother, Magan. Basically, Magan was idle and a drain on the funds of the rest of the family. He and Kuverji were often in dispute.

Kuverji vanished in January 1966 and his disappearance reported to the police by Magan. Initially he was treated as a normal missing person. His wife became concerned and the police made further enquiries. Traces of blood were found in the family home and some money was found to be missing. Magan was suspected of a serious crime, but no body had been found and Magan was admitting nothing.

A week after his reported disappearance a human arm was found by staff in a locker at Gosta Green Technical College (now part of Aston University). Initially the arm was thought to be just rotten meat, perhaps a student prank, but as it was dumped in a large waste bin it became apparent that the object was in fact a human arm, and part of a thigh. Following that discovery a number of officers, myself included, from Steelhouse Lane were sent to the college to search all remaining lockers. We did that and DS John Shaw discovered a severed human head in a parcel. It was the head of Kevurji Gordhan.

Magan was seen again. He had studied at the college and knew his way round. He had the motive and he had the access but was it him we were looking for? A lot of things pointed to him. He had money. That was in itself unusual. He had opened a Post Office account a few hours after the disappearance was reported. He was charged with the murder of his brother. His father had arrived from South Africa and Magan spoke with him after his Court appearance.

Magan then volunteered that he had been out during the afternoon in question and on returning home he had found his brother dead and two black men standing over the body. He had been threatened and had cut the body up to conceal the death. He had hired a driver for the family van and had then delivered the body, in parcels, to colleges around the City. The weapon was recovered from a locker at Handsworth Technical College, my old school.

Magan took the police to a room at Suffolk Street College and pointed out the parcels containing his brother's remains. His own writing was on these parcels.

It is interesting to note that he appeared before Birmingham Assizes less than two months after the crime. Such a time scale would not have been possible today. He pleaded 'Not Guilty' to the murder, but was convicted and sentenced to life imprisonment.

When I saw Magan in Court I wondered what sort of a man it was who could murder his own brother for a few hundred pounds, dismember his body in the family home and dispose of sacred remains in such a manner. I concluded that it could only be a man with an intense hatred.

On the completion of the attachment I verbally reported to Mr Wanklin my feelings about CID postings. He committed my comments, plus his own, to paper. He agreed with me. Others did also because very shortly afterwards the entire structure of the CID was changed and control returned to divisions. I know of one chief inspector who posted one of his uniform carriers to the CID in the knowledge that he would be transferred out of his way to hide, as he put it, in the grey-suited sea of mediocrity.

Midway through the year I was sent to the Force driving school to undergo a Standard Driving Course formerly known as the Standard A. I had previously been assessed to undertake the Standard B course direct, but because of a higher accident rate among younger drivers the Insurers had demanded a restructuring of courses in line with Home Office policy. The A and B courses were abandoned and renamed as Standard and Intermediate. The Advanced and Advanced refresher remained unchanged. This meant that I would have to complete, successfully, two full courses, totalling eight weeks, to drive an area car, instead of three weeks as previously. As early as 1963 I had been assessed as a motorcyclist and without further instruction given authority to ride lightweight motor cycles and in the same morning did the Standard B test successfully.

I was pleased that I had been given the course, but felt much disappointment that area car work would be delayed. That sphere was my next natural progression.

The Standard Course was good. The first week was taken up with elementary mechanics and Roadcraft and Highway Code theory. The rest of the time was spent on the road learning to drive to the police 'system'. Fortunately, Cockney Bill had taught a lot of 'system' in my driving and I was to benefit greatly from that. My crew was comprised of Full Licence holders but one crew was entirely learners. At the end of the course I was successful, leaving with a Grade 4, the lowest of the low, but at least past the first hurdle.

Eight light-hearted weeks followed. I was chosen to drive the dispatch van. I was to be the divisional postman! This function was normally reserved for an older officer and was considered to be a very cushy number indeed. In a strange sort of way I enjoyed the break. The routine was fairly simple. The first function of the morning was to collect the post from the PO Box office at the Postal HQ and deliver it to Police Headquarters.

The internal post around the division took two journeys. The canteen had

Youngest Area Car Driver, 1966.

to be stocked because firms charged delivery then. Crime circulations were delivered to the Transport Police to be put onto trains to everywhere. Fax had not been invented, and telex could not transmit pictures. In the afternoons more runs to the local stations and finally the post from the post room to the Postal HQ.

The little van also had one other very useful function. Transport. The 'A' division did not have many residents but it had an awful lot of visitors and any trivial enquiry was made a little cumbersome by distance. A quick ride out in the dispatch van resolved many things. It also gave me the opportunity to learn from the way other officers did their enquiries. I was now detached from my own shift and working some part of my day with fresh faces. Despite the routine of tasks, I arrested a car thief, and a man stealing from a building site.

I was suddenly found a place on an Intermediate driving course at very short notice, due to injury to the nominee. That course was excellent and I was particularly thrilled to have finished top student with a recommendation for early advanced training. I became, at twenty-two, the youngest at that time, but not the youngest ever, area car driver in the City. However, on duty in the vehicle I had to be accompanied by a Grade 1 driver, and that experience was surely no hardship.

On the domestic front Penny was now pregnant and happy, but her mother was far from keen. She described me as 'an animal' for such behaviour. Pregnancy was a dangerous state of life and childbirth could kill. Her idea of marriage was celibacy! I felt that there might be difficulties ahead and thought back at what Sue had said, just a year earlier!

I also had the sad task of having to bury my dog. He had suddenly died at home whilst apparently in good health. He had been a faithful friend since I was fourteen and I had trained him as a gun dog, by use only of a starting pistol and a few dumb-bells and decoys. The burial was not a job I relished and I was quite upset about doing it.

I found area car work the most challenging so far and I enjoyed it beyond imagination. The Land Rover was my favourite. We had two on the division, one used as an area car and the other by the vehicle removal squad. I quickly became very skilled with that vehicle and undertook a two-day course at the factory learning just what it was really capable of. Apparently I should not have been sent. The course was only offered to advanced drivers who had not previously received Land Rover instruction. I was not advanced, and I had received Land Rover tuition! The world was kind. I was the last City officer ever to attend that factory course.

One character above all from my early days at Steelhouse Lane was Neil Fletcher. Neil was about fifty-two when I joined. He was a native of the Shetland Islands and was the only man on the division allowed to take all his annual holiday at once because he always returned home and it was three days travel in each direction.

Like all men from that region he was big and strong. He was also very fit by any standards. He would think nothing of walking twenty miles for an afternoon stroll. He also threw the hammer. He had learned at school and had competed in Highland Games, and whilst in the army. At this time he was the Police Athletic Association champion. By way of training he would cycle or walk to Marston Green or Coleshill to friends and would play loud Scottish music and from the safety of a field he would hurl the hammer vast distances. There was a mental hospital at Coleshill and one Sunday morning he caused great alarm, because an old lady phoned the police to say that a madman had escaped and was throwing his ball and chain around the field. The police rushed there to find Neil training.

Neil also had an enormous appetite for alcohol, much of which he managed to solicit whilst working. It was one of the reasons he never learned to drive. It was also one of the reasons he was entrusted to me one afternoon when I was working on the dispatch van. He was to compete in the Regional Sports day, an elimination event for the National.

My instructions were to take him, keep him out of the beer tent, see him through his event and bring him back to work. It sounded simple; it wasn't. When we arrived Neil was thirsty and cleared his throat with about three pints of mild. His event was timed for about 3 and at 2.30 I found him and took him to the pit. There were five other competitors. They were quietly warming up in their tracksuits. Neil was still in half-uniform. I asked him to get ready and he said he was ready, he didn't need to pose about; when his turn came he would throw.

The first two competitors threw, good throws. They were applauded by the other competitors. Neil went forward, and I was amazed. He had tucked his trousers in his socks, and his collar was still on its back stud; his tie was in his pocket. He jumped up and down and started to shout and bellow then he picked up the hammer and hurled it some twelve feet further than either of the other two. He looked at me and said, 'Stay here, if anyone beats that, come and get me.' He then walked off to the beer tent. I didn't need to fetch him back. He won the event comfortably.

When he retired on age limit at fifty-five he still stayed in touch with us. He worked as an usher in the Magistrates Court. He eventually retired to his beloved Scotland.

CHAPTER 7

Aberfan and Beyond

PRIOR TO LEARNING THAT Penny was pregnant I had volunteered to undergo training with the 'mobile column'. This was a Civil Defence orientated project and was a statutory requirement of Chief Officers. In essence it consisted of 132 police officers, a superintendent in charge, a deputy and couple of inspectors, a handful of sergeants and the remainder were constables. The course was for a week and was conducted on a regional basis. The plan of things was that the unit should be fully self-contained, with its own mobile kitchens, offices, communications and accommodation and in times of war it would be sent into areas where bombs had fallen. You went somewhere, probably a disused RAF or Army base and invented a disaster, which you played around with. In the ten years in which it existed it was used in anger once. I was to experience at first-hand a major civil disaster.

At 9 am on 21 October 1966 the 132 police officers from the Midlands reported to the column commander at Kingswood Camp, north of Wolverhampton. Thirty-three of those officers were from Birmingham City. The camp had not had military use but had been a boys' camp run by the local authority. We were split up into units, given duties and introduced to our equipment and vehicles. The theory was good.

At about 9.20 that morning in Aberfan, South Wales, two million tons of black, sticky slime fell from the top of a mountain, slid half a mile down the hillside and engulfed the village and its school, killing 144 people. That was more than there were of us. The news reached us at lunchtime. There was no request for our attendance and we continued with our routine of war games. By teatime there was still no request. Older members suggested that our existence was probably unknown to the Chief Constable of the tiny Merthyr Borough force, so therefore he was unlikely to ask for us. Somebody, for Christ's sake, use the phone, and offer us as a unit. That was finally done, but not before we had all been stood down to go out on the town, if you could go 'out on the town' in Albrighton.

We were later rounded up and returned to camp. We were being sent. Sir Derrick Capper, Chief Constable of Birmingham and Chief Constable designate of the column, had kicked some bottoms and we would travel overnight. The stiff upper lip was still in place though; the convoy could not

81

travel until midnight because of the possible disruption to traffic! The deputy of the column was a big man from Worcester who was a cross between Yogi Bear and Fred Flintstone. He instructed that we could not take all our possessions, as limited as they were, and could only take what would fit into our issued holdall. The rest would remain at Kingswood, with a sergeant left to guard them and the camp. He had a telephone and would maintain our HQ. We would only be away a couple of days; the problem down there would soon be resolved.

We arrived at some ungodly time in the morning. Or most of us did. Some vehicles, including two of the Pathfinder motorcycles, would not run on the water from the jerry cans. Somebody hadn't checked the cans or their contents and had used the cans from the kitchen truck. The bikes were loaded onto the supply truck, by hand! They were later replaced with two patrol motorcycles from Birmingham, which were ferried out to us.

The briefing was attended by three Chief Constables, from Merthyr Tydfil, Glamorgan (on whose territory the disaster had occurred) and Birmingham. The situation was very serious, we were told. The coal tip had come down, and more could follow it. The school and about eight houses had been cast aside or buried, we didn't know which; the slurry was deeper than the roof of the school. The death toll would be high and many of the dead would be children. We would remain here until the job was done and that could easily be a fortnight. Our task would be to police the incident, which would leave the local officers free to deal with all other aspects of it, including the incident room and their own community. Our accommodation would be the local grammar school. Sir Derrick wished us well, thought three Chief Constables at one incident was three too many, and left.

The next day a truck was sent back to Kingswood Camp to collect the luggage, which we should have taken with us in the first place. The sergeant could close down the HQ. We needed all the help we could get.

My first impression when I arrived at the scene was one of total and utter disbelief. I was staggered by the magnitude of the disaster. I had a mental picture of what to expect but what I saw made that picture so unreal. There were men, thousands of them on their hands and knees digging with their bare hands and small shovels, looking for signs of life or even bodies. When they were sure an area was clear the excavators moved in and loaded the tippers. There were dozens of mechanical diggers and even more lorries. Only twenty miles away, and in two places, there were major roadworks schemes taking place on the M4 and the A40. All the plant from both these places had been sent to the scene. Even more was to follow.

A one-way system had been created to ease congestion and our first task was to police this. Trucks came in with all manner of tools and equipment. Any which were tippers were loaded before they left. Some of the drivers had been at the wheel for thirty-two hours. One went to sleep and his lorry overturned, blocking the road. A bulldozer was used to shove it aside. It stayed there for the rest of the week. Fortunately, many of the soldiers who had been sent could drive the lorries, and they did so whilst the drivers snatched some sleep.

Bodies were now being recovered quite quickly and a mortuary had been set up in the chapel. I was one of the officers chosen to work there. A number of factors decided staff for that task. Medical advice had dictated that staff should be chosen around certain criteria if possible. They should not be parents, they should not have younger siblings, and they should have no relatives in the area. I met all three conditions. The task was not one I would have chosen but it was made all the easier by the fact that so many of the corpses were intact. The children hadn't been smashed to pieces by the landslide, but had survived that only to suffocate under their desks where they had apparently taken refuge.

The system we set up for their identification was very simple and worked well. The clothing was removed and sent to the Hoover factory for washing and ironing. It was carefully and accurately itemised and placed in a plastic bag and it was given a number. Each body was given a number to match its clothes, and the body was placed in a white linen bag. Parents generally knew what the children were wearing, and identified the clothing. Names were added to the numbers and identification was complete. Parents who wished to see their child, or some cases children, were allowed to do so, but discouraged.

One major shortage existed, coffins. The ones for adults were easy but coffin makers and undertakers do not hold a large stock of children's sizes. We sent out a nationwide appeal and the response was marvellous. One undertaker drove down from north of Aberdeen with two.

Once the mortuary was closed down we prepared for the funerals. Some would be private but there was to be a mass grave for about eighty and that would at least be emotive, if not explosive. Ten thousand mourners were expected.

The media had been both a help and a hindrance and at one point there was a news blackout. I remember one reporter from the *Daily Mirror* leaving his car in the way of the trucks. He ignored good advice and returned to find it out of his way upside-down on the sports field. Irresponsible journalists existed then as well.

The funerals went as well as could have been hoped. We dealt with two

Royal visits; Prince Philip visited twice, the second time accompanied by the Queen, and there was a visit by the Prime Minister, Harold Wilson. Sightseers and ghouls were a nuisance.

As with all major incidents, an enquiry followed and a finding announced. For my part I spoke to the local people as I worked alongside them. The tip had moved on two previous occasions, in 1959 and 1964. It had also caused flooding. But still nothing had been done, other than to keep adding to it. The tip was a waste product and should have been better supervised. I was not allowed to dump my waste outside my front door but the National Coal Board could dump theirs outside everyone's and even on their own roof. There was a spring under where the tip stood. That pumped out 100,000 gallons an hour, but its existence was apparently unknown. I was led to believe that it was known about in 1910 but had long since been deleted from maps.

I suspected that as long as coal came to the surface and the miners kept their jobs very little else mattered in Aberfan until . . .

We left Aberfan by Merthyr Corporation buses and screamed up the M50 at 40 mph. The vehicles had low-ratio gearboxes and were designed for use in the mountains. The offer by Midland Red to bring us all home would have been more comfortable but the gesture from Merthyr could not be ignored; the town wanted to say 'thanks' to its visitors.

The official enquiry report on Aberfan was that the disaster was foreseeable and preventable. 'Decent, honest men led astray by foolishness or ignorance or both in combination are responsible. The disaster is a terrifying tale of bungling ineptitude by many men charged with tasks for which they were totally unfitted, a failure to heed clear warnings, and a total lack of direction from above,' was a part of what it said. That sounded like manslaughter to me, but the Coal Board was owned by the Government.

That is not a lot different from what locals said at the time.

Lord Robens, the then Chairman of the National Coal Board, suggested that there should be in existence a permanent disaster force with special vehicles, maintained regionally, to provide communications systems and twenty-four hour canteens for rescue workers at such incidents. There was the Civil Defence Corps and the Mobile Column. Neither now exist! We also at that time had a very efficient army.

One year later, almost to the day, we returned. I attended a refresher course. A guest speaker, to talk on Major Incidents, was the deputy of the Aberfan mobile column, the Yogi Bear look-alike. He incurred my considerable wrath when he described 'the idiots who left their personal property at their base in their hurry to leave' and 'a vehicle had to be sent

ABERFAN AND BEYOND

from the scene of the disaster area to recover over a hundred suitcases'. I disrupted his lecture with my version of those events, which was a little more accurate. He was not a happy man, but did not contradict me. I felt much better!

The experience of Aberfan, I believe, made me a much wiser person, but that wisdom created within me an intense dislike of incompetence and inefficiency at all levels.

It did not however improve my domestic circumstances, which in my absence had deteriorated beyond all measure. I had been away for our first wedding anniversary. My mother-in-law was now making demands that I leave the service, and take a proper job so that I could be at home to look after my wife. How I could possibly take a proper job and remain at home was a mystery I never solved. Neither could she understand how I would lose my house if I left. Her interference had got to stop. I felt that in one ceremony I had somehow married two women, not one. She had been given a key to the house to facilitate entry whilst I was on nights but I discovered that she was in fact visiting in the absence of us both and doing housework, washing and snooping.

Work continued around domestic turmoil and between Christmas 1966 and New Year I was working at Bridge, but having meals at the Lane. Sometimes I caught the bus back to Bridge but if I was on one of the beats nearer town I would walk straight out into the beat. One evening I walked along Loveday Street and found a brand new Rover 2000 parked at the kerb. This car was so new that it wasn't even registered. It had number plates and a tax disc fitted but neither came into force until 1 January 1967. It was showing an 'E' suffix.

I wasn't over sure of what to do. This was a Motor Taxation matter, but the normal form didn't cover this eventuality. In the end it was decided that both the sergeant and I would make appropriate entries in our pocket books, sign each other's entry and then let the Inspector sign both entries. I then submitted a report to the Motor Tax officer for his information.

It came back from them with details of the owner and I went to see him. The end result was that the numbers, tax and insurance were invalid until 1.1.67. He went to Court for those matters and was fined. He was not a happy man. He was less happy when the Motor Tax officer withdrew the 'E' suffix and allocated a 'D'. He now owned a 1966 vehicle which was worth much less second hand.

The interference in my personal life continued when I was confronted by mother-in-law with a letter from my American pen-friend. She and I had been writing since we were thirteen. The letters had been frequent whilst at school but were now only an accompaniment to Christmas cards. The letter had been in the pocket of my coat and had been there since I had collected it from my parents' address. She had been going through my pockets and had found it. She ripped it up in front of me. She also made me very angry one morning when she woke me up shortly after 9. I was to rise, immediately. The sheets had got to be washed. I explained that I was on nights and therefore slept in the day. The reply that I should not work nights resulted in me having back the door key and her being sent out of the house.

Solicitors' advice was now very much on the agenda and at the first opportunity a consultation was sought. From then on I kept a full diary of all events involving my in-laws and my wife. At the same time I still had to work to save the marriage from total collapse, although, at this time, that seemed, sadly, an inevitable result. The baby was due in March 1967 and it was to be hoped that the birth would calm both women. Penny had started to smoke again and that gave more potential for strife. I was aware that smoking whilst pregnant was not advised, and said so.

At about this time, Bob Wanklin received an anonymous letter. That said that I was having an affair, that I was having it in order to wreck my marriage, and force my wife to leave the matrimonial home. It went on further that it was my intention to install this unnamed woman in the matrimonial home. I did not recognise the writing. The contents of the letter were untrue. I trusted my boss and confided in him that all was not well at home but I was making huge efforts to remedy the rifts. He was satisfied with my explanation but would, for the moment at least, keep the letter. I was later very glad he did.

My daughter was born on 17 March 1967 and christened Shirley Helen. I was on nights; but as she was born late in the afternoon I was able to see her and Penny before I went to work. The 17 March is St Patrick's Day and always very busy in Birmingham so the chance of having an evening off was out of the question but I had a very enjoyable shift.

When mother and baby came home matters got notably worse. I was in constant dispute with mother-in-law and she increasingly took my wife and daughter to her house whilst I was at work and would only return to my home when convenient to her.

Protests failed and in the end I sought an interview with Bob Wanklin asking to be given a job away from shift work. It was a bloody cheek, but I had to try. He had been mindful of my work record and my domestic situation and was in fact about to offer me a twelve months transfer to the divisional plainclothes squad. Not CID but a job that allowed uniformed staff to work on projects in plain clothes such as indecency between men, licensing, and gaming for example. I accepted that instantly. Not only had I received the help I sought but I had been given a career move as well.

The job was excellent and my partner, we had to work in pairs, was a man I knew well, Roger Graham. Roger was two years older than me but we had attended the same school and had both been brought up in Handsworth. Roger retired on the pension of a Chief Inspector. I liked Roger's approach to his duties and we quickly formed a repartee. We also added to our arrest tally on our first day out together: a suitcase salesman, fly pitcher, unlicensed street trader, call him what you like. The City had dozens of them and they were very difficult to deal with in uniform, especially if the lookouts were well placed.

The new job did not suit mother-in-law. Nothing short of resignation would come close to what she sought, whatever that was. Finally the crunch came. Penny and I had arranged for some friends to visit us on a Thursday evening. During that day a message was left for me at work saying that my wife and daughter were at her mother's and I was to collect them on the way home. Difficult as my car was at home. I cancelled the friends, went home, collected the car and then called on mother-in-law. Owing to the time I had taken to call for them the baby had now been put to bed and would remain where she was. Also they had people coming tomorrow to see their granddaughter, and Penny and the baby would remain there until at least Saturday evening. My patience finally exhausted and I made my ultimatum.

'I will be home tomorrow by twenty past six. If Penny and the baby aren't at home then, I won't be living there when they return.' I was quite positive.

Mother-in-law's reply was, 'You wouldn't dare to do it. You would get the sack. I would see to that personally. You would not risk your precious job.'

Penny said, 'That would cost you everything you've got.'

My reply to her was the last words I would say to her before we went to Court, 'You have already cost me everything I had.' I turned on my heels and left.

At 7.30 the following evening, 12 May 1967, I left my matrimonial home with all my personal possessions, my uniform and all other things which I was legally responsible for. The home and the furniture I left intact, as the solicitor had advised. I was out of the battle, but not the war.

I moved back with my parents and occupied my old room. I became aware that a lot of sentimental items had been removed from my things whilst they had been at my matrimonial home including the letters from Claudine and Lorna, together with the photo of Claudine, pictures of my dog and other items of no value to anyone but me. I was angry with myself for putting those things in jeopardy, but surely, I thought, they were in my own home, they should have been safe. Claudine had taught me a lot about trust and honesty in a relationship. I had now witnessed the opposite.

At the earliest opportunity I reported my change of address and new circumstances to Bob Wanklin. He was very decent about the whole thing and assured me that provided my work continued to be satisfactory and I kept my nose clean my job would be safe. He also reminded me that I had previously lost my warrant card in Sutton Park late one evening.

'Once before I told you to be careful when you took your trousers off. This time I would advise you to keep them on. Adultery can be very expensive.'

I thanked him for his help. He was a man's man and a first class policeman. He also knew his men.

Roger and I had settled at our job and I was disappointed when we were split up. Roger was to transfer to the divisional CID. It was what he had worked towards so I wished him well and settled to train a new partner. This time it was Bob Jones. Bob was destined for high office and keen to learn. We also worked very well together. Our first arrest together was for a series of serious indecent assaults on boys.

A young lad of about eight had started to behave strangely at home and his father sought our advice because he suspected that he had been assaulted. The end result was that a woman officer in plain clothes would spend some time talking to the lad each day until we had an idea, one way or the other. Sure enough dad had been right. The lad had been buggered, and the doctor confirmed it. The lad showed us where the house was and described in detail the room. When we arrested the man responsible we showed him a plan of the room which the lad had helped make. It was accurate, including the pattern on the rug.

The young policewoman was June Robinson. June had just finished her local training and had been released onto the 'A' division from the Police Women's Department. She was a cheerful, friendly girl of twenty. She was a former cadet and a hockey player. She had been born in the City. Her father was a pharmacist and her mother a farmer's daughter. The family still kept two farms and June spent most of her childhood holidays at one or other of them. We had a lot in common with our love of the countryside.

The man got three years for that offence and he admitted others for which we were unable to trace victims. That lad's father had done us well. I did not know it then but that woman constable would one day be my wife.

As anticipated I was summoned for maintenance. There would be no simple way out at Court. Penny, aided by her mother, had got a story worked out which bore no relationship to my account of events. It was going to be a

June's Initial Training Course, Ryton on Dunsmore, 1966. She is far right on centre row.

long, unnecessary, costly fight and I was not entitled to legal aid. In the interim I would have to find £4 per week: £2.10s for the child and £1.10s for the wife. One fact that they had not known was that by vacating the police house quickly she had left me eligible for a lodging allowance to live at home, so some of that amount came straight back. I also expected that Penny by now had found another man, which was why she had left the police house in a hurry. After all it was next door to others and policemen are trained to see things.

Once I had established that there was another man I obtained proof and went back to Court to get some money back. I had the Order amended to £3 for the child, nothing for the wife. I had clawed back another pound. Despite the Court granting me access to the child this was never possible and was never permitted.

The family had certainly not liked my counter-action and a couple of weeks later Bob gave me a message which said, 'Phone Lorna Goddard, urgent.' Lorna's address was on her missing letter but her phone number had been sent later. I had a sheet of paper on the inside of my locker door and on it were written no end of names and phone numbers which had no other place. Fortunately I had written hers there. I called it.

'Lorna, Ralph Pettitt.'

'Thank God, are you in the shit?'

'No, why?'

'I've had a woman DI [Detective Inspector] here asking about us.'

'I haven't seen you for years.'

'That's what I told her. She asked about the caravan.'

'What, Arley?'

'Yes.'

'Got it. Did you know that since then I've got married?'

'You, married? No.'

'Yes and separated. The problem is that mother-in-law has read through loads of my letters and kept most of them. She is now stirring the shit. That letter was never dated so she won't know old it is.'

'Anyway, I told her I hadn't seen you for three years.'

'That's about right but it could be more.'

'She asked if you screwed me.'

'What did you say?'

'I said you bleedin' hadn't. The cheeky cow.'

'How's Jack?'

'Lovely, thanks.'

'You got anyone else?'

'Not as such, I'm sharing one at the moment. He's married and drives a lorry so when he's this way he stays here. He's OK, he's good with Jack and nice to me but I'll only ever be a bit of spare to him.'

'I can't say too much on the phone, can I take you for a drink and tell you the full story so far?'

'Lovely, when?'

'When can you get a babysitter?'

'Got one, Mum's here for a few days.'

'Tonight then, 8 o'clock.'

'Yes, yes, OK, you don't mess about, do yer?'

'See you tonight then, 'bye.'

''Bye.'

Bob looked at me a bit askance, 'Are you about to burn your fingers?'

'Bob, mate, that bird has just told me that bloody mother-in-law of mine is a thief. I knew it before, but I can prove it now. She raided my letters and one from that bird has just turned up. I ain't about to spoil my chance of stitching her up.'

Lorna looked a lot better than when I had last seen her; she had kept her flat spotless and little Jack, now four, looked happy; as usual he was asleep. I thought that she had put on a little weight as well and that was no bad thing for her. We ended up at a pub in town and she listened intently as I told her the full story of my marriage.

When I had brought her up to date she said, 'You poor bastard. What a couple of cows.'

She was not impressed by what she had heard.

Then she said, 'Change of subject completely. You know Izzy Cox.'

That was not a question. It was a positive statement.

'Yes, how do you know her?'

'She used to live round the corner in Newtown. I knew her then. She lives over here now. I met her the other day. She came over to the flat the next day and we had a good natter. Your name came up in conversation because she is getting married to a copper.'

'Is she divorced then?'

'Just, like about six weeks.'

'Izzy was great fun, we had a good time.'

'So I believe. You'd be surprised what girls talk about.'

'I wouldn't,' I joked. 'Who is the lucky copper?'

'Martin something, plays hockey.'

'Atkins?'

'That sounds right.'

'Nice bloke, on the bikes at the moment. He's a right ram so she'll be well away.'

'How do you know?'

'That, my dear Lorna, is for me to know and for you to imagine. Come on, let's get you home.'

We decided that the evening did not exist. We had imagined it all but it had been a nice break.

Working in close liaison with the plainclothes squad there were occasionally temporary teams, wearing plain clothes, to target such things as car theft. Two lads who had a lot of success working together were Pip Scrivener and Eddie Lees. Both these men were very fit indeed; Pip was a near professional class footballer and Eddie was a cross-country runner.

One afternoon they disturbed two youths breaking into a car on a car park in Hurst Street. On being challenged the youths ran off in opposite directions. They split up, and each was pursued by an officer. Pip chased his up the Pershore Road and arrested him outside Cotteridge police station. He was exhausted and grateful to be locked up. Eddie chased his through the City Centre and eventually caught him outside the Aston Hippodrome and literally 'ran him in' to Bridge.

A few days later Bob and I found another cache of stolen scooters in similar circumstances to my previous success. This time they were all Vespas and none had to be got out of the canal. We had been walking between calls when I spotted the first scooter on false plates. We followed up that lead in an identical fashion to that which I used on my first scooter enquiry.

Towards the end of that year Bob Wanklin moved to higher places and was replaced by Bill Donaldson. I could never bring myself to like him, but I was soon to meet him. Another letter had been sent in and this time it named a person. I was told, by the Admin. Inspector, that Donaldson was not in the best of moods.

He started abruptly, 'I would have thought that in your domestic situation you would keep your dick in your trousers.'

I said nothing. There was nothing to say.

'Mrs Owen, you've been fixing her up.'

'I don't know a Mrs Owen.' My reply was honest.

'I am in possession of a letter which says you are having an affair with a Mrs Owen,' he insisted.

'I don't know a Mrs Owen, but are you aware that there has been a similar letter before?'

The police service keep personal files on each officer, a full one at

Personnel Office and an abridged one on Division. The local one is about a dozen pages and covers information needed to allocate courses and the like without reference to a great sheaf of papers.

'Nothing on your file.'

'Mr Wanklin said he would keep it. It's probably at Personnel.' I made no mention that I suspected that there was a third communication relating to Lorna.

'This Mrs Owen might be a photographer, does that ring any bells?'

Suddenly it all fitted in place but I said, 'No, not at all.'

By telling Donaldson that there was another letter I had taken away some of his fire. He obviously wanted to see that before he addressed the matter further. I was sent away and given an appointment for the afternoon.

The lady photographer was formerly a Miss Irene Owen. She was now a Mrs Ballard. I had met her first in 1964 but had not seen her since I had been married. Her car had had a puncture one evening about 8.30 and I had changed the wheel for her. I had noticed her wedding ring and said something like, 'If you weren't married that would cost you a date.'

The reply was, 'Don't worry about the ring, you're on.'

When I finished work that evening at ten we went for a drink together. She was working for her father as a photographer, but she was also attending Art College to qualify. She later took a number of pictures of my Raq and myself for her portfolio. We had spent a weekend together in a cottage at Clent.

She was married to Phil but was awaiting a quick divorce on the grounds of his adultery. Her father was also Phil and traded as Phil Owen. When she sent me some of the photos they had been in Phil Owen folders and there was a letter saying that the divorce was through, Phil was happy and that anything she now did was legal.

Those photos were missing and I imagined that the letter was with them. In the letter sent in, the writer had obviously got the two Phils mixed up and assumed her to be a Mrs Owen. I never corrected that assumption.

Instead I went back to my solicitor. The late George Brown had been a policeman before turning solicitor and he knew how the police ticked. He sent a letter to Donaldson making an allegation of the theft of my photographs and letters. It stated that the service was in possession of information which could only have come from the thief or someone with knowledge of where the letters now were. The letter invited an investigation.

In the meantime the first letter was found in a sealed envelope on my personal file. Appropriate notes had been made, as promised by Mr Wanklin. There was also a second letter giving details of Lorna. This had been followed up and there was no cause for further enquiry in relation to the first two. The first and the current one were on the same paper.

I was asked, 'Where do all these women [all two] fit in to your life now?'

'They don't. I don't know a Mrs Owen.'

'Somebody thinks you do.'

I was sent away to continue my duties.

There is no doubt in my mind that the previous notice of such letters saved a further and unnecessary enquiry into my conduct being undertaken. How fortunate they had been filed away.

A few days later my solicitor's letter landed on the division. It was not the most popular piece of correspondence received that morning. I was sent for. I was told that the chief superintendent was almost beside himself with rage. When I saw him it was most apparent that he was indeed very cross. 'What is the meaning of this?' he shouted, tossing the letter at me. 'The police force is not here to sort out your private war with your wife.'

'Sadly my private war, as you call it, is no longer private. A fact you well know. I have been advised to contact her only through a solicitor. It is obvious that property which was stolen from my home is now being used to cause problems. They want me out of a job. I cannot investigate the loss of the documents but the service can. Hence the letter.'

'You don't give me instructions. I am the Chief Superintendent, understood.'

'I am advised by my solicitor. He has invited an investigation into an alleged offence. If it can be proved that documents which have been unlawfully obtained are being used to cause me problems with you, then there is an avenue open to you to have the original documents, and thus stamp on this nonsense once and for all.' I was quite frank and candid in my summary.

'I will not authorise that.'

'Please, then, write to my solicitor and tell him so.'

'You tell him. He's your solicitor.'

'The letter is addressed to you. I am sure he would like a reply. Especially one which is a refusal to investigate an allegation of theft.' I felt I had won my argument. I knew when he bellowed, 'Get out, get out,' that I had. I left quickly before he changed his mind.

At the same time that George Brown wrote to Donaldson he also wrote to Penny's solicitors. For whatever reason the letter had worked. It is fair to state at this juncture that our divorce went ahead, albeit slowly, without further hindrance and was finalised in November 1970. The maintenance payments remained at £3 per week, without any application for variation, until March 1983. The child's name was changed and I was unable to trace her. Penny had shot herself in the foot. By changing the child's name without my consent she had done two things: she had denied me access in contravention of the Court Order, and she had also prevented herself ever receiving any further monies from me.

There suddenly arose a spate of indecent exposures in the City Centre. They were mainly in the evenings or late afternoon in the region of subways. Many of the complainants were nurses travelling between the hostel in Ludgate Hill and the General Hospital. Most of the offences were committed by a man, of similar descriptions. We had to work on the possibility that they were being committed by the same man. It was becoming too frequent to ignore and we decided to set up a little operation in an effort to catch him.

Moves were afoot to move the police headquarters from Newton Street to a new building, Lloyd House. Lloyd House was owned by Stewart & Lloyds, now swallowed up into British Steel. The building was tall enough to give us a good view over the area we wanted and we approached the caretaker for permission to use the roof.

With the assurance that we could have the access we needed we arranged for two policewomen to dress in plain clothes and wander around the area. We would have two officers on the roof with binoculars and a radio and the other officers would be placed handy to make an arrest, should we detect an offence.

I was posted to the roof. With everything in place we waited for action. Nothing happened. Suddenly I saw a man of the description we wanted walking out of a subway. There was not a woman near him but two had just gone into the subway. I was able to get a message to one of the men on the ground to speak to these women. The reply came back. Positive. He had 'flashed'. I relayed that information and we found our man in the adjoining subway. The policewomen went through twice, without any sign of a problem. Just as they prepared to wander through again, wearing different cardigans, they heard a scream. He had 'flashed' to someone else.

The policewomen arrested the man, but I often thought that they were disappointed at not being the 'victims'.

He was a persistent offender and had convictions all over the place. We added to his total.

CHAPTER 8

The New Approach

1967 WAS INDEED A MILESTONE in police history as it saw the introduction of a system of teamwork known as Unit Beat Policing. The scheme had been pioneered in Birmingham, based on the Sub-Divisions of Belgrave Road, in Balsall Heath and at Erdington. The strategy was that one permanent beat officer would be allocated a beat and he would remain guardian of it for as long as possible, working as varied a combination of shifts as possible. A unit beat car, nicknamed a Panda, would be overlaid on four (or two if they were very large) permanent beats, but on twenty-four hours, rotating shift. A detective constable would be allocated to two beats to assist the beat officers and the car drivers with their enquiries and to assist with paperwork. There would also be one or two women constables working on the team. At last personal radios were in force-wide use.

On a sub-divisional basis there would be twenty-four hour cover from a traffic patrol car. To allow for this the strength of the traffic department was increased by almost 200 per cent. This increase was made up from top grade advanced drivers from divisions. The divisional area cars ceased to exist in the form in which we had known but the Land Rovers would remain.

All officers would be in contact by way of personal radios, and sub-divisions set up their own miniature control rooms. The cost must have been enormous. For use as unit beat cars some 120 Austin A40 Farinas were purchased, in Panda colours. For reasons no one can give they were all fitted with two-tone horns and blue flashing lights. Each of the six divisions received a new Land Rover and the traffic car fleet was increased to around fourteen white Austin A110 Westminster saloons. These had previously been supplied black, and all black ones were repainted white. For use by CID officers on the teams, a number of black A40 cars were supplied. Finally the existing black area cars were sprayed Panda colours for use by supervision staff. The Pandas were not to be used for enforcement of speed limits, but the former area cars, 'Giant Pandas', had calibrated speedometers fitted and could be so used.

Later, to combat a problem with motorists overtaking a Panda car, two Austin 1800S traffic cars were also painted as Pandas. Somebody told the Press that the Pandas were not to be used for the enforcement of speeding

96

offences, so that was *carte blanche* to overtake them all. Finally, officers working shifts but not allocated a specific function were sent to patrol a permanent beat on foot, usually when it was not being covered by the regular man. The system remained in being for many years.

I was on plainclothes duties when the scheme was launched but upon completion of that attachment, in April 1968, I remained at Steelhouse Lane, driving a UBC around the City Centre, not a task that particularly fired me with enthusiasm. Parking was difficult enough without adding to it by having a glut of police cars to park. The parking problem was eased a little with the implementation of 'diplomatic squares', a white cross in a white box, painted on the road, usually at the end of a row of parking meters.

On the suburbs, the system must have been an absolute godsend, though it was a little over the top for the City Centre, but it worked well at Bridge.

Obviously the outlay had caused cash problems elsewhere, and as if to claw some cash back the system of divisional canteens run by and for the divisions were scrapped. The 'A' Division kept the huge canteen facility there because it was a 'Force canteen' but the smaller shift one and the single quarters ones closed. We were not left without food though. We had vending machines and micro-wave ovens. Permitted adjectives do not allow discussion of this vile, tasteless, and unimaginative junk food. Suffice to say it was soon phased out, and a few years on some canteen facilities were restored to stations. I took to having a standard daily packed meal, which varied little in style for the next two decades.

The City centre had always been like a magnet to young men in smart cars. One Saturday night the Unit set up a roadside check on these lads. We chose Snow Hill Ringway, opposite police HQ on the out-of-city side. There were about six of us including the Inspector. Before the ban was put on cars using Bull Street they used to crawl through it surveying the bus stops for young fillies, before zooming down Snow Hill to complete the lap of dishonour and start again. The art of success was to be selective. I was on the central reservation, calling which to pull over. Real poseurs only used smart cars. We really only needed to stop them once. When they had been checked we picked whatever was left, including those on whom the first message had been lost.

We were in phase 2 when a new smartie came through Bull Street a bit quick. I called, 'Cortina, fast,' as a Mark 2 GT approached with tyres screaming. As he screeched to a stop the driver was laughing. I was also safety officer, watching their backs, so I resisted the temptation to speak with him. I then heard him say something like, 'I'll get you next time.' With that I quickly organised a relief safety officer and had the Cortina driver parked up at the kerb. Except for the Inspector I was senior man there so any flak from the stop ought to come my way.

This lad was just twenty. He had bought the car during the Saturday afternoon. In other words he'd owned it all of twelve hours. Whilst reading this lad my version of the road safety riot act, one of the team stood behind him with a message on a clipboard, 'He's a Pro Con.' So our irresponsible man was a Probationary Constable. There would now certainly be flak. He was unable to produce any documents so I presented him with a certificate to produce them at his nominated station. I also specified my option for full details to be recorded on production, not just a note of validity. He lived and worked at Bordesley Green, and had nominated to produce there.

Within the hour he had. A copy of the form would come to me anyway, but I phoned Bordesley to forewarn them. That news prompted me to collect the form. Details of the insurance supported my worst fears. He probably hadn't got any. The certificate was an annual one, with an 'any vehicle' caption. That would only be valid if the insurers had approved the new vehicle. I doubted whether a company would cover a twenty year old in a GT at fully comprehensive. A requirement of the finance houses is comprehensive and I knew this car was on finance.

Monty Phillips was our Inspector and we sat down afterwards and sorted out a strategy. We were on nights, and would have the following Monday and Tuesday on leave. He arranged for the early turn Inspector on Monday to check with the insurers the validity or otherwise of the insurance. According to how that panned out we would go from there. The other, minor, and internal, problem, was that Mr Cortina was posted to earlies on the Sunday morning and should have been in quarters by midnight, instead of swanning round the town at 3 am!

Wednesday revealed all. There was no valid insurance. What he had was for an A35 van. Monty arranged for the lad to come and see him and I was there as well, and would do the deed. Very simply, he was reported for driving a car without insurance. Monty then took the papers up to Bill Donaldson. To his credit he recommended prosecution, but asked that the papers be forwarded to Chief Superintendent 'E' Division, Ron Pickard. This was as a courtesy to Ron, so that he was aware, officially, of the situation.

By Friday afternoon I was expected at Acocks Green to see Ron Pickard. Pickard was generally pretty forthright, but he was also very protective of his staff. Tea and biscuits were on so the situation was not fraught. He browsed through the papers and said, 'Is there anything that's not in here, that I should know about?'

'Like what, sir?'

THE NEW APPROACH   99

'Like any fucking thing not written down here.'

I then mentioned the manner of driving, his manner when he first stopped and that the lad was out after curfew.

'Now we're getting somewhere. You have been very fair with this prat. He is far from one of the best I've had. He has been on thin ice for a few weeks. Now he's just fallen through. He can have a Regulation 8 and he can see Their Worships afterwards.'

Regulation 8 is the clause allowing a probationer to be sacked before the completion of two years service. It's not used often but is very useful if someone is not up to scratch.

I went back to the Lane. Monty had expected that result. I lost no sleep over it.

A relic from the Area Car days still remained. Half the Pandas changed over an hour later than the bulk of the shift. At around 6.30 on a weekday morning I was sent over to the Bridge patch to search for an escaped prisoner. The little toe-rag had been locked up by Joe Public who had found him trying to hot-wire his car. In true Newtown style Joe had banjoed the kid and then dragged him up the road to Kenyon Street nick, which was an outpost of Ladywood, much as Bridge was to the Lane.

Kenyon was an old nick, by any standards. It had been condemned as unsuitable in the mid 1920s but still stood bastion to the 'C' Division boundary, less than 100 yards from the 'A' Division. Its greatest asset was the huge coal fire which dominated the front office. Some of the best toast ever had been cooked on that fire. Young son didn't like the place and escaped.

That was not very bright. He was well known to all Bobbies in the area, as were most of his family. He was a son of the Dane family. They were a family of professional, career criminals. He, though, was a bit distinctive. He had alopecia, and didn't wear a wig because he had been teased at school.

He had been chased along Constitution Hill, past the Cedar Club and into Bond Street. He turned left and was last seen in Mott Street. I parked up in Great Hampton Row, right at the end of Mott Street. I had a good view and all the time in the world. I saw movement. He of the shiny head was peeping round the cab of a drop side lorry. He was in the back and had he laid low and still he would have remained unseen. I radioed in and we closed in a bit. Ken Tyson was in a new traffic car and this had the usual public address system on it. As Ken drove up Mott Street he called over the system for Dane to give himself up. Ken would have had more success in selling a pork sandwich to the Chief Rabbi!

The Dane family did not give themselves up. Once inside they were fine to deal with, but you had to work hard with them before you got that far.

The lad jumped out the back of the lorry, scrambled over a fence and was then onto a partly built factory. He was over the scaffold, down the other side and away into Buckingham Street. I went in from the Great Hampton Row end and Ken blocked Hampton Street. Ken then did something absolutely brilliant. He sent a couple of chirps out on the two tones and then announced to everyone in earshot that the bald headed lad was an escaped prisoner.

They were building St George's School and the entire workforce were just assembling for a 7 am start. They flocked off the site and grabbed the lad. He'd already had one smack off Joe Public this morning and swiftly got a second when he kicked one of the builders. I'd dumped the Panda and we shoved Dane into the back of Ken's traffic car. This time he went to Ladywood. Everyone except Ken seemed fairly happy. Dane left dirty building site footprints on the nice clean mat in the back of the Westminster. Had he not been prone to escaping Ken would probably have got him to clean the mats before he left.

I digress a little now. Kenyon Street had always been a busy nick staff-wise. Full shifts worked from there to cover the Jewellery Quarter. The territory was mainly factories and commercial premises, again much like Bridge. Obviously the lads had their favourite hiding places and one of these caused a problem. It had obviously been the preserve of an older man for many years. Somehow one of the newcomers had stumbled upon it and taken full advantage of everything on offer! They were on different shifts. One day, on lunchtime changeover, the matter came to a head in the middle of Kenyon Street in full view of half the Cannings Chemicals workers. They had a round of fisticuffs in the street in full uniform.

The Chief did not take too kindly to reading that in the *Evening Mail*. The discipline court was set up and punishments issued. Neither stayed as police officers for long after that.

However, the mass evacuation of top grade drivers to traffic had left chronic shortages on the divisions and I was very quickly sent back to the driving school for advanced training.

The Home Office advanced driving course is probably the best of its kind in the world and is much sought after. There are many members of the public who would pay vast sums of money to undertake one. They are not available.

It is the only driving course where the National speed limit may be breached, but all other limits must be obeyed, rigidly. The course was of four weeks duration. The first two days were used to brush up the theory and the rest was on the road, much of it on the open road. We travelled thousands of

THE NEW APPROACH   101

miles all over England and Wales. I passed the course but to my personal annoyance I failed, by just one mark, to obtain the top grade.

My theory marks were the best on the course and had I received a first grade I would have been top student. Within a few days of completing the course I was to work full-time with the Vehicle Removal Team Land Rover. The team consisted generally of three men: a sergeant, who gave the orders for vehicle removal, the Rover driver and the removal driver. I had previously done this on a temporary basis but this was to be my job for the next few months at least.

The police were given powers to remove vehicles which were unlawfully parked or causing obstruction. They were then impounded and the drivers charged a fee to have the vehicle returned. We also recovered stolen vehicles for safekeeping and as a sideline we also moved broken-down vehicles to safer locations. The whole operation was actually quick, sharp and got better.

On paper an early-style Land Rover is capable of towing around two tons but on my course at the factory it had been proved that over short distances they were capable of much more. We carried a towing eye to screw into the front of Corporation buses and these were regularly moved quite some way if they broke down. Two memorable feats I achieved were on weights way in excess of expectations.

One afternoon an articulated lorry, laden with steel sheets, snapped a half-shaft as it crossed Newtown Row. Newtown Row was the main A34 north and a major arterial road into and out of the City. Within minutes we arrived and found chaos, with more to come. Nothing was moving. Once we had established the problem it was obvious that the lorry would have to be moved before it could be repaired. The gross weight was 26 tons and the sergeant and the removal driver said the Rover would not move it.

The road was dry and I said it would. We used a very thick nylon rope for heavier vehicles. I found it far more successful than a chain, in that it gave a certain amount of stretch as it took strain; kinetic energy from the rope was the secret. The rope was attached and tension taken up. With the Rover in low-ratio first I set off very slowly indeed with 26 tons moving behind. I cleared the junction and stopped to a round of applause from the stranded drivers and gasps of amazement from the crew. The little girl had moved the monster.

Some months later the team created one of the strangest road trains seen in the City. Before the inner ring road was fully completed much heavy traffic used Suffolk Street and Easy Row to traverse the City. The route was from Holloway Circus to Broad Street and was up hill and had cobble sets as a surface. The surface was very slippery in the wet and totally unsuited to modern traffic. The road dated back to the age of the horse and cart. At the top of the hill was a pedestrian crossing, which was usually manned at peak times to assist traffic flow. On this particular evening it was staffed by two females, a WPC and a Traffic Warden. Neither was a driver.

Moving very slowly up the gradient towards them was a refrigerated fish lorry, a six-wheeler. Unbeknown to them it was towing a similar lorry, which had broken down. Both were empty. Seeing a break in the traffic the Warden decided to stop the traffic and let the pedestrians across. The lorries stopped and there they remained. I arrived with the Rover but I hadn't enough power to assist. I couldn't get the necessary grip. I called on the radio for two more Land Rovers and with all three roped together, like a string of beads and the front lorry pulling as well we cleared the hill. Another reminder of how versatile the little Land Rovers were.

The next day I was rushed into hospital for an urgent and immediate appendix operation. I'd had belly ache for a couple of days and I thought it was probably due to too much social activity.

At about this time we had a dark cloud over our Land Rover drivers. In a sad and very unfortunate incident a pedestrian had been killed in a collision with our Removal Land Rover in New Street. Sad for two reasons: the victim had done it on purpose and the driver Alec Coupland was in the last few months of his service. Alec was distraught. He had never damaged a firm's car and was doing no more than 10 mph with this accident. The initial gut reaction on the division was one of real sorrow, especially for Alec. When we thought about it more it could have been any of us. I was still off sick from my appendix, or it might easily have been me.

There were often opportunities for overtime away from the Removal Team and one event, which always generated its share, was the Remembrance Day Parade in November. On that Sunday in 1968 I had been lucky enough to be selected for duty. I had always enjoyed the spectacle of the event and had taken part both in the air cadets and as a policeman. It gave me a great sense of pride to share the street with some of the brave men and women who had fought for their country over two World Wars. It was also my opportunity to pay my homage. The weather on this day was cold and crisp with a little sunshine. It was an ideal morning to be out.

When the march-past and the ceremony were over I was clear to leave, once the crowds had dispersed. As the people left I heard a voice say, 'Good morning, Mr Pettitt.' I spun around. I knew that voice. It was Claudine.

Despite me being in full uniform we hugged each other warmly for a few seconds, 'You look radiant,' I said. 'How are you?'

She said that she was well and said, 'Can you spare a few minutes?'

THE NEW APPROACH

'For you I can spare the rest of my life, let alone a few minutes.'

'There is someone I want you to meet.'

We eased out of the crowd and she walked me towards a group of men in bowler hats and Crombie overcoats; each carried a rolled umbrella. These men were officers. One broke away from the group and walked towards us. 'This is Cyril. Cyril, this is Ralph, my policeman.' Cyril wore a row of medals including the Military Cross. He was a tall, upright gentleman, probably just into his early fifties. Instinctively I saluted him, and we shook hands.

'Cyril and I married in the summer,' Claudine said.

I felt a degree of disappointment with that news but at the same time I was thrilled for her. She was far too nice to remain a widow.

'Congratulations are the order of the day then. I am so pleased for you both.'

Cyril was an absolute gentleman. He was well worthy of such a splendid wife. After a few minutes he suggested, 'You walk Claudine back to the car. I'll say my fond farewells here and join you there.'

As we walked away Claudine looked at my numbers and said, 'Still a constable, I see.'

'Yes, but I have passed the exams, and I thank you for your contribution. I'm moving round different departments for more experience.' I hadn't the heart to tell her that I had a broken marriage and a baby daughter.

'I see the shop has closed, do you work now?'

'No, only at being a wife. Madeline had the business off me and she moved it to Stratford. Doing very well she is too. I am pleased for her. I have a new hobby, flying.' She beamed at me.

'How come?'

'Cyril uses a Cessna 310 at work and I went with him sometimes and got the bug. I have just got my PPL on a 182. I fly three times a week at the moment out of Halfpenny Green.'

'Lucky girl, well done.'

We had obviously walked slowly because Cyril got back to the car almost at the same time as we did. We spent a few more minutes talking together before we shook hands and went our separate ways. What a super surprise to meet Claudine again.

At the start of the next year, 1969, I was attached to traffic patrols for training in enforcement with the vehicle. I was posted with Bob Keeling. I had worked with Bob on the 'A' division, both on foot and with the area car and we got on well. I even did my first prosecution under his guidance.

Unfortunately, Bob's Westminster had run out of miles and had been replaced with a Mini Cooper 'S'. Two of us in that, together with kit, which would not go in the boot, proved to be very crowded, and quite noisy for long periods. The firm had fitted two tone horns to everything and on traffic cars they were on the box on the roof.

The cars were very quick and would have been great as urban traffic cars if they had been reliable. They were highly tuned and could not cope with stop-start city motoring. The service had always been particular about crews being familiar with the cars they drove but the Coopers arrived and were in use before anybody had practised with them and in the early days some were quite extensively modified following impact with street furniture. They had a strange habit of going straight ahead if one was too heavy with a combination of right foot and steering.

The garage at Duke Street was a legend in itself and the garage sergeants were some of the most miserable and unhelpful individuals one could wish to meet. There was more to Duke Street than the garage though, and the comradeship was second to none. There was also intense rivalry between the motorcyclists and the car crews. The motorcyclists' attire of the day was dated in style and a little untidy; they were nicknamed the 'scruffies'. By contrast, many of the car crews were just the opposite and considered themselves almost male prima donnas.

The main sport of the traffic men at Duke Street was Tug-o-War. The activity was encouraged and Frank Parkes, an ex-'A' division man, and Jock Edgar worked very hard at promoting the teams and they enjoyed considerable success at a high level. Training was undertaken on a Sunday morning at Tally Ho! sports ground. A gantry had been built there and the teams trained by hauling an old water tank, filled with concrete blocks, up the gantry and holding it suspended for as long as possible.

Not everyone was interested in that though and Nigel Fleming was a shooter. Nigel was a traffic motorcyclist. He initially shot pistol and competed against the best in the country. He retired from that as champion and directed his attention to full-bore rifle shooting with almost as much success. To his considerable credit he once arrested a man who had discharged a shotgun at him. For that act of bravery he got a Queen's Commendation.

The Chief Inspector at the time was Don Enstone. He was in charge of the whole set-up and his pet hate was cars parked in the wrong bays (each bay was numbered) or even worse, in the central gangway during the day. At shift changeover there was no choice as the garage wasn't designed to cope with the number of vehicles that were now operating from there.

A motorcycle shift started work at 10 am and shortly after then one morning Don found a Cooper parked out of its bay and in the central gangway. Obviously he didn't check before moving it. He jumped in the driving seat, started it up, slammed it into reverse and hurtled it backwards into its bay. As he did so the passenger door flew open and smashed into the central pillar. The din was sickening and the whole door was wrecked. Suddenly there was not a motorcyclist to be seen. Don was red with rage. He had, in fact, fallen victim to a trap set for someone else, the sergeant.

One Saturday evening in the summer Bob and I were out and about using a loan car, a Vauxhall Ventura, supplied by the factory for evaluation. There was no two-way radio fitted to the car but we had the benefit of a portable. We picked up a call directing officers to what was thought to be a shooting. The 999 service was less efficient then than it is now and the call was from Smethwick and the incident was in the former Staffordshire area. The call had been received at Birmingham and relayed to Smethwick, but because of the serious nature of the incident Birmingham cars were sent as well.

When we got there an ambulance was just taking away a hysterical woman wearing only her dressing gown and slippers.

There was also a motorcyclist in attendance. He was at the front door smoking his pipe. 'Nothing we can do in there,' he said. 'Both dead.'

The story which had been related by the woman was that she had been in bed with a man when her husband came into the room armed with a shotgun. As her lover tried to get out of bed he was shot dead by the husband. The husband had then said something like, 'Watch this, bitch', put the muzzle of the gun under his chin and pulled the trigger. She had seen both her lover and her husband die before her eyes.

The aftermath was very gory and messy; what she witnessed must have been horrific. I imagine that every time in the future that she thinks about a man that incident will come flashing back to her like a bad dream.

At the end of the four months all attached crew were re-tested to ensure continued ability. It was an ideal opportunity to up-grade. My test was a personal disaster. Conditions were awful. I had used a Cooper for most of my work and I was now being tested in a Westminster. Not a driving school one though. It was one which was up on its miles and being prepared for sale. It had cross-ply tyres instead of radials and was a dreadful beast to drive. The end product was four months valuable experience but no top grade.

Before the Driver & Vehicle Licensing Centre was established at Swansea, virtually all local areas had their own Motor Taxation Office. The offices carried records of all vehicles registered in their area and also Driving Licence records of the inhabitants. The information was invaluable to the police.

As these were manual records and not on computer, access to the information was only possible during office hours. If urgent information was required it was necessary to 'turn out' somebody with the keys and obviously this was expensive.

In Birmingham the keys were entrusted to the traffic patrols and carried normally by the sergeant. Thus, the entire records were open to scrutiny, by arrangement with the sergeant.

I had a good working knowledge of the Birmingham office because I had worked in there during the Cannock Chase murders. The suspect vehicle then was an Austin/Morris Cambridge/Oxford derivative. So all the records were checked by a team of cadets and police officers and the necessary notes made. I had been in there when unfit for full duty following an ankle injury.

Because of that knowledge I was often sent with the keys to do urgent searches. One night we had a request from the police at Nuneaton to verify ownership of a vehicle in which the driver had been killed in an accident with a tree. The tax disc had been issued at Birmingham and thus they should carry the records for the car. As I wrote the number down it rang a bell with me but I didn't know from where. When I looked at the file I realised that I had recently had dealings with the driver, a West Indian. I also checked out the driving licence records and phoned Nuneaton.

The result was a request for me to verify the identity of the driver and to notify relatives of his death. We went to the house and got abuse from the female occupier. I asked whether John King lived at the address and she told me that he didn't.

'He lived here three weeks ago.'

'No. Nobody that name live here.'

'Are you Mrs King?'

'No. Nobody, that name here.'

'I think you are Mrs King. You were in a car with John King three weeks ago.'

'No.'

'Do me a favour will you?'

'I might.'

'When Mrs King comes home tell her that her husband is dead.'

'Ma husband, ma husband, him dead, where?' I gave her the information and left. I find it very hard to have sympathy with persistent liars, and that is what my twenty-five minutes on her doorstep at 4 am convinced me she was.

It was during my first attachment to traffic that I became aware that there were a number of Porsche and Mercedes cars in a police vehicle store at what was then Sheep Street. It was just round the corner from Duke Street and was used to store new vehicles prior to kitting them out for work and gutting kit from those which were due for disposal. These cars, I was told, were the subject of a very interesting enquiry being undertaken by the Regional Crime Squad and the force Stolen Vehicle Squad.

The basis of the enquiry was that information had been received that a number of cars stolen in Birmingham had found their way to an area near Düsseldorf in West Germany. The gang involved had cut their costs by returning to the UK with a vehicle stolen from West Germany, for ultimate disposal in this country.

As a result of observations carried out on the given address a man, Christopher Schirle, had been arrested. He was then thirty-three years of age, a native of Warsaw and a mechanical engineering graduate from Heidelberg University. He also held two passports, one British and one West German! He had left a much-travelled stolen car outside his flat.

When the flat was searched it was easy to connect him with a number of thefts of cars. As a result of the interview with Schirle two Porsche cars had been recovered. These were part of our cache at Sheep Street.

Schirle's German passport was the key to much of his movement as then the Immigration Authority kept records of the comings and goings of foreigners. If the number of visits to this country represented a stolen car then the case was very big indeed. This proved to be so. In one week members of the gang left the country in a Mini Cooper on Monday, returned on Wednesday in a Mercedes and left in a MGB on the Friday.

To the amazement of all the same set of number plates was used on all vehicles.

The enquiry extended to Germany, but like so much of bureaucracy, the Interpol communication system was, even if thorough, slow and a more direct approach was needed. That direct approach was probably now too late, because news of Schirle's arrest had reached his German accomplices and much had been swept under the carpet.

It is probably not a well-known fact that many of Germany's senior detectives are also legally qualified. All detectives are trained shorthand typists and all interviews are typed up at the time and a seal placed on them. The authenticity cannot then be challenged. Very useful, it must save so much time.

At this time, all crime in West Germany involving a British connection was jointly investigated by the Special Investigations Branch of the British Army and the German police. The army was able to assist the enquiry with the provision of interpreters, and a shorthand typist and a driver.

One aspect of the enquiry which worried the German police was the apparent ease with which the impossible was happening. In theory, at least, it was impossible to import a vehicle into West Germany. Only a vehicle for tourist purposes could be brought in. Each time a car is sold in Germany it is given a new number plate, which incorporates the equivalent of a tax disc.

The procedure is carried out locally and this appeared to be the weakness in this case. Before an imported vehicle could be licensed it had to be seen by a Customs Assessor. His duty was to examine the vehicle, satisfy himself as to its identity and the validity of the ownership of the person importing it. Usually the logbook was required. The Assessor was obliged then to complete an official Customs form with all those details, plus make, colour, engine and chassis numbers and current registration number. The current speedometer reading was also listed.

With this procedure complete the vehicle was then taken to another Customs officer who assessed the amount of duty payable. This done, a number plate was issued. The registration official then had to fill in a similar form to that completed by the Assessor (to verify that the same vehicle was used at both procedures). There then followed a road-worthiness test before the vehicle could be driven.

With that procedure in operation it is not surprising that there was genuine concern by the authorities at the ease with which stolen vehicles were being absorbed. It was later discovered that the Customs official who carried out the procedure in respect of many of the vehicles imported into Germany by the gang was in fact the father of the girl friend of Schirle's legitimate business partner. That partner was killed in a car crash before any prosecutions could take place in Germany.

Most of the cars leaving Britain were stolen from in and around Birmingham and on a few occasions from the car parks at Silverstone and other racetracks. Schirle was a brilliant engineer and a competent racing driver who was well known in racing circles.

The stolen vehicles were driven to a garage in Germany where they were fitted with old tyres and had the speedometers advanced. All means of identification were removed and new identities substituted. This process was so efficient that even under forensic examination the original numbers were not discernible and the new numbers were as good as originals. The vehicles were submitted for assessment in a dirty condition and thus import duty was minimal, even though the cars were but a few months old.

Once assessed the vehicles were taken back to the garage where they were cleaned and serviced. Each was converted to left hand drive and the speedometers re-adjusted. They were then presented for registration.

THE NEW APPROACH

Because the customs forms had never been completed correctly not all the vehicles were traced. Of the forty-two cars stolen in Britain only fourteen were initially found in Germany. One vehicle is known to have been sold in South Africa and another to Italy. It was as a result of a press appeal by the German police that they were found. It also helped the enquiry that many of the people who bought the cars were known to each other and good police questioning put them in touch with another buyer.

The Mercedes and Porsche cars imported to Britain had been registered and sold simply through laxity or neglect of some taxation authorities whose employees did not insist on the production of the appropriate Customs clearance documents before so readily issuing the log books.

In the meantime Schirle escaped from police custody whilst being taken between Court and prison on remand and was at large for nine days. To his credit Schirle admitted his guilt in Court and was imprisoned. All the cars recovered in Britain were returned to Germany. Technical and legal reasons prevented the return of those found in Germany.

The enquiry was assisted by members of HM Customs & Excise who in turn had their own success from it. They discovered a lucrative smuggling operation involving vehicle spare parts from Germany, involving nearly £100,000 in lost duty.

Whilst not personally involved in any part of the enquiry other than moving a few vehicles about I learnt an awful lot about the import and export of vehicles from conversations with the staff involved and talks given on refresher courses as a result of the enquiry.

The spectacle of a smart body of men and women marching is something which one either enjoys or dislikes. Personally I find it very pleasant indeed. I also found it equally enjoyable to be a part of such a body, and Birmingham City Police held two annual events where the public could witness the spectacle of their Police Force on parade.

In June of every year the Force held a large parade and inspection. It always coincided with the visit of Her Majesty's Inspector of Constabulary and was held in Cannon Hill Park. The visit by the HMI was a requirement of the Home Office to assess the efficiency of the Force. The parade was merely a public relations exercise. It must have been popular. It was always well attended. For many years the Parade Marshal was Ron Pickard, and when he was replaced by Superintendent Flannigan it lost a little of its sparkle.

In the autumn there was a Church service in St Martin's in the Bull Ring followed by a march through the City behind a military band.

The Force had a splendid male voice choir and they held an annual concert in the Town Hall, on a Saturday in October. A military band always

HMI Inspection 1968. Cannon Hill Park, Birmingham.

attended as guests and accompanied the choir. The same band would then lead the march past after the church service. I often listened to the concert knowing that next day I would march with the band.

There was also the 'official' parade route. Marches and parades usually followed the Colmore Row, Victoria Square, New Street, Corporation Street, Bull Street, Colmore Row theme. There were many reasons for this, most more sensible than historic. At weekends there was ample parking for coaches and the like in the Cornwall Street area and the Council House is in Victoria Square. If the parade involved a saluting base then where better to host the dignitaries and build a dais outside.

There was a lot more to being a Bobby than locking people up. The parades gave the public an immense feeling of well-being. To the Brums we were their own Police Force and they could come and see us in a different guise if they wished.

The late 60s finished on a very sad note for Birmingham City Police. On 1 July 1969 Prince Charles was invested as the Prince of Wales, at Caernarfon Castle. About a dozen officers from Birmingham went there as reinforcements for the local Force. Many other Forces also sent officers. None stayed in official accommodation.

Typically of the Tourist Industry, prices for accommodation for special occasions went through the roof, and most of our officers were out of pocket. Police Regulations dictated specific amounts for subsistence and lodgings. Nothing extra was available. In an effort to re-coup their losses some apparently resorted to creative accounting.

When the claims were crosschecked some were found to be bogus. Officers went to Court and were convicted. Dismissal from the service followed.

Sir Derrick Capper had to accept the situation, but vowed that it would never happen again in his Force. Any claim for expenses which exceeded guidelines would be paid, if justified. All that was needed was the receipt and a report to explain the circumstances.

I put this to the test very shortly after the decision. Two of us went up to Bolton to escort a prisoner back. The M6 link was not complete and this made Bolton a fair trip in a day. When we got to the nick up there, there was no canteen and no food locally. The area was under the control of Ruston Bucyrus demolition balls and men in hard hats. The best we could do was a Berni Inn.

A mid-range main course and a coffee put us over the official amount. I claimed and got paid the full claim. Sir Derrick had been true to his word. No doubt had the Investiture claims been made at home instead of in Wales he would have pre-dated this policy.

CHAPTER 9

Troubled Times

I WENT BACK TO BRIDGE at this time as a permanent beat officer. It had changed dramatically from the area I had worked just a few short years ago and created a totally different environment. The heart had been knocked out of the area.

When I had been here first it was drab and dingy. Everywhere was lit by gas lamps. Or nothing, if they'd blown out. It was drab and dreary then but it was a happy place. The same people were probably still about but they now lived in tower blocks and we were out of touch with them. There was no more chatting on doorsteps; that, sadly, had gone for ever.

There was grass, there were trees and lots of new houses and new people. There were still criminals to be arrested though. I had a good memory and I remembered a Mini van which I had seen parked whilst working the Land Rover. The pound was based on Bridge, hence we called at the station many times a day. I had always looked at this Mini van with a curious feeling, but never knew why and never did anything about the feeling. Recently this Mini van had been re-painted and looked pristine. It looked too good. Late one night I lifted the bonnet and obtained all the relevant numbers. These I checked with the vehicle index file at CID HQ (no computers then) and sure enough the van was stolen and running on the lad's old numbers.

Armed with the knowledge that the van was always in the same place I planned to arrest the driver when he returned home on Saturday evening. The reason for this strategy was simply to have Sunday to tidy up all the loose ends before Court on the Monday morning. Sergeant Ernie Evans agreed to assist at the arrest. The driver came home much later than expected and the vehicle had obviously been in an accident. There was damage to the front and the windscreen was missing.

The driver stopped in the usual place. When he stepped out I told him that I knew the van was stolen and I arrested him. I told him how my suspicions had been aroused but he wasn't entirely convinced. For the previous four hours he had been at Aston police station being interviewed about the accident he had been involved in. A drunken man had staggered into the path of the van and had died. He was surprised that he had not been arrested for the stolen van there, but clearly that enquiry dealt only with the accident.

112

The fact that the accident had occurred concerned me quite a bit. I had had some sort of suspicion about that van for weeks and had slowly pieced my enquiry together in the belief that it was straightforward and not urgent. The day I chose to act was the day that a man died because I had not shown enough urgency. Ernie reassured me. The accident was unforeseen and therefore an act of God. The loose ends would now extend well beyond Sunday.

The Inspector dealing with the fatal accident was very unhappy with my actions. His enquiry was complete, there was no blame on the driver for the accident and only the file for the Coroner was necessary. There were now untold complications and the criminal matters would have to be dealt with prior to the inquest. The entire accident file was transferred to me in order that I could compile the prosecution file. He would complete the Coroner's file from a copy of mine.

Tom Sommerville was the Inspector concerned and I was to have dealings with him again into the future. He had had a varied career. He was shot as a young man in 1951, and made a recovery. I had no problem with the fact that he was awarded a King's Commendation afterwards. He was however not very friendly with anyone and had collected for himself the unflattering nickname of 'The Snake'. To show his anger about this van he reported my 'neglect of duty' to Donaldson. He in turn pointed out that had a proper examination of the vehicle been conducted after the accident, either by him or his staff, the theft would have been detected at that point and my enquiry would have remained a secret. No action was taken against me.

The prosecution papers were a pleasure to prepare and at court the driver was convicted and fined heavily. Amazingly I received a commendation for my work.

Just as I was about to finish shift one morning at about 2 am I saw a lad of about nine walking along Summer Lane towards me; he was carrying a policeman's helmet. I expected him to run away, but he came to me with the helmet asking me to hand it in. Apparently his mother had asked him to take it to Bridge as 'the policeman had left it behind when Daddy came home!' Well, some things hadn't changed after all. That's refreshing. The owner of the helmet had a real good ribbing about the incident.

One evening when I had not been back at Bridge very long I was involved in a very nasty incident in which a number of police officers were assaulted, in circumstances which could have been far more serious that was actually the case.

John Seddon had called at a house in Miller Street to speak to a family about an assault, which had taken place earlier in a pub. He was invited in and the door was bolted behind him, although at this time he was unaware of that fact. John was sure that the person responsible for the assault in the pub was in the house and was allowed to search it. Whilst he was upstairs he saw the wanted man in the back garden, trying to climb over the gate.

John ran downstairs and found that the settee had been placed across the door to the stairs, locking him in the stairway. He forced his way into the downstairs room and was able to call for assistance. His radio was then taken from him and thrown into the garden. As John followed it into the garden, he was attacked, by two men, the one he had come to see and his father. There was no way out of the garden and John couldn't get back into the house.

I heard the call for assistance and got to the front door at the same time as Brian Rogers. Brian was another typical 'A' division man, tall and big. Between us we smashed the front door down, encouraged by the fact that John had now been reunited with his radio and was saying that he was being attacked in the back garden. More help arrived and other officers were able to climb into the back garden by way of some dustbins in the alley at the back. Once Brian and I had got into the house we still had our way to the garden blocked by furniture. I opened the sash window and got into the garden to give John what help and support I could as two more officers climbed over the fence. The problem with the fence was simply that it was a six-foot wooden one with about five feet of chicken wire on top of it. Eventually all attackers were subdued and arrested. John required hospital treatment for a lot of bruises and a cut lip.

There was never any doubt in our minds that it was the intention of the occupants of that house to assault John, having invited him in. Why else would they have bolted the front door and blocked his way out of the stairs? One can only fear what might have happened had John not been able to radio for help.

Early in 1970 there was a change of policy with the Removal Land Rover. The three-man crew would remain. The sergeant would be replaced by a paid acting sergeant. All the crew would be first grade drivers. The biggest advantage as far as the job was concerned was that two vehicles could be moved at once, because in the past the sergeant had not of necessity been a driver. I was to be placed in charge of the crew, subject, I was told, to an up grading from the advanced refresher course I would undertake from the following Monday.

I had a great course. There were six students, all advanced trained already with four going for an up grading. Finally, I got what I was after, Grade 1. The test had gone like a dream. I knew I'd succeeded long before Ron Cato told me. That qualification would open doors which had previously remained closed to me. I was henceforth eligible for transfer to traffic, crime squad driver, vehicle removal driver, driving instructor's course and other duties set aside from the less able. Only a grade 1 driver could drive a traffic car on his own; any other had to be accompanied by a grade 1. However, that would not be for me for some time.

I now had to make sure the new shuffle would work. The other full time member of the team would be Barry Tottle; the third member would be, where possible, a short term posting for training. My thinking behind that was simply to have a trained nucleus to fall back on. I knew Barry, I had worked with him briefly before and had found him an excellent partner, and I was looking forward to working with him. He had a reputation for being a hard drinking, hard fighting womaniser, and not much fun to work with. Barry did not suffer fools gladly. He was about sixteen years older than me; a former Royal Marine and a very experienced policeman. He had been a Crime Squad Driver for many years.

The vehicle was to be on patrol between 8 am and 6 pm Monday to Friday and from 8 am to 2 pm on Saturdays. Between 8 am and 10 am the crew would be two men only. That cover represented a fair amount of overtime for us all. That was the carrot. With it there was the stick, results. The City Centre was becoming more and more congested, much as a result of bad parking and poor loading access to premises. The pound had been refurbished and a permanent post had been created to monitor its use and function. The documentation procedure was also modified to speed its efficiency. Lastly the crew had to be efficient.

Barry went to Hendon to learn how the Metropolitan Police coped with volume. We were too slow in our removal technique. If we were going to be licensed car thieves, we had to be as quick as the unlicensed ones, and still cause no damage.

Barry came back with the answer. That was jigglers and master keys. We had a vast array of keys but each lock probably required that we tried up to sixty keys before we were in. With just seven master keys we were able to open and move the entire ranges of British Leyland, Ford and Vauxhall cars. A set of jigglers gave us almost everything else. Such was the unacceptable face of these keys being in use that they were purchased from the petty cash of the then stolen vehicle squad, for their use. Politics!

There was one man who thought it was great sport to watch us struggle with the old keys with his Rover. We had it open once but he then came out of his shop, and got dealt with without the removal of his car. We had, of course, noted the key number for the door and the one for the ignition was stamped on it. Once the door was open we could get that number as well. Sure enough he was there one afternoon, as usual, right outside his shop. Barry walked down the road, opened the door and had the car away before he was out of his shop. I drove down slowly towards the man and he said his car had just been pinched. He was a little peeved when I told him that the thief was a policeman and he had just got a bill for £6 to repatriate his car. Strangely enough he was more co-operative after that afternoon.

It was for years a standing joke with Barry about how many wives he had had and his reply was always, 'Only two of my own.' He never referred to those he had borrowed from other people and as I got to know him it became apparent that those of other men were still falling for his charms. I was into a steady routine of courting June and I often met Barry socially after work. I never knew who he would have with him. Then it all changed. He stopped going out on the town.

The morning he bought a Brownie uniform from the Guide Shop and a Cub uniform from the Scout Shop I knew Barry had finally found that which had eluded him for so many years, a family. He was courting a shortly-to-be-divorced wife of a shortly-to-be-ex-policemen. I was very happy for him. The wedding reception was one hell of a party. June's mum did the photographs, and a friendly licensee the catering. Barry is still married; that little Brownie is now a mum.

At about this time we had quite an unnerving shock. We were contentedly driving around the City Centre when the vehicle suddenly filled with smoke, or so we thought. We didn't hang about. We both jumped out as the motor rolled to a stop. I just cut the ignition and jumped out. After a few seconds there were no flames and further inspection revealed that it was not smoke but steam. The heater had split. The immediate cure at the garage was disconnection. There was no spare in stock and the next few days were quite cold in the cab.

Barry did have a short fuse though and on a couple of occasions he moved very fast to surprise me. The most notable one was when we had been sent to bring a vehicle in for safety. The driver had just been sent down the steps for forty-two days for non-payment of maintenance, much to his dismay and surprise. His van with all his tools aboard was parked in a cul-de-sac near the Courts and we were to move it to the pound until its removal from there could be arranged. It was the last one in the line on the right hand side of the road. We had the keys for it and it should have been easy. For some reason it wouldn't start so we planned to tow it. As I drove back to turn round a car was driven into the space in front of this van and locked up. Barry was sitting in the van and spoke to the car driver.

When I reversed to alongside the van I heard Barry about to explode. 'I've asked you twice to move. Now I'm telling you.'

'Fuck off,' was the reply.

Barry shouted, 'Door,' and carried the car driver to the back door of the Land Rover, threw him in the back, followed him in, slammed the door and shouted, 'GO.'

I drove quite quickly to Steelhouse Lane. Barry had used his power of arrest for wilful obstruction but I was unaware of the full circumstances.

The driver was locked in a cell and we went back to our task. Barry told me that whilst I was turning round the man he had arrested had parked in the space in front to prevent the removal of the van. Barry explained what he wanted to do, and offered the driver the space the van was in once it was available. The driver obviously didn't trust Barry because he then suggested that when he came back he would find his own car gone as well. He ignored Barry's requests for him to move his own car and Barry had lost his rag and arrested him. It seemed very fair to me. We also removed the offender's car, but that went first to be sure of the revenue. The van was only a favour so it went second.

The second occasion was even more amusing but potentially more urgent. Barry was driving the Land Rover, I was in the passenger seat, writing up some notes, and Dave Millichamp, I think, was in the back. Dave shouted, 'Behind!' or something like that and both he and Barry were gone. The Land Rover was in the middle of the road, driverless, with the doors open. I quickly moved the Rover out of the way. Dave had spotted a skirmish behind us and Barry had seen, through the mirror, a helmet on the ground. Because there were no windows in the side of the Rover I had seen precisely nothing.

When I was aware of the brawl I went to assist. A young bobby had arrested a man for fighting and his mates had jumped the officer in an effort to release him. They were just putting the boot in when Barry got them. He grabbed two and butted them into each other. They lay down and counted the stars. He then dropped the original on top of them and he and Dave took two more. I helped the officer to his feet. That is all there was left to do. Another car arrived and the conference was moved to the Lane. The men had all been together earlier in the day but had split up. There had then been two fights close together. The one who got locked up at the original fight had already come out second-best there. By chance his mates had seen him. They sorted out that fight and then went to look for their mate, only to find him being arrested. All were well battered from their brawls before they met Barry.

All the men were locked up overnight, a very effective ploy that was standard procedure then. At Court in the morning they looked a very sorry bunch, black eyes and split noses all round. They all pleaded guilty to assaulting the young officer. None had a solicitor. They elected one of them as spokesman. His mitigation was excellent. In a rich Irish voice he said, 'We're all very sorry. We got pissed and then had a fight, or was it two. When he got arrested we didn't think it was fair, 'cos he lost his fight. Suddenly a fokkin' giant give us all a good hiding, but it was a fair fight, the coppers won.'

There was much laughter in the Court from the police and the public. However, from the dock there was some dismay because they all got twenty-eight days, forthwith, and no fines.

Another very messy accident happened just behind us one afternoon when we were parked in Corporation Street. A young WPC had just exchanged greetings with us and had walked away when we were aware that there had been an accident yards away.

A woman had walked out into the traffic from between parked cars and slammed into the side of a bus. As she fell the bus ran over her causing a terrible head injury. Cath, the young WPC, had seen this happen and gone to her aid. Cath was instantly violently sick, but ignored that and did what she could for the woman, which in reality was unnecessary. She had died instantly. By the very nature of the work we were doing it was expedient that someone else should do the paperwork for this incident. It was not going to be a five minute job. Cath really didn't need to get any further involved. She had done her share at the scene. We took her back into the Lane for coffee and the shift dealt with everything else.

We were lucky to have very few mishaps with the vehicles we moved. I remember two which we damaged and caused the service some expense. One car, an early Cortina, had an ingenious anti-theft device fitted. It was also unannounced, because we didn't spot it. It was a variation from the dual control system used on driving school cars and caused the brakes to lock on once the foot pedal had been operated. I was driving the Rover and Barry steering the Cortina; we slowed down at traffic lights and when they changed I accelerated away, removing half the front of the Cortina as its brakes locked on behind me. The device had worked well. That was reports and fingers rapped.

The second occasion was a reversal of the first. We were moving a Morris 1000 van which had been stolen. Again it wouldn't start and was being towed. Barry was driving the Rover. I was on the piece of string. As we descended a hill I ran completely out of brakes and sat there with the Rover getting closer. I used the handbrake and got the van into gear before it hit the back of the Land Rover. Fortunately there was a spare wheel on the back door and that cushioned much of the impact. No hassles from that one.

Barry nearly modified the Land Rover one Saturday morning. Mini skirts were the fashion and a woman wearing one was leaning into the back of a little van. Whatever she wanted caused her to lean in further and thus bend over more. She was not wearing pants and the hairs round her honey-pot were well exposed for all to see. Barry pointed and shouted, 'Haircut.' I shouted, 'Brakes,' as the driver in front of us stopped for a better look. The woman took no notice at all.

I did make one contribution to the Rover that was not discovered for about three years. There used to be a turntable at the Lane, to make moving out of there a lot easier. It was very close to the fire escape and one day someone moved the Rover whilst we were in the station. I hadn't noticed and I gave it a good shove to spin the table round only to hear a rending of metal. I was relieved to find damage confined to the bumper, which had pulled forward around the girders of the fire escape. It was pointing forward. That was repaired without reference to official sources and was welded and painted to look as good as new. Ages later somebody at Duke Street noticed it and could find no record of a repair. That wasn't surprising as there had never been one. The truth was known only to those involved. Anyone who was asked about it said, 'It's been like that for ages.'

Barry motivated himself to sit and pass the promotion exam. His wife's former husband had failed it on previous attempts and that was why Barry so much wanted to pass. When I moved on Barry took over the team and made a splendid job of it.

Under new divisional management I was invited to join the Accident Enquiry Squad, with a special responsibility for complex and time consuming enquiries generated locally and from outside forces. I wasn't sure. I enjoyed what I was doing. I had to look towards the future though, and that was an offer of yet another type of work of which I had little experience. I remained with the Land Rover for another four months. The job I had been asked to consider was due to commence on 1 April, and I took it.

My father died a couple of days before Christmas 1969. Bill Smith was the Chief Inspector at the Lane at the time and I went to see him asking for the rest of the day off. It was a busy time and I hoped he would agree. He was brilliant. Clear off home, sort out what has to done, keep in touch and he'd see me after Christmas. I was even offered a loan of funds from the Benevolent Fund for the funeral. That was genuine staff care.

The function of the Accident Enquiry Squads was to take from the Unit officers any partly completed accident reports and to continue the enquiry to a conclusion. They were time consuming enquiries and were an unnecessary drain of resources, which could otherwise have been used on the beat. I would also undertake any enquiries from fatal accidents which had not been completed by the officer at the time, and return them to an Inspector. All other work was submitted through the sergeant.

I missed the outside work and regularly volunteered to work on Saturday night's anti-hooligan patrol or the removal Land Rover, which was now being employed to curb unlawful parking in the vicinity of nightclubs. One night on the Land Rover, with the duty inspector at my side, I spotted an MGB being driven slowly round the City Centre. From my knowledge of car numbers I assessed the number on the car to be false. To this day I remember the number; it was POP 200 D, a Birmingham combination but one which had never been issued. The two lads in it didn't seem aware of our interest and I waited my chance to stop it. Good sense dictates that vehicles should be stopped from behind, but not a stolen MG with a Land Rover behind it.

As I got alongside it in Snow Hill Ringway the driver must have lost his nerve and decided to make a run for it. I squeezed him tight and we finally stopped with the passenger door of the MG against a bus shelter and the driver's door kissing the Land Rover. The din had been enormous but there was only superficial damage to both vehicles.

The car had been stolen from Newcastle on Tyne the day before and its correct number was PUP 200 D. On that number the car could have driven round Brum with impunity. I knew nothing of Durham numbers. The lads in the car never knew how they had been detected. They were both Newcastle United supporters and had used the car to come down for a football match in London. It was only by chance that they had come to Birmingham at all.

The owner of the car was a doctor from Newcastle. I spoke to him on the phone and he got a lift down to Birmingham with the police who came to escort the lads back for Court. He was well pleased to have his car back and not bothered about the minor damage.

The damage to the Land Rover was mostly paint deposits from the MG and a very few scratches. I polished most of it out before I went home. I told Barry about the damage the following Monday and he then had a little joke with his partner. Norman Collinson was very fastidious about the old tub and he kept it immaculate, inside and out. In fact he used to get quite humpy about Barry and me having our lunch in it. He had apparently collected it from the garage that morning and had been the only driver. Barry looked at the damage, shrugged his shoulders, smiled and went to wind Norman up. He succeeded. For about a quarter of an hour Norman flitted to and fro, clucking like an old hen around her chicks.

Try as he would he could find nobody who knew anything about it and in desperation he came to the AES to check on weekend accidents, just in case. Yes I knew about the Rover having a bump, I'd done it. It was recorded in the Logbook, and really he should have checked that before using the Rover. Barry knew all about it, anyway. The look that came over Norman's face said it all, but he was too polite to swear. He walked off shaking his head and muttering something about 'childish'.

A couple of weeks later I was in the same Land Rover doing the same job. This time I was alone. I had just dropped the crew off with a prisoner and was on my way to pick up a key-holder, who wasn't duty man so hadn't got his car. In front of me was an Austin 1100.

The number flashed up in my mind but why? We stopped at traffic lights and I had a quick rummage through the papers on the seat; there it was, non-stop accident in the evening and circulated. I'd read it on the board when we sorted out the Rover. As a 'just in case' I called up on the Force radio and then moved off to stop him clear of the lights. He didn't want to stop. He went off like a bat out of hell along Constitution Hill and out towards Hockley. Sod him! A single crewed Land Rover was not much use with a chase but I could keep him in sight whilst I shouted for help.

Help came in the form of a small traffic jam and I got out of the Rover, opened his door and grabbed his keys. I had once before been dragged up the road, albeit slowly, and it wasn't a nice experience so it was now keys out first. This man was obviously drunk and I expected problems until I could get some help. I was right. As I went back to the Rover, with his keys, to update the Room he drove off with a second set of keys.

Back in the Rover, foot down, this time two-tones and blue lights on. If I needed help then Joe Public might as well hear about it. Left into Key Hill, left into Icknield Street, under the bridge then right, Pitsford Street, a dim dark road with no residents. Not ideal. He slowed down to about 20 mph. I could do him easy but was it safe to stop him? I got alongside and didn't like it. Neither did he; he shot off backwards, tried a handbrake turn, got it all wrong and came back at me. This time I would stop him. I was now broadside on across the road and he couldn't get behind me!

He obviously didn't want a Land Rover in the driver's door because he stopped. I moved forward across his bows. His only way out now was backwards, and he had messed that up last time. I picked up the radio handset and indicated to him that I was using it. There was a car on its way to me. Good, things were looking up. I was very wary of getting out; I much preferred safe cat and mouse. When the car came it was, in fact, two, one from each end of the street. A Panda came from one way and a traffic car the other. He leapt out and started to run away from the one behind him. He probably thought that we had blocked the road and that the car couldn't get past. As he ran past me I backed off and the Panda had loads of room through. He was now between the traffic car and the Panda and on foot. He was going to stay on foot. I upped his bonnet and pulled a few plug leads off.

Breath test was refused so it was in custody for court on Monday. Fined, banned, job done, or so I thought. The next Sunday I saw him driving the same car on Soho Road, Handsworth. He hadn't seen me. That was enough. Into a phone box and three nines. Inside twenty minutes we were both in Thornhill Road, me on foot, and him in a Traffic car. The next day he got three months. I was going to Thornhill to get June's car to take my mother out.

My first serious enquiry with the new squad concerned a fatal accident where the second car had at first stopped, but had left the scene before the police arrived. The dead driver had driven through a red traffic light into the path of a car going through on green. They had crashed at about the middle of the junction. There was one witness who was waiting at the red light, facing the opposite way to the one involved. Whilst he had gone to phone the other car had vanished. At 3 o'clock in the morning there was not much passing traffic. He thought it was a black A55 or similar.

I first went to the site to familiarise myself with it, and got an up-to-date plan from the cartographer. Then I begged a car and had a ride round. Within ten minutes I had found the vehicle, neatly abandoned in a line of others. They were all bangers and I hope that is the only reason it was not found during the night. The fact it was on the D Division probably meant that their iron curtain had gone back up.

With the car to hand I had it removed to the pound and went through it. I knew that the current listed owner had sold it and a name and address was shortly forthcoming, but it had been sold on from then. The boot was full of working clothes and, sure enough a pay slip. I was looking for a building site worker. I had his name, I had his National Insurance number, but I didn't know what he looked like. He had never been in trouble and I had no photograph. Another interesting point was that the widow of the dead man had no idea why he was where he was at that time of the morning. He should have been at work in a nightclub, miles from there.

The media, I thought, will run this. I sought approval for an appeal for witnesses and got it approved. Then I drafted what I wanted said. In effect I wanted a building site worker who had taken a flat in the last few days, and who was called Peter and had a black Austin A55. I also wanted to know anyone who had seen the dead man in the hours before the accident. That bit was questioned but I explained to the boss that not all married men always told their wives the whole truth. Perhaps he was not working at a nightclub, perhaps he was entertaining at one, and I didn't mean on the stage.

Within twenty-four hours I had got a response. I had got an address for Peter. The landlady had phoned. He had been out late on the night of the accident and had come home without the car. He had told her that it had been stolen. I had also spoken to a girl friend. She was distraught.

I found Peter at home that morning. It was his car and he was in it at the time. He was well drunk then, and his mate had been driving. His mate was banned, but he was sober. He had driven away and dumped the car. They took a taxi home, but he had spewed up in it and the driver had kicked them out. It was a black cab so it should be easy to find. His mate had apparently gone into hiding but Peter would try and prise him out. We found the taxi and the driver gave us a good description of the two lads. One was obviously Peter and the description of the other agreed with how Peter had described him. The witness, to some degree, described the driver and I was certain that Peter was truthful.

The girl friend was a real good-looker. She was also very upset. She was seen, in the comfort of her own home, by Sue Gunner. Sue was working with the squad in her own right. The girl had known the dead man for two years and they enjoyed a very intense affair over that time. He had never worked in a nightclub, but it was excellent cover for the affair. When the dead man had left her home, twenty or so minutes before his death, he was on a high. They had wined, dined and made love. He had decided to leave his wife and marry his mistress. They had celebrated that decision earlier. Yes, he had been drinking but no more than usual and he had seemed quite able to drive.

The woman never attended the inquest but her statement was read to the coroner. She, at least, was spared that ordeal.

Armed with her statement I was fairly sure that the dead man was so elated with the events of the evening that he had suffered a momentary loss of concentration as he approached the traffic lights, or more probably that he had simply fallen asleep. I would never know for sure.

Peter had promised to contact his mate. I still hadn't got a name other than David and that wasn't a lot to go on. A few days later I had a phone call from David. He wanted to give himself up, to me, alone. Not totally what I would have wished but at least it was a start. We agreed a place, a park bench in Highgate Park at the back of the Rowton House men's hostel. I guessed then that that was where David was living.

By the very nature of that establishment the police were well known there and the staff were fairly helpful and more importantly discreet. I knew an officer who had an excellent working knowledge of their registration system and at my request he came back to me with two possible men who had recently booked in. I was able to check them out and only one of those was a banned driver. Hopefully he was my man, David Richardson.

I kept my appointment at the park and I was indeed joined by David Richardson. He was very much as described, gangling, scruffy and with a shock of very ginger hair. He was genuinely sorry about the accident, it had not been his fault, other than that he should not have been there; the car had come through on red. I agreed. He had got out and found the other driver half out of his wrecked car, obviously dead. There was nothing he could do for the man so in his own words he had 'fucked off, quick' before the police came. The rest we knew.

David could not be arrested, I had no power, but he accompanied me to Bradford Street police station and the formalities were dealt with there. I got summonses issued very quickly and the sad business went to Court. Both men were fined and the papers filed away. The events surrounding the accident and the subsequent enquiry convinced me that the concept of the newly created post was a correct one.

I remained in that post for sixteen months.

The City generally enjoyed good results in the promotion examinations. In November 1970 290 Birmingham candidates sat the papers and of those 69 passed (24 per cent). That might not sound high but it compared well with other forces in the region: Thames Valley 14 per cent; West Mercia 19 per cent; West Midlands 15 per cent; and Warwickshire & Coventry 12 per cent.

When the Unit Beat system had been in operation for three full years a working party was set up to identify the benefits, or otherwise, of the new method of policing. The findings proved interesting to us all. After all we were involved with it, warts and all.

The first fact which came to note was statistical. In 1960 the City had a strength of 1,882 officers. Allowing for leave days this meant that in a twenty-four hour period no more than 1,478 officers were available.

In 1970 the strength of the force was 2,528. There had been an increase in the number of leave days permitted and the new figure left 1,828 officers available for duty during the day. In ten years that made a net gain of available strength of 350.

That sounds a lot until workloads were taken into account. The table below gives an indication.

	999 calls Per day	Crimes reported Per day	Violent Crime Per day
1960	81	62	2.5
1970	202	126	4.8

Any boss in industry would be pleased to note that with a modest increase in staff of 350 that production had more than doubled. Unfortunately it wasn't as easy as that. Crime was on the increase. The daily workload on the service was on the increase and would probably not lessen into the future. The manpower shortages caused by poor pay only manifested the problem.

The major recommendations of the working party were only really a re-run of the original concept of Unit Policing. The system was here to stay until it could be improved upon. Minor adjustments could be made to the selection of the Resident Beat Officer. It should not be a post for probationers but should be treated as a specialist job. The Pandas should be double-manned, where possible. It should be introduced immediately, at least with one vehicle, in areas of violence. There should be a better integration of women officers and CID into the system. Finally the Specials should be used as observers on the Pandas when a regular officer was not available. That was to be the way forward.

At the start of the 1970s police pay was very low compared with virtually every other trade or profession. The service does not have a trade union and the Police Federation was having a major battle with Whitehall to improve pay and conditions. The plea was falling on deaf ears. Many officers were frustrated by the lack of urgency shown by the Government. A number of meetings had been held around the country by the Federation to keep the members informed of negotiations. One such meeting was held in Birmingham in the autumn of 1970. The meeting was opened by Sir Derrick Capper, and he quoted from an American magazine the following:

> What is it, after all, that we ask a Policeman to be?
> We ask that he be swift in doing his duty, but not so swift as to become hasty.
> We ask that he be forceful in exercising his vested responsibility, but not so forceful as to become oppressive.
> We ask that he be calm regardless of the circumstances that surround him, but he must not be passive to them.

We ask that he be bold but never brash; fearless but not foolhardy; dauntless but not reckless;

He must be resolute, but he must not be stubborn.

He must be self-assured, but not so much as he becomes arrogant.

He must be dispassionate, but not distant; impartial but not impersonal; sympathetic but not gullible; thoughtful, but not uncertain.

He must be compassionate, but he must not become emotionally involved.

He must be friendly, but he may have no friend to put before his duty.

He must be virtuous, but not self-righteous.

He must accept violence as the everyday order of things, but he must not be violent himself.

He must deal with humanity at its ebb, in its poorest moments, but he must not become calloused or embittered by it.

We ask that he be all things to all people: protector, servant, guardian and mediator.

Meeting these expectations sometimes calls for the supreme sacrifice.

Sir Derrick then told the Federation to take that to the Government and ask, 'How much is a man like that worth?'

He had right to be concerned. In that year 110 officers had resigned from the City.

Within a few weeks of that meeting the breakthrough came and the service, nationally, received a pay increase of around 23 per cent, across the board.

Towards the end of 1970 the then Special Patrol Group flooded areas of the City with officers in an effort to combat crime and also to reinforce the depleted manpower on divisions. It was a variation of an exercise known as 'Capper's Commandos', which was saturation policing. On 29 November they were involved in one of the most publicised events of the time. It was the capture of four illegal immigrants, and the arrest of some of the conspirators.

It all started so simply. A routine road check was being carried out in Coventry Road, Small Heath, without much success when the team stopped a Dutch registered Volkswagen pick-up being driven by a Dutchman. The officers thought it unusual that he was accompanied by two Pakistani men in the cab. Being unhappy with explanations given by all concerned, officers decided to check the internal luggage compartment and found two more cold Pakistani men.

All were arrested and it became apparent that there had got to be a rendezvous point in the City and enquiries were made to locate it. This was found to be a corner shop in Alum Rock and it was raided later that night. An intelligent piece of action by John Seddon in using broken English when he knocked at the door had been the key. It was dark and it is assumed that the Pakistani occupant believed that he was speaking to the Dutch man. He opened the door and had no escape.

The arrival of the immigrants in the pick-up had been made possible by a sea journey from the Continent aboard the MV *Maren C*, a freighter crewed by Germans, and moored at this time in the Thames at Battersea. The ship was impounded immediately and the crew detained for questioning. Two were later charged.

The case was dealt with at Nottingham Assizes in April 1971 and terms of imprisonment imposed. The four immigrants were repatriated, probably wiser and poorer for their experience. It will never be known how many other immigrants had reached our shores by that method. What was sure was that the route had been cut.

The value of the services of an underwater search team should never be underestimated in relation to the detection of crime. The City force did not have such a team in their own right but they had the next best thing. They were the Warley Underwater Diving Club. The club was founded in 1967 by Arthur Smith. Arthur was a businessman and a special constable. He had learned to dive whilst in the Royal Navy and it was a hobby of which he was passionately fond.

Because of Arthur's connections with the Police Service the club had as members a number of special constables and members of the regular Force. From early beginnings in the swimming baths the club, with a lot of help from its members, gradually purchased more equipment and extended from the swimming baths to lakes and the open sea, depending on the skill of the individuals involved.

June and I became seriously involved in the sport in 1968. It was the one thing we could do together without fear of recrimination from the Service. Married men were not encouraged to have girl friends, not even when separated.

The services of the club were often called on by police forces and June must have been one of the few policewomen in the country to have taken part in an underwater search.

June and I had set a wedding date for 24 April 1971. She by now was working from Thornhill Road, Handsworth and was well established in her career. She had passed the promotion exams and was certain to be promoted within a year. We had sorted out all our finances. We could afford our own home in the near future, and in the meantime we had been allocated a police property in the grounds of the training centre, at Tally Ho! Ideal. We also bought a new car, a first for either of us. That was in the February.

Diving. L-R: SC Arthur Smith, Harold Moss, SC Bob Cottrell, PC Graham Harbidge, PC Ralph Pettitt, John Hopcroft, DC Syd Hobson.

One afternoon in March, June and I met in Birmingham City Centre to finalise details about some furniture. The weather had been wet and I would travel home with her, leaving my motorcycle at work. The weather brightened up and I decided to ride home. That decision may well be one of the luckiest I have ever made. As June drove along Soho Road, Handsworth, slowly in heavy traffic, she was involved in a serious accident. A lorry, towing a tar boiler, stopped abruptly and the towing pin sheared. The boiler, all 5 tons of it, veered into the opposing traffic and smashed into June's car. The car overturned 2½ times, across the footpath and smashed into a shop window.

The impact destroyed 180 square feet of plate glass, which showered down as the car rolled back another complete turn to finish on its roof. The traffic jam as I followed June's journey was almost impossible. I blessed the motorcycle for its usefulness; I was making good progress, but nothing else was moving. I little knew then what had caused the traffic congestion.

As I neared the scene I recognised our car only by its number. It was totally wrecked and on its roof. I feared for June. I knew the two policemen

Diving. Courtesy of Oz 1970.

dealing with the mess. Bob Jones, my partner from plain clothes, was the local beat sergeant and the late Len Whitcombe was the traffic officer. Both assured me that June was reasonably all right. She was conscious; despite the glass being out of the car and the windows, she was not cut; she had some sort of leg injury. I was now on the other end of my own job.

Len was kindness itself. I had worked with him on the 'A' Division, where his sense of humour had kept many of us amused on dark and cold nights, and again during my brief spell with traffic patrols. He organised the safe

The tar boiler hit June's car. (With credit to the Birmingham Post & Mail Ltd.)

removal of the car. He collected me from home and took me to the hospital; he made sure that everything was done right. That was Len, always. He died very suddenly just after retirement.

June had broken her pelvis. The trailer had smashed into the driver's door and had in turn hit her. The A frame of the trailer had fortunately lessened the impact, which had been confined to the lower part of the door. If the trailer had hit the car higher up it would have crushed it; as it was it had flipped it aside, like a puppy hitting a ball. The rollover had saved her life. The motorcycle journey had probably saved mine.

June was transferred to a recovery hospital, the Forelands at Bromsgrove. She was confined to bed for six weeks, under traction, and was off work for about five months. She was out of hospital two days before our wedding, on two sticks, but out. My stag party went ahead, jointly with three other mates who were getting married on the same day. The Midland Red Club in Digbeth was the venue and from what I remember of it, it was a good 'do'. The wedding went OK and her father walked her up the aisle, I walked her back. The sticks helped her round the reception. We had a honeymoon in Spain with 140 policemen and their families. Our travel club had chartered a complete aircraft and we filled every seat. It was indeed a different holiday.

Tally Ho! offered the best sports and social facilities in the City with grass pitches for soccer, rugby and hockey. There was an excellent cricket square, tennis courts and two top-flight bowling greens. There was also a bar and a ballroom. The Training Centre was modern and very efficient. It had excellent lecture facilities and a conference suite.

The cadet year seemed to rotate around the academic one and towards the end of the 'year' the cadets always had an end of year disco. It was always well attended, and properly supervised on the booze side, like they weren't served any. The first summer we were there the disco happened the same day as both bowls and tennis. Superintendent Jack Barnes lived in the same block of flats as us. He was a good neighbour but a bit of a worry-gut. He also played bowls, big time, to the point you would think he owned the greens. Jack and his wife left at about the same time as us, closing time. We would probably have all walked back together but Jack noticed a huddled heap on the edge of the bowling green. Jack stopped and said something and the good lady carried on alone.

I knew what Jack had seen but he didn't. What he thought was a coat somebody had left behind was in fact two cadets in number one sexual position working up a head of steam.

Jack stuttered, 'They're, they're, they're on the bowling green.'

I smiled and said, 'Don't worry, boss, they won't be there much longer.'

Here was a senior police officer worrying about a bowling green when we had two teenagers, entrusted to our care by their parents and who were being supervised at a disco in police premises, in coitus on police property. That's the stuff of lawsuits, and he was worried about his bowling green! On the way back I stopped at the ballroom door and spoke to their PT Instructor. I knew he would deal with the problem without worrying about it. It would probably be Coitus Interruptus!

Dave Millichamp had been a crew member on the Land Rover on a temporary basis and we were both Grade 1 drivers. In the summer of 1971 there were two jobs up for grabs: Crime Squad Driver and Traffic Patrols. The division had an option on both posts. Dave was offered first choice and he chose the Crime Squad job, to start in July. Both were likely to be permanent and he had got his first choice. That was fine by me.

In August, I was offered a six-month attachment to Traffic Patrols. This was not like the four month one I had done previously. This was for real. After a satisfactory six months I would join the permanent staff of this elite team. I was thrilled and accepted the offer at once. It was the one job, above all others, that I wanted to do. I know that Dave's decision was a correct one for him. He is now a Detective Superintendent.

CHAPTER 10

Traffic Patrols

WHEN I WENT BACK TO Duke Street, it was really like going back home. The Land Rover had been kept at Duke Street and I knew many of the men working there. Since I had last worked there, though, the M6 link had been completed through the north eastern side of the City and more officers had been transferred to the Motorway team. Hence there were some new faces.

There was also a responsibility to back up Motorway crews in the event of a major incident. I was fortunate that I had a good knowledge of the theory, at least, of current Motorway policing. When the M6 link was completed it encompassed the notorious so-called Spaghetti Junction, the link with the A38 and the A38 (M). Because of the complexity of the junction and the network all emergency services held familiarisation exercises prior to the roads being opened to the public, and the police also had lectures and talks from officers from other forces who had complex motorway networks. The motorway was policed by a regional team known as the Mid-Links Motorway Group, or simply as Mid-Links. They were equipped with the newly released Range Rover for accident work and the sleek Jaguar 4.2 litre, XJ6 for enforcement.

Duke Street was allocated a fleet of Austin 1800 S saloons. The Coopers and the Westminsters had long gone into retirement.

Alec Black had been a legend at traffic. He had just retired when I went back and I had fond memories of him, right back to area car days. Very shortly after he finished he took a job with an insurance company as a vehicle loss adjuster, a job he was well able to fulfil to advantage. It is said that old habits die hard and Alec regularly had his lunch at the Duke, across the road from the garage. He was in there one lunch time when I had just finished work. The pub was more crowded than usual and this we attributed to a new intake of students at the college, in the womb of whose campus we had latterly found ourselves.

It was obvious by our dress that at least some of the customers were from the police garage and one particular group decided to fling a few insults out about the police and us in particular. Alec was a man of few words and great strength and when one of them said something like, 'I don't think I'm going to like sharing my pub with policemen,' Alec reacted rather strongly. He dragged two of them into the street and they protested loudly, 'We will complain about you. We can, you know.'

Alec said, 'Two things, drink somewhere else and tell your mummy you've been thrown out of a pub by a pensioner.'

Nothing more was ever heard about that incident.

My new partner was to be Jack Manifold. Jack was an unassuming man, then in his early forties. His specialist subject was braking systems. He was also a very fine, experienced driver. All the officers on traffic tried to have one specialist field, and that was his. Mine was later basic suspension systems.

Under the Unit Team system Jack's allocated Division was the 'F', which for traffic purposes was the wedge of the City which fell between the A41 Warwick Road and the A441 Pershore Road, a good and varied chunk of the City. Ironically it was the same area that I had had with Bob Keeling. Bob was still there but I was now posted to a different shift.

June was soon to go onto the same shift on the other end of the radio. She was making good progress and was probably fit to go back to her old job, but it was decided that she should, at least for the time being, have a desk job. The old Information Room was no longer adequate for its task and a new, computer assisted, Control Room was soon to be completed. There would be a need there for more staff anyway. She went to work in the old Information Room in Newton Street and transferred to the new Control Room later.

Jack was good to work with and his enthusiasm for his duty was a tonic. Our work-rate was one of the best at the garage. Very early on we received a commendation together for the arrest of two burglars. A storeroom on Frankley Motorway Services was broken into and the offenders had been seen to leave in a very distinctive Mini, white with black boot and bonnet. Part of the number was probably 13. When the description of the car was given over the radio it rang bells. We had seen, regularly, a car like that, but where? City Centre? Possibly, give it a try.

All my service there had been a mobile kitchen in the vicinity of the all night buses and at this time it was in Colmore Row. It was like a magnet to car poseurs. It was also a magnet to police cars because there were by now no canteens at night. No one bothered when a police car drew up. We had a drive round what the senior officers called the parade and march route. The constables called it the crumpet run, because of the large numbers of women around during office lunch times. When we came back, sure enough, there was our Mini, but was it the one we wanted? There was certainly a 13 in the number. I had a walk to the kitchen and looked into the Mini and saw two lads in it; there were also toolboxes on the back seat and that is what had been stolen.

We gave it a try and the lads were arrested. They were the ones. They were initially taken to the Lane and then we transferred them to Halesowen to be dealt with. The Mini went along as well. The Superintendent there was so pleased with the result that he sent a letter of thanks to Sir Derrick Capper and he in turn gave us a commendation for our 'alert and prompt action'. That was a very nice start for the new team.

We had more than our share of bad accidents to deal with and having come from the AES I made a point of being as thorough as possible. I did not like the attitude of 'leave it to the AES'. The AES was formed to enquire further into an event which had already been reported upon, not to elicit information that was available at the time. I was pleased that not once did a divisional AES complain about lack of detail from one of our reports. The main roads through our segment of the City were fast and there was quite a lot of speeding, despite enforcement. The speed reflected in the severity of the accidents, particularly at night.

I remember one very sad situation, not related to speed but to wind. In the early hours of the morning a brand new Reliant three-wheeler had been blown onto its side and the driver killed. The Reliant was of fibre-glass construction and was known as the 'plastic pig'. (I drove one once whilst on the removal team and I must confess to not liking it.) This car had been driven quite normally until the accident. When on its side it had slid across the road and the driver had struck his head on the kerb as the car came to a stop. He died at the scene.

When Jack's car was due for replacement we were quite chuffed to find that we had been allocated a new Triumph 2500 PI. That was what I called a police car. It looked the part as well. It was the first one in the City to have the red stripe along the side. The vehicle was 'up market' to what we were used to and had adjustable back rests and steering column. The fuel tank held a sensible amount of fuel and did a full shift on less than a tank full of petrol. It was comfortable and very safe. I did a private survey later to prove that. Where possible a car was allocated to one man on each of the four shifts. It helped to work like that because you got to know not only the car well, but its kit as well.

The fact that the car was the first in the City with the red stripe was not in itself particularly useful, especially when shift inspectors on divisions had not been aware of the changes. We were chased at high speed one night by two inspectors from adjoining sub-divisions, in the same semi-automatic Austin 1100. We were on our way to an accident and their intervention was not helpful to our cause. The two men should not have been together. The car was unmarked and unsuited to high-speed work. The driver was not trained for fast driving. However, it was us who were at fault! He verified by radio that we were permitted to be where we were before he allowed us to continue. They said they didn't know that their division had had twenty-four hour traffic car cover since 1967. I did not forget that incident in a hurry. The incompetent prats . . .

I was to have more than one brush with those men in the years to come.

One Saturday evening we were just about to go 'off air' to do a quick documentation enquiry when we heard a call on the radio for observations on a particular vehicle which was being driven by a man thought to be drunk. It could well be coming our way so we abandoned the enquiry for the moment. Within minutes there was another call that the same vehicle had scooped up a pedestrian and that he was still under the car as it drove away. We were now less than half a mile away.

It was stopped before it got to us so we went anyway. The driver was obviously 'out of his tree' and was immediately arrested. Suddenly there was a change of plan. This driver was to go into Steelhouse Lane. Do not take him to any 'B' division station. Strange! But more would soon be revealed.

The body of the pedestrian had been recovered about half a mile from the scene of the impact. That was not good news. This might now be a murder enquiry. We stayed with the car until the photographer had 'snapped' it and then I took it into a dry store for Forensic. It was a weird feeling driving a car which had been involved in such a macabre incident just an hour before. It was not a feeling I enjoyed.

The full circumstances of this evening then started to emerge. The driver had already been stopped by a traffic car and had given a positive breath test at the roadside. He had been taken into Longbridge police station. Here he gave an apparently negative one. He was obviously drunk so a more complicated procedure should have followed. For reasons I never knew he was then kicked out, and drove away. That was when the traffic man put out his call for observations. Knowing the traffic man I can understand his frustration.

To put not too fine a point on it someone had dropped a bollock. It seemed at the time that either the equipment at Longbridge was duff or it was used incorrectly. At that point, had it been me I would have disabled his car, even if I had later had to justify it. Years on I thought about it and still think I would have doctored the car or binned his keys. I had done that, ages before, but in totally different circumstances.

Christmas Eve 1965, I had seen a car park itself in the middle of a traffic island. I was off duty, it was late at night. I had not had a drink and was the way home. This bloke was legless. I took his keys off him and chucked them over a garden hedge. At least he wouldn't hurt himself or anyone else, even if he found it a bit cold to sleep there.

Once my six months was completed I formally transferred to the traffic department and gave my 'A' division numbers back. The end of a era. I was now on the 'R' Division.

I was allocated a new Austin 1800 S from a batch of six. It was the worst car from the batch and it spent more time off the road than any of the others. It must have been assembled on two consecutive Friday afternoons. The gearbox on it was never right and it was always a bit of a lottery as to which one you would find after a change. The other cars were fine. Mine never reached its operational target mileage and was sold alongside its brothers in due course. It had reached the age of five when I found it in a scrap yard in Small Heath. There were 5,000 more miles on it than when it was sold. It never reached 50,000.

However, when it was running it was quite quick and I had a few high speed runs with it in the pursuit of stolen vehicles (we were allowed to chase them then) and also whilst escorting ambulances. It also received body modifications, one as a direct result of the gearbox problems.

I remained Jack's partner on the division. We both usually had observers from the attached pool, but if we were without a partner we would work together. It was Jack who had the first bump in that car.

I had found a Ford Escort van parked on wasteland in the Warstock area. It was on an impossible number, but as I had an appointment I left it alone. When I came back it had gone. A few days later it was parked in a different place, but in the same area. We decided to set up a small operation to catch someone with it. On a Saturday morning I went out for a sortie in an unmarked car and found it again parked in the locality. It was obviously being used furtively. The plan was that I would keep watch on the van, and Jack would be a few streets away, in the traffic car and in a position to stop it, should it drive away. We had arranged with the Information Room to have 'talk through' on the radio as soon as we had action. Other vehicles could then also monitor our work.

Shortly before noon a man came to the van, jumped in and drove off towards Jack. I followed at a distance. The driver must have spotted Jack parked on a garage forecourt because he drove twice round an island, so I had to pull in. We asked for 'talk through' but an ambulance escort was using the spare channel so there was no facility for us. I eventually caught up with the van and when I saw Jack in the mirror I started to overtake the van, in order to make that the meat in the sandwich. The van driver must then have realised that mine was a police car and he braked and went into reverse. He rammed the front of Jack's car as Jack did his best to avoid him. I handbrake turned and faced the van as it rammed Jack for a second time. The driver then ran off, through a garden, over a fence and along the canal towpath, never to be seen again.

The van had been wrecked in an obvious attempt to disable the traffic car. That in turn was well dented to the front but still able to be driven. Jack was unhurt, but angry. He had been unable to select reverse to protect the vehicle from the second ramming.

The van was never reported stolen, or if it was the chassis number had not been recorded. We had a van on false plates for no reason. It was speculated that it had been got ready for use in crime, or terrorism; it had been cleaned of all fingerprints and was empty except for a scrap (now, anyway) television. We never knew the answers about that van. It went into history as another vehicle abandoned at the scene of an accident. That was all we had at the end of the day.

The second crunch was mine on a dull, wet, Saturday afternoon in January. I had spent all afternoon at the Social Club at Tally Ho! assisting at the Christmas party which we ran every year for the Spastics Society. The car was there to give the more able children a drive around the grounds. I left at about 5.30 and headed into City along Pershore Road. Coming the opposite way was a Austin 1300 GT without lights, I flashed my lights to remind the driver and he ignored me. I decided to turn round and follow him. As I turned round the car sped away, still without lights.

I called up on the radio and set off after him. As we neared the traffic lights at Priory Road they were showing red. There were already three lanes of traffic waiting. Traffic was heavy; Birmingham City had been playing at home and the traffic from there had joined the shopping traffic. The 1300 then went onto the nearside footpath and carried on as though this was normal. I put the blue light and two-tone horns on and as the traffic moved forward it parted like magic. The 1300 continued out of City travelling at about 80 mph, still without lights.

It was of no comfort to either of us that June was on the other end of the radio listening to the chase. She had the benefit of a commentary from other cars, which I did not have. She was also aware that I had probably dropped my handset, because there was no communication from me but I could hear my set. I understand that she was on the edge of her seat when she heard the commentary from the vehicle behind me. The speed we were doing was apparent by the distances we were covering in the time.

Word of the chase had spread and near to Dog Pool Lane a Panda driver had stopped both lots of traffic on the straight road and had created a chicane. The 1300 slowed a little but weaved through. As the driver struggled to keep in control he smashed into the nearside kerb. I drove through a cloud of sparks and debris, and some of it hit my car. The two-tones went dead, except for a panting noise. A hub cap had hit the roof box. By now I had all my lights on full and I was right behind him. Suddenly, at around 60 mph the driver hurled the car into the junction on the left. Dog Pool Lane. I knew that this junction was an acute angle back and I slowed very quickly. The 1300 lifted the rear inside wheel, and then both left hand wheels came off the road.

It bounced off a grit bin and stayed upright. It was now getting very hairy and I considered calling it off. However, now I had dropped my radio handset on the floor and radio contact was no more. (The safety of single-manned cars was a hot potato.) That brush with the grit bin slowed the driver down and he took another sharp left very shortly afterwards. He then used full acceleration and veered left into a parking space. Without lights he had not seen a parked motorcycle under a sheet. That finished up under the car as it stopped. As I screeched to a halt beside it, the driver opened his door, and I took it off with the traffic car. I struggled to get the driver out of the car by way of the passenger door and then he tried to escape.

The commotion had brought out a number of the neighbours and one of them punched the lad with a pugilistic special. The lad went quiet for some time, even after he came round.

The car was, again, on false plates. The driver worked at a car sales site and had a duplicate key made for the car which was one his now ex-employer had on sale. It had vanished a few nights before from the site.

At Court afterwards the lad was fined heavily and banned from driving for a year. I was very proud to have been commended, by the Magistrates, in open Court, for my action.

Within six weeks, and before his eighteenth birthday the boy died when a stolen car he was driving crashed in a ball of fire after it had been driven over a very steep hump-backed bridge, at high speed. The car bottomed as it landed and ruptured the petrol tank. Sparks from the impact ignited the petrol and the car exploded.

At the time the car was being followed by a traffic car. I knew the officer well and he was very shocked by what he had seen, and lucky not to have been involved himself.

My second attempt to modify that car also led me to my first personal confrontation with Tom Sommerville, the Inspector who had complained about my actions with a stolen van years before. I was on patrol, single-manned again, in the City Centre when I was called on the radio as 'Traffic car, Carrs Lane.' I replied with the call sign and was told that the blue Austin van I had just waved at was following a Ford Capri which had just been stolen. The van was from the 'B' division and was the observation vehicle, used by their Vehicle Theft team. The crew had seen the Capri get stolen by two men. They were following it until it could be stopped by another officer.

I set off after them and I caught up with both vehicles as they waited at traffic lights on Newtown Row at New John Street. When the lights changed I went away like a rocket and went to the right of a very short section of dual carriageway, then pulled back in front of the Capri which swerved onto the grass on the left, hit the side of the traffic car, bounced off and sank in the mud. It had very little momentum and stopped abruptly after bouncing into the side of my car. That was the first time that driver realised there was a police car near him. They were so surprised that neither of them tried to run off.

The damage to both cars was very slight, but all accidents involving police cars had to be dealt with by, in those days, an Inspector. 'The Snake' arrived, and demanded that I took a breath test. I had no objections. I hadn't had a drink for about three days. Then he couldn't find a kit. I didn't volunteer mine. He then found some skid marks on the road, which had clearly been left by a heavy commercial tyre, and associated them with my car. I measured them for him, I then measured the width of my tyre. Try again. I would be reported for ignoring the traffic signal. The man had no idea what had taken place, and he didn't bother to find out. His report suggested that I should be grounded, and returned to the driving school for a re-test. Neither happened. The enemy was not always on the outside. To my surprise he was later a pleasant bloke to work for.

The driver of the observation van that night was my good friend Bob Osborne. He was a very good driver and had miraculously survived a horrific motorway accident. He owned a Triumph TR4 and a front tyre had burst causing the car to go out of control. It had then overturned several times before coming to rest on its roof. He had made a wonderful recovery but his good looks had been dimmed by much facial scarring. Sadly, Bob died as a result of infection to a broken leg. He had been a passenger in a car involved in an unfortunate accident and died, quite unexpectedly, in hospital.

It was a very sad day indeed when six friends gathered at Ross-on-Wye Parish Church to bear Bob's coffin to his last resting place. That was in the summer of 1975, just three short years on.

That traffic car was also hit by a stolen vehicle whilst it was parked at the scene of an accident. I would stress though that all damage to this car was not major, and was repaired before it went back into service.

If you have ever wondered what a hearse carries under the coffin, I can tell you. Generally flowers, but quite often another coffin. I had never paid much attention to them although I did know that there were also small seats behind the front ones. We went to assist at an accident one morning, involving a funeral cortege. A Transit van was awaiting a Give Way sign to join the main road. It started to move out and then for good reason stopped. As it did so it was hit in the back by a Ford D Series truck. The Transit driver was in gear and the van shot forward and cannoned into the side of a hearse which crashed onto its side.

That was on its way to Brandwood Cemetery with a body and had two carriages of mourners behind it. Fortunately no one was hurt. Undoubtedly there would be a delay, but with lots of help from many sources the matter was resolved fairly quickly. One of the funeral directors used a phone in a nearby house and quickly had a relief hearse on site to continue their journey. The mourners were wonderful. The last journey of a loved one or dear friend is never enjoyable. To have it disrupted in this manner must have been heartbreaking. Apart from a few tears from the widow everyone was so calm and behaved with utmost dignity.

Very quick thinking by one of the directors had a police car up to the cemetery to collect the vicar who was to conduct the burial. That was a stroke of genius because he was able to comfort everyone who needed it. We were quickly made aware that there was a second coffin in the cellar of the hearse. Apparently this was not an unusual event then because the hearse usually cleared from a funeral before the coaches and would team up with another cortege to do a second run, without going back to base. In simple terms it was a logistical exercise. In fairness the mourners really didn't need to know that. On the pretence of making room at the scene they were all moved on a little further up the road.

With the second hearse at the scene, the coffin and flowers for our event were salvaged and everything put back as it should be. As soon as that had continued on its journey the lower coffin was transferred to the back of a black A55 van and, with our traffic car to assist, it was speedily moved to Canterbury Road nick. Here it teamed up with a hearse loaned or hired for the occasion and a fresh cortege set off for a second funeral at Perry Barr crematorium.

It was kind that even in grief, a few mourners wrote in and asked that all the officers who had played a part at the accident be thanked for their kindness and reassurances. As an aside the Perry Barr funeral was still conducted on time.

The next brush with one of the 'F' Division inspectors happened at the scene of a serious accident, which Jack and I were dealing with on Stratford Road. To protect ourselves, and the immediate scene we had set out reflective 'accident' signs and a set of cones on the approach side. The inspector came to satisfy himself that all was well, and whilst he was with us we were aware that there had been another accident at the same location. His car was parked so as to obstruct our reflective sign and another car had run into the back of his. He had been too lazy to get out, move a cone, and park in comparative safety. For his trouble he now had some work of his own.

During the winter I had a serious dispute with the other. I was working nights on a one-man car. At around midnight all Pandas were grounded because of a heavy fall of snow. The traffic cars and Land Rovers were put in at stations and would be sent to incidents as they arose. My first call was to an accident in Acocks Green village, but this had been resolved long before I got there and I found nothing. I was then given a second job to fit in on my way back. By this time snow was sticking well and was about four inches deep. I was sent to Moseley Village where there was a car up a tree.

When I got there I found the car, but just as I was about to report my arrival I heard that the bump was apparently being dealt with by the division. I was not happy with that message. There was no one with the car I had found. I made sure that the car was unoccupied. There was a lot of blood about and the driver was obviously bleeding profusely. The accident had also happened at quite a high speed, and the car, an Audi, was a write-off. I followed a trail of blood, at first on foot and then in the car. It led me past the local police station and into a quiet residential road.

I found the inspector rendering first aid to a man with a cut head. The man was clearly drunk. The inspector had arrived in a Panda and there was another Panda there as well. The man with the cut head was obviously the man from the car. The inspector told me to leave the scene. I offered him a breath test kit for the driver; he swore at me and told me that the injured man was too ill to take a breath test. I now decided that I did not like what I had seen and heard. I suspected, and quite rightly, that the man and the inspector were known to each other. I also suspected, and again correctly, that they had in fact been drinking together prior to the accident, that the inspector had found the wrecked car, recognised it, and gone in search of his friend. He had called out a Panda to clear the paperwork, which would read like, 'Unattended vehicle found damaged. No trace of driver.'

I couldn't prove it but I knew it to be true. I went back to the Audi, checked the tyre patterns and went to outside a pub where I thought they had probably been. There were three patches in the snow where cars had stood whilst it was snowing. One set of tracks in the snow matched the Audi.

I committed to paper my thoughts about the events of that night. When the matter was looked at further the accident had never been recorded. The inspector had recorded his dealings with a man. The details in the inspector's book were not those of the owner of the car. The injured man went to hospital by police car. The false details were given there. The car owner/driver had a criminal record and from his photo I knew that he was the man I had seen with a cut head. No action was taken against anyone.

One of the 'advantages' of Traffic cars was that they had either Multi-Force or Force-wide radio channels and quite often we were sent to major incidents such as murders so that the Information Room could keep in touch with us, and an incident, direct. Because of our City-wide role we also got sent to collect all and sundry who were needed at major jobs. Photographers and SOCO workers (Scenes of Crime Officers) in particular, were regular passengers.

I was soon sent on a Traffic Patrol Officers course for six weeks. This is a specialist course and invaluable to anyone engaged on full time traffic law enforcement. It is akin to a City and Guilds in Construction and Use. To my surprise I went straight from that to an Accident Investigation course. This was very advanced and covered the investigation of accidents by way of science and mathematics. It became such a specialist field that a full time team was set up and a basic requirement was 'A' level maths or even a degree. (The 'A' level I couldn't attain at school seemed not to matter here.) Investigation is now also computer assisted.

I went to a serious accident one evening involving a stolen car, which had been chased into Birmingham from Wolverhampton. The driver had been recognised as disqualified, by the crew of a traffic car. The car, an Austin 1300 GT, had been reported stolen from Walsall. They tried to stop the car but the driver decided to give it a run and sped off along the A41 towards Birmingham. The crew were well acquainted with that part of the route and gave a good commentary on the chase. They had multi-channel radio and as they came into the City they changed to our frequency. It made good sense that they dealt direct with our Control Room. With the talk-through facility working there was soon a Birmingham car in on the act and that car took over the commentary.

I was working with the traffic sergeant and we made our way across the City towards the party. The chase came straight through Handsworth and then into Villa Road towards Lozells. At this point everything slowed down a bit. Speeds of over 90 mph had been recorded. They were now down to sixties. The chase then moved through Aston, up and down parallel roads and eventually out onto the A38 northbound near to Ansells brewery.

There are traffic lights here and rather than stop at red the driver went through. He brushed a vehicle on his way across and this caused him to swerve slightly. He crashed head on into a black taxicab at about 55 mph.

The impact wrecked both vehicles. The taxi was a substantial beast and stood up well. The driver escaped with minor injuries. The stolen car was completely smashed apart. The engine was literally on the driver's lap. He was seriously injured and trapped. The driver was cut out of the wreck by firemen using the latest equipment, conscious and in agony. He died in hospital, within the day.

The events of that night brought some criticism to the police. The question was asked, 'If you knew who he was why give chase?' Had I been the officer involved I would have done the same thing. I was paid to do a job; I had a mandatory responsibility to enforce the law. The citizen has a duty to uphold the law. If the citizen is found to be in breach of his duty, in other words offending, then it is the duty of the officer to deal with him.

In this instance the offender had decided that he did not want to be dealt with. He was given the opportunity to admit defeat and detection but he refused. He then continued to commit further offences, including driving at dangerous speeds. He ignored a red traffic light and it cost him his life.

Sad that may be for his family but he was a volunteer. He volunteered to break the law by driving whilst disqualified. He knew he was banned. He stole a car. He knew that to be wrong. He drove dangerously to avoid capture. Those were all actions committed by him alone. Why therefore, should the police be blamed because he was killed? He caused his own death by his own actions. Fortunately he didn't take anyone else with him.

I had been faced with high-speed chases involving non-stolen vehicles and the decision whether to continue must remain with the individual officer. We had all been trained to a very high standard. We were professionals in the true sense of the word.

I remember following two vehicles, in separate incidents, where I came close to abandoning pursuit. In both instances the drivers were unaware of my presence and both were in legitimate possession of the cars.

The first was on a Sunday afternoon in Moseley. I followed a sports car along Queensbridge Road and Russell Road at up to 85 mph. These roads are subject to a 30 mph speed limit. They are residential and at one end there is a hospital and a school and at the other there is a park. When I finally stopped the driver he was unconcerned. He hadn't had an accident. Therefore what he had done was not dangerous. The fact that he was driving at over the legal speed limit both for that road and for any motorway was purely academic.

The Court was not amused. He got banned for six months.

The second was at about 5 in the morning. It was raining cats and dogs. It was evil. I was just about to come back into the City Centre along the A38. As I emerged onto Bristol Road South at the Travellers Rest I saw an Opel Manta literally flash past me. I guessed then that he was doing a ton, at least.

I set off after it and kept it in view all the way along the Bristol Road, through Bournville, through Selly Oak and Selly Park. I finally stopped it, after about five miles, near to the old Bristol cinema. At no time had I travelled at less than 60 mph and in places I was doing 90 mph. I made no ground on that Manta at all.

He must have eventually looked in his mirror and seen my blue lights because he slowed down and then stopped. We stood out in the rain together until I was sure that he was aware that it was raining, then we sat in my car. His explanation? He was angry that his girl friend had not allowed him to have sex, he having spent a lot of money on her. He was also fined and banned.

On another occasion I chased a very fast speeder. I knew the car, but the owner was not the driver. I went after it and the driver started to drive even faster. Then the car went onto a housing estate and was then driven quite normally. I didn't like that. It looked as if the car was making its way back to the owner. Eventually the driver stopped and got out. He told me that the car belonged to his father. Well, I at least knew that it wasn't nicked. His father was a sergeant who I had known for years. He had worked at the Lane and Duke Street. By now he was on the Driving School. Whoever his dad was, it had to be done. He went to Court.

There was another instance in which the presence of a police car may have caused a driver to have a serious accident. On this occasion I was the driver of the police car. It was in the small hours of the morning in Alum Rock. I had just dealt with a minor accident and was on my way to drop off the paperwork at the local station. As I went past the 'Jig Saw' club I saw five people getting into an Austin 1300 GT, identical to the one the man from Wolverhampton had died in.

The club had a reputation for late drinking and had been the subject of raids previously. It was my belief that the driver would be a good candidate for a breath test. I slowed down and as I did so the car was driven off, quite quickly. By the time I had turned round and gone after it, it was almost out of sight. I saw it turn right into Nechells Place and then I lost sight of it altogether. I hadn't got a number. I hadn't any real evidence of wrong doing so I carried on with my original task.

I suppose that by the time I had concluded my business at the police station about thirty minutes had elapsed since I had first seen the 1300. I had probably even forgotten about it. As I got back into the car I heard a radio message asking for a traffic car to assist the division at a fatal accident in Rocky Lane, Aston. I was not the nearest and I was not sent. I elected to go to assist if necessary.

The accident involved the 1300 from the 'Jig Saw' club. Rocky Lane is undulating and winding, not a road for high speeds. What appeared to have happened was that the driver had lost control on a bend. The car had gone through the wall of a factory compound, dropped into the compound and crashed into the doors of the factory. There were no known witnesses.

The impact had caused the factory burglar alarm to activate and that in turn had called the police. The alarm was one to which response had been limited because of false calls and was visited quickly, but not as a matter of urgency with a number of vehicles. When the officer had arrived at the factory he had seen the crashed car. To his horror there were five people in it. Three were apparently dead and the others injured.

When the dead and injured had been removed from the car we then had the job of trying to piece the evidence together and get relatives notified. That took most of the rest of the night.

The post mortem revealed that all the deceased, including the driver, had been drinking and were well over the drink-drive limit. Witnesses from the club had also confirmed that, when they were seen the following night.

Whether that accident would have happened if I had not seen the car outside the club will never be known. It is probable that given the sort of car involved it would have been driven quickly whether or not the driver had seen the traffic car. For my part my conscience was clear. I had not chased the car for the simple reason I had no realistic chance of catching it. If I had given chase and not seen the accident happen I would probably have been unaware of it because the car had gone completely off the road and was out of immediate view. He had chosen to drive. He knew he'd been drinking. So did his mates.

I continued my work but was increasingly called upon to stand-in for an absent sergeant. This gave me a greater freedom of movement and my responsibilities were for the whole City. It was customary for the sergeant to have a partner and I changed mine regularly to share out the 'perk' and to get to know the members of the shift better. One evening I shared a car with the motorcycle sergeant. That was no 'perk'. 'Peb' Stone had a little more service than me but was quite a lot older. He loved his motorcycles but occasionally he relished the change and drove a car.

On this particular evening, with other officers, we were sent to Coventry Road, just down the hill from the bus depot. A car had crashed in flames and two people were trapped. When we got there the fire brigade had things under control. The driver, a girl, had been taken to hospital, badly burned. The passenger was still in his seat, very dead, very badly burned and barely recognisable as human. When all necessary tasks had been carried out the body had to be removed, first from the car and then from the scene.

The fire brigade cut the seat out and the body was part of it. Peb and I tossed a coin to assist in the removal of the body from the seat and into the coffin. I won. When it was over Peb looked pretty grim. 'That,' he said, 'was the most fucking horrible thing I have ever had to do. Yuk.'

I drove Peb back to the garage, parked the car up and took him down the road for a pint. He had earned it.

The car had not crashed, as such. They had been for petrol at a garage which was making large price cuts in a war with its competitor. The car had taken on eleven gallons. The tank held only ten when empty. Some had leaked into the boot and was running out when the car left the forecourt. Despite having this knowledge they continued the journey, but within half a mile the car had exploded in flames. Passers-by got the girl out but they could not reach his seat belt. The girl died three weeks later.

One peaceful Saturday afternoon turned out to be far from quiet after 3 o'clock. I was working as sergeant when I heard a car being sent to an accident in New John Street West, near to the Lucas factory. The location was not precise but I guessed where the scene was. I was less than a minute away and I went.

The accident was on a perfectly simple, wide, open crossroads and involved two cars. The first car had been driven over a 'Give Way' sign and had crashed into a car on the main road. The driver of the first car was hanging out of it and was unconscious. He looked in a bad way. My partner went to his aid. The other car was a police car, an unmarked Allegro. I recognised it by its number. It was the 'A' division policewomen's car.

I knew both the girls. The passenger was Allison, she had terrible cuts to her face. The door pillar had come back and she had gone forward into it, put her head through and then bounced back, hitting the pillar with her ear. She was not well. The driver was Polly Evans. I had known Polly since she had joined some five years before. She was relatively all right. Her seat belt, and lack of damage on her side had seen to that. She had bruises to her chest.

Once everyone had gone to hospital and the scene cleared up I went to collect Polly's flat mate and Allison's husband. That done I set about the papers. The local inspector was happy to be relieved of it.

The other driver was prosecuted. He surprisingly made a very quick recovery.

Allison was left with permanent scars, but the hospital had made a good job and thought that they would disappear with time. Polly had quite an unusual injury. She had been wearing a wired bra and the seatbelt had used that to disperse the impact. In consequence the whole of the front of her torso was badly bruised and she was in some considerable pain for some time.

I used her example to many of the fashion conscious young ladies who drove cars over the coming years. It also helped to stamp out the habit of personal radios being stuffed down the front of tunics. A remote carrier was fitted to the Pandas and the radios were then used from them.

The traffic sergeant often dealt with accidents involving police officers from divisions. The duty rested, in the main, with the division but on occasions they had no staff available and Traffic dealt with it. One such, I attended on nights, whilst acting the rank: a very minor incident that would not have been reportable had it been with a private car. A Panda driver had driven downhill on a dual carriageway in Billesley. As he got to the end of the dual carriageway he had slowed to go over a narrow bridge. He had then skidded slightly and grazed the kerb. The car was an Austin 1100 and the front nearside wheel had been knocked slightly out of alignment.

The incident was on the 'F' division and my favourite Inspector was on duty somewhere, but could not be found. Knowing this I breath tested the officer. It was a negative test, but those were the instructions. Just as the garage was about to remove the Panda by trailer the Inspector arrived. He blustered about and ordered the Panda driver to take a breath test. He refused. The Inspector got angry and threatened to arrest the officer for refusing.

I intervened. He had already provided a negative test. There was no power for anyone to offer him another. The Inspector insisted that I had exceeded my duty. I had no right to use the equipment without his approval. I regret that I did not offer the Inspector a breath test that night. The result might have been interesting.

The concept of single crew on the cars suggested that we looked for something altogether more compact, but not as tiny as the Mini. We tried an

Escort Mexico but that was a coarse beast, almost straight from the Rally scene. I went to the Triumph factory at Coventry and collected a Dolomite. I was very impressed with it. However, I was the only person ever to try it. It was used by a senior officer for a few days whilst he was out of the City. When he came back he declared it to be 'useless'. It was, he had decided, too small for two men to sit in all day. Odd. The car came to us to evaluate for one man crewing. It went back to the factory. They seemed disappointed. So were we.

One Monday morning in April 1972 I was having breakfast in the canteen when the phone rang. There was never an urgency to answer it because it usually meant that whatever was on the plate was about to be put in a sandwich and stuffed into your pocket as you were sent out. It was answered. 'Ralph, for you,' came a shout. I left my breakfast and answered it; it was June.

'Guess where I am?'

'No idea.'

'Headquarters.'

'Why?'

'I've just seen the Chief.'

'Why?'

'I've just been made Sergeant from Monday. Going to the "B".' She was obviously very pleased.

So was I. She had done it. She had been close before her accident and now, a year on, she had recovered enough to take on a completely new challenge. I went back to my breakfast and told my pals the news. They all seem pleased for her. She had become one of the team simply by being on the end of the radio.

June was working in the Information Room and her sergeant was the duty Press Officer. He decided that the event of a WPC being promoted ahead of her PC husband was newsworthy and spilled the beans out to the Press. The next morning I was told to bring a Triumph traffic car up to HQ and meet the Press. They went to town. June and I were interviewed and loads of pictures were taken. The story was big news and made the *Evening Mail* and the *Birmingham Post*, their morning broadsheet.

Jack's news wasn't so good though. His younger brother Des, also a policeman, had been arrested. Des had apparently been recorded offering to obtain some private information in return for cash. That obviously is not allowed. Jack was shaken badly by that event and the news hit him very hard.

I don't think Des was criminally corrupt, more naive. None the less he was convicted and went to prison. Worse was to come. It was never known

June's promotion to Sergeant. (With credit to the Birmingham Post & Mail Ltd.)

whether what followed was coincidence or resultant upon that conviction. There were suddenly allegations of widespread corruption within the traffic patrols. Bribery was rife and things had got to be done, it was said. Things were. The Chief Constable ordered a full enquiry and asked West Mercia Police to undertake it. The enquiry was to be headed by Superintendent Pugh.

The basis of the allegation was an imbalance in the number of offenders reported for offences and the numbers who were finally dealt with, either by prosecution or caution. That was a black and white statement and there could be no grey areas. The inference was that by whatever means many offenders were being let off. The main, and certainly the worst, allegation was that money was changing hands to achieve these ends. This was serious stuff.

To set the scene it is necessary to place the characters and the records in context. The traffic department had no specific territorial leadership. It was a department staffed by officers from HQ strength, the 'R' Division performing their duties on the territory of a Divisional Chief Superintendent. In consequence all decisions to prosecute were his responsibility. We had the authority to caution or advise at the time but once it was on paper it was up to him. In order to keep a record at our end there was a large ledger, a sort of index in which all process decision papers were entered. We also completed work sheets.

The register contained the recorded name of the offender, the brief details of the offence, the officer and the date the papers left Duke Street. In addition each officer kept a brief record and an index, in his pocket book. The index usually contained the eventual result. The system was not bomb proof but it had worked well for years and had never been questioned. The annual statistics for the department came from that sole source.

The imbalance in the final numbers was, in general terms, easy to account for. Not everyone who is stopped by the police gives his correct details. If they were never traced again the papers would be filed, and available. If they were traced there was no facility to cross-reference and the original surname would show no result. The papers would be forwarded under a new name.

Similarly, many of those stopped were persistent criminal offenders, stopped many times, all over the City. Quite often a number of sets of papers for these people would be amalgamated and dealt with by way of one decision only, not of necessity on the division where the offence happened.

If an accident was involved the papers would all finish up with the accident books and these were recorded separately. They were also filed at HQ.

That is the scene.

Pugh decided that he would first interview all officers in the department in an effort to ascertain the addresses of those offenders who had apparently got through the net. The interviews went OK but he was chasing shadows and had very little help from the information he had got. He then took a different stance. He would interview all officers who had a name in the ledger for which he could find no result. I was one such and the interview was most unpleasant, I was invited to smoke. I explained that I didn't and he said, 'You smoke a pipe.'

'No. I don't smoke at all and never have.'

'Are you sure?'

'Certain.'

'Do you keep an index in your pocket book?'

'Yes.'

'Do you keep it up to date?'

'Yes.'

'You have six cases in the ledger for which I can find no result. Can you explain that.'

'Try me.'

'Number one is such-and-such.'

I looked in my book. 'Convicted.'

'Are you sure?'

'It's marked off.'

The next two were the same.

'Number four, so-and-so.'

'Convicted under another name.'

'How do you know?'

'Went to Court with him.'

'Five.'

'False name, never traced, filed.'

'Six.'

'Still outstanding, no result here.'

'Right. So where are the papers?'

'No idea,' was an honest answer. I vaguely remembered the man but nothing more.

'He is in prison at the moment. He is singing. He says there is a Mr Fix-it. Any idea who?'

'No.'

'You are living beyond your means.'

'Pardon?'

'You are living beyond your means. You have your own luxury flat. You have a brand new car and you have a brand new motorcycle. How can you afford all that?'

'You have obviously done your homework, Sir.'

He seemed smug, and liked that comment. 'Of course.'

I had to be a bit careful here. Although the bike was only a few months old I was the second owner. I had recently bought a '68 Bonneville and loved it. However, Eddie Lees had just bought a new and similar machine. He then found the girl he was going to marry so had no time for motorcycling. The bike was on HP. My deal with Eddie was that I gave him a cash sum and took on the payments. To change the HP agreement would cost an arm and a leg so I continued to pay the instalments using the original book. I knew that having sold the '68 bike I only needed to make about three payments and pay the rest off from the cash from the old bike. That worked, but Pugh might not have been too amused, because it wasn't exactly standard practice.

'In which case you will know that I am married to a sergeant. The car is paid for through an essential users allowance. I travel to work by motorcycle. Our joint income exceeds that of a superintendent and nobody would question you having a new car.' I was quite curt.

'That is insolence.'

'No, fact. My wife and I had to wait three years to marry. That gave us a chance to save. Before we married she had a serious car accident. There was compensation. Some of that has already been paid. We can well afford our lifestyle and you are out of order with that line of questioning. I am not even under caution. If you think I have committed an offence you must caution me.'

I got up and left the room.

The rules of interview, as they were then, dictated that once an officer had grounds to suspect that an offence had been committed he was obliged to advise that person that they didn't need to answer further questions. A failure to give that warning rendered the answer inadmissible in Court. It was my view that Pugh's questions implied a suspicion and I refused to say any more. If he wanted to see me again he knew where I could be found.

With the increase in the number of cars now based at Duke Street it was decided that one of the garage sergeants should be promoted to inspector, and be deputy to the man with overall charge of the complex.

That new inspector was 'Porky' Lewis. Porky was probably the most miserable of the lot and promotion did not mellow him. It was forbidden to use the car wash for private vehicles, but that rule certainly didn't apply to older and more senior members of the staff. At night it did not cause a problem but in the daytime the garage was busy and the rule was understandable. I incurred his wrath once.

June and I were on afternoons. We had been to the family farm at Leek in Staffordshire overnight and had come down the M6 in time for that shift. As I drove through Great Barr, on the elevated bit, I hit a swarm of bees at about 70 mph. The effect was astounding. The windscreen just blacked out. The wipers were just not enough. I was forced to stop on the hard shoulder and scrape off what I could. I went straight onto the car wash at Duke Street and set about cleaning the screen. I wasn't bothered about the rest of the car, although there were some dead bees in the radiator.

As I was scraping the bodies off Porky came out of his office almost beside himself with rage. 'What do you think you are doing?' he demanded.

I told him the truth.

'Get it out of the garage.'

'Sir, are you telling me that you want this car to go on the road with half an inch of dead bees on it?'

'I don't care what you do with it,' was his reply.

I carried on, commenting, 'If you insist that I move this car before I consider that the screen is safe I shall report to the Chief Constable the full circumstances. He will not be pleased because he pays for the use of this car on allowance. My wife uses it at work.'

Porky made no reply and walked off. I finished with his precious water and June took the car to work.

Somewhere about now I worked a Saturday afternoon on a day when Birmingham City were at home. It was handy to have a traffic car working 'short' around the ground to assist with traffic matters. I got something far different. I was parked up writing out some notes when a kid came to the car and told me there was smoke coming out of a house and he was just going to call the fireman, and ran off.

I went round to the house, and sure enough there was some smoke coming out of the front downstairs. I looked in, but there was no fire. I ran round the back; the back door was undone and inside the fire had fallen out and had set the rug alight. That in turn had set fire to an armchair. It didn't look like anyone was at home. So I went to the front and found a neighbour with a ladder up the front.

The old boy should be at home, and probably in bed. He liked a drink at lunchtime. He went up the ladder and said that the chap was in bed. He couldn't get the sash window open and was going to smash it. I told him not to and went round the back again. By now the chair was well alight but the door beyond was open and that door gave me the stairs.

That had to be the way forward. I shut the door behind me and went up the stairs. I got the window open just as the fire brigade arrived. One went round the back and washed the back room over and others came to us at the front. They then lifted chummy out of his bed and took him outside. We were all safe and there wasn't much damage to the house. I went back to the car and the radio is going barmy. I'm not answering. Then I realised that at no time had I told the Room where I was or what I was doing! I had forgotten the basics. Thank God, the young son had called the brigade. Why I had just got stuck in without telling anybody I would never know. However, there were nice comments in the *Sunday Mercury*, the next day.

When Balsall Heath was being redeveloped many of the existing roads remained in use, at least for pedestrians. There was usually a 'road closed' board up but it was possible, with care, to drive through. One morning one of the building site huts was reported as broken into and a Panda was sent. The driver went along a closed road to the office. He didn't get that far. As he drove over a filled in trench the front of the Panda disappeared into it and stopped abruptly, with its belly on the road.

I was sent as traffic sergeant and found it quite amusing. The driver had assured me that he had been going slowly when the incident had occurred. I knew him well as he was married to one of June's policewomen. The next task was to get the car out and check it. I sent the driver to deal with his original job, and set about finding volunteers to lift the car out of the trench. I didn't want to tow it for fear of causing further damage. Sure enough, as the site workers came to clock on they were sent to the Panda. About ten of them lifted it bodily out of the hole. The car went to Duke Street and when it was on the ramp we were satisfied that there was no damage. The car stayed in service and there was no report, just advice about driving down closed roads.

The City was by now being bombed by the IRA. The attacks were random but generally the bombs were left where they would do some damage but cause major chaos: the steps of the Rotunda, a signal box at New Street, shop doorways, always lots of glass broken.

At one stage it came fairly close to home. The MP for Small Heath then was Dennis, later Lord Howell. He was a near neighbour and we were on speaking terms. Whilst we were on a short holiday in Ibiza we saw in the *Daily Mirror* that his car had been bombed on his drive. June's mum also heard about it on the TV and came over to check our place out. She couldn't get anywhere near it but spoke to some senior officer nearby who arranged for our flat to be checked. To her relief, and ours, it was OK.

Such was the concern that a team from the Ordnance Corps was based in the City with a twenty-four hour police escort of traffic officers to speed them to any suspicious incident. It was with great sadness that on Monday 17 September 1973 the escort witnessed Captain Ron Wilkinson suffer a bomb go off in his hands. Ron died on 23 September, in hospital. I had been in the company of Ron and his wife Pauline the very night before. Little did we know then that Ron would be murdered. That Sunday night is always remembered fondly.

Shortly after Ron's death I did a few days, a holiday relief, with an army team as driver of the van filled with their kit. We went to one or two false, but with good intent calls. One was a night job. The team leader at this time was a man I'll leave as just Chris. He was very experienced, and didn't like working in the dark. He had seen a mate killed disarming a new device, at night. A few days later he had been faced with an identical device. Apparently, it needed to be dismantled to find out more about it. Chris had a video of the work up to the point of detonation. He played this all the time he was working on his. He eventually disarmed the device successfully. He was highly decorated for that action, and rightly so.

On the night we had our call a 'suspicious package' had been found in the middle of Acocks Green bus garage. By the time we got there the mechanics had moved all ninety-six double-deckers into nearby roads. We thus had an entire, empty garage in which to play. Chris gave the box a look-over through binoculars and then deployed 'Willie'. Willie was a small fully tracked work platform. It was battery driven and remote controlled. This particular model was fitted with a TV camera and a shotgun. The gun was loaded with a single slug 12 bore cartridge, familiar to all who have seen movies of US Sheriffs shooting engines out of cars.

Chris sent Willie to look at the package. There was no obvious sign that it was anything other than a box, so Chris decided to let fly with the slug. The box disintegrated and we went to investigate. We found pieces of mosaic. If the contents had been in military stores they would probably have been labelled, 'Tiles, ceramic, white, Pilkington, Gents toilets, for the use of.'

It looked very much as though one of the mechanics had decided to 'borrow' a box of tiles from the contractors who were refurbishing the gents toilet. He would probably have moved them out in a bus later, had someone not found them. Chris issued a few words of advice and went back to bed.

An awareness of danger was embedded in us all by now but was it enough? The powers that be thought not and all refresher courses around this time encompassed a lecture and demonstration of explosives awareness. The lesson was brilliant. The soldier who gave it knew his stuff. He demonstrated a number of detonation techniques used by both the army and terrorist organisations. During the talk he insisted that nobody smoked in the classroom. He then gave us a break and asked smokers to go into the corridor. As one lit up a detonator exploded in the room. He had made his point. Smoke actuation was another way of setting off a bomb. This simple mechanism is now used in every household in the land. It's called a smoke alarm.

The Pugh enquiry lingered on for two years. I believe that he had made his mind up that somebody would have to drop to be his scapegoat. He had got to find something. If he couldn't find anything after two years there probably wasn't anything!

Virtually the entire staff were questioned along the lines of my interview. He then turned his attention to garages. He had a whiff that accident damaged vehicles were being directed to garages of the officer's choice, instead of that of the owner. The officer was then being rewarded.

Certainly, before the adoption of personal radios (circa 1967) some direct contact had been made in some areas, but that had long ceased. The system was now on computer and garages were directed to accidents by a single source, and all dealings closely monitored.

Next interviews were about who we knew in the garage trade. As traffic officers that was a good many. They were our bread and butter. A false name and address enquiry usually started with the garage where the car had last been sold.

I must confess to knowing only one of the many I was asked about. I had met him once. I didn't like him. He obviously knew a lot of policemen, and dropped names as if they carried a status. Most were from the CID. His name was Don Parsons.

As if the shadow of the enquiry was not enough there was more bad news. The Force was to be amalgamated. Rumour was rife, as the final details were not known, but come 1 April 1974 we would be in another Force.

The Pugh enquiry ground on, the amalgamation loomed nearer. That event would have a more profound effect on the police service as a whole and Birmingham, in particular than any previously. We would have a Force stretching from the northwest of Wolverhampton to the Leicestershire boundary in the southeast, from Halesowen on one side to nearly Coleshill on the other. More than 6,000 men and women officers plus civilian back-up staff would be affected. No control room would be big enough. There would be three centres of control: three little Police Forces under one umbrella.

1966 had seen amalgamations, lots of them. In the Midlands alone the borough Forces of Dudley, Walsall and Wolverhampton had already been swallowed up. West Bromwich and Smethwick had been part of Staffordshire. Oldbury had been part of Worcestershire. These had all been joined together as the West Midlands Constabulary. Warwickshire had been amalgamated with Coventry City. The counties of Shropshire, Herefordshire and Worcestershire had joined with Worcester City and had become West Mercia.

Now there were to be more. The West Midlands Constabulary and Birmingham City would merge in their entirety. The former Coventry City and the boroughs of Solihull and Sutton Coldfield from the Warwickshire Force would join them. Also to be included would be the borough of Halesowen and the town of Stourbridge from West Mercia and previously Worcestershire. Warwickshire would be left with a smaller Force than ever, and it had suffered before because it was too small! The whole thing sounded stupid then. It sounds no better now when written down like that. To oversee the mergers there would be a new County and a new County Council. It was to be The County of West Midlands. Similar mergers were to happen in Merseyside and Manchester as well.

Plans were drawn up. Traffic would be a division in its own right, broken into four sub-divisions. Western would comprise the old West Midlands plus Halesowen and Stourbridge. Central would be Birmingham and Sutton Coldfield, Eastern would be the rest of the bit stolen from Warwickshire and Coventry. The fourth would be the Mid Links Motorway Unit. The Birmingham Divisions would lose their Land Rovers to Duke Street and they would then be exchanged on a one for one basis with Eastern and Western for two patrol cars from each.

There would be three sergeants and an Inspector on each shift and a Superintendent and a Chief Inspector on each subdivision. A Super-intendent! There wasn't enough work for a Chief Inspector. One sergeant would be a full-time motorcyclist. The others would work with the car crews.

The thought of the whole thing appalled me. I could foresee a rapid decline in standards all round. Most of the officers involved in the first shake-up had become embittered. Their experience said not to do it. There was probably room for change, but to embark on such a radical and far-reaching project with so little consultation was courting disaster. The public didn't want it, the police on the ground certainly didn't, but everyone was assured that it was the way forward.

My personal feelings are that the amalgamation of the constituent Forces in the West Midlands was at best a serious misjudgement. It was probably an unmitigated calamity. Or even a regional disaster. The other emergency services also suffered as a result of the same reorganisation.

Because the City Force had a very successful Sports and Social Club there was also an excellent infastructure of sections and groups within. Traffic had always maintained a social fund without actually having any club premises. In effect we used the parent club at Tally Ho! or outside venues for our functions. All the Social Clubs were faced with the problem of impending rule changes so we decided on a party to mark the end of the Traffic Department.

The social committee decided that we would have a stag evening at a suitable venue. They chose the Custard House at Bordesley Green. That regularly staged Boxing Evenings so they had the staff and expertise to cope. We would lay on a short film show of the 1973 Formula One Grand Prix season and the 1973 Isle of Man TT races. That would be followed by a supper of faggots and peas or bangers and mash, an after dinner speaker and a cabaret and a couple of strippers.

At this point it was obvious that anyone on duty would miss out and we really needed it to be for everyone. Because it was the end of the financial year, and indeed the current funding arrangements, we still had a few shillings in the overtime pot. Such was the sense of loss at the department closing, that the bosses actually suggested that we hire in drivers from the territorial divisions to provide cover between 6 pm on the chosen evening and 6 am the following morning. The bikes would come off the road at 6 pm and surplus divisional drivers could elect to plunder our overtime pot, and drive the traffic cars. A ballot was organised as the offers way outstripped the vacancies. That way everybody was free to attend.

The evening was hugely successful. Many of the wives and/or girlfriends arranged to deliver and collect their loved ones and some organised various things for themselves. The motor sport bit went down well. The after dinner speaker had us falling off our seats. The band for the cabaret had a topless drummer. That wasn't unusual. The fact that she had tassles on her nipples and could contra-rotate them as she played her drum-set, fascinated everyone.

The strippers gave an excellent routine and had a hard time repelling randy motorcyclists who wanted to strip with them. Quite a few had pints of beer poured in their laps to dampen their ardour. All in all it was an excellent and fitting way to close the pages on one of the largest, and most successful, traffic departments outside of the capital.

On the last day of Birmingham City Police, PC Dave Sewell from Digbeth sponsored a special postmark to commemorate the sad demise of a proud force, struck down by the sword of bureaucracy, in search of economy, to the knowing detriment of the very community it had been created to serve. It was a very sad Sunday indeed.

I signalled my contempt with the arrest of a young motorcyclist riding a stolen machine. When he went to Court in the morning I was in a different Police Force.

CHAPTER 11

Amalgamation

NOTHING CHANGED OVERNIGHT, for me, except my number. No letter 'R', just four figures. A lot changed for the drivers speeding in Tamworth Road, Sutton Coldfield. The road was subject to a 40 mph speed limit and had been a source of concern to Warwickshire because they simply could not enforce that limit effectively. That morning Sutton was 'D' Division and two radar crews set up camp and prosecuted over a hundred drivers on Tamworth Road. Some were so angry at getting stopped that they sped off into the second trap.

That process was repeated all over the borough, sorry ex-borough – Sutton was now a suburb of Birmingham – and the Magistrates Courts had to become far more efficient. They had to run a Court every day. Another hidden cost of amalgamation.

The police station at Sutton also had to buy a lock for one of the gents' toilets. There were identical sets of porcelain in two adjoining rooms. One was marked 'men', the other 'officers'. There was a third, marked 'ladies'. I walked past the ladies straight into the officers. Whilst halfway through my pee the superintendent came out of a cubicle and said, 'What are you doing in here?'

My simple reply was, 'Having a pee.'

'This is the officers' toilet.'

'I am a police officer.' I washed my hands and walked out. He stood there with a stunned look on his face.

The first good thing from my personal point of view was that one of the F division inspectors who had been such a pest to work with was transferred to the other side of the Force. He lived in a police house and they moved his family as well, and they paid for the move. Word must have got through. He sure upset someone.

There was a light-hearted moment one afternoon towards the end of that first month. I was posted as sergeant and the only vehicle available was one of the Land Rovers, which had become resident on 'that day'. I happily took it out for a drive, and useful it was to prove. I was outside Dudley Road hospital when I learned that a local Panda, with a woman driver, was in pursuit of a Sprite sports car very near. I set off to assist and within seconds

160

had both in sight. I was amazed when the Sprite went onto the car park of the Tower Ballroom. That was a dead end.

The driver knew his way round and got onto the perimeter road of Edgbaston Reservoir. Still a dead-end, provided the park gates were shut. The procession continued; there was no room for me to pass anyone. About three parts of the way round the road followed the water to the right, and there was a large grassed area on the left. The Sprite stayed on the road and I took to the grass to head the Sprite off. It was quite wet and four wheel drive was the only way to go. There was a little stream across the grass and constant speed here was vital or I might hit a problem. I went out of the stream like a steam train and got back on the road to halt the stolen Sprite.

I was able to arrest the two lads from the car and then I saw that the Panda had followed me across the grass and was totally bogged down. The driver was in tears, standing beside it, ankle deep in mud. She did look a sad and forlorn creature. I felt very sorry for her but I couldn't help but to smile. The lads from the car were very amused about it, but not their own plight. They were taken away in another car and I went back for the Panda.

It was stuck firm. The mud was up to the hubcaps. Angela was still crying. I told her where the towing rope was and how to fix it on to both vehicles. She had never been towed before and it was her first day out in the car on her own. She got back in the car, started the engine and I saw the front wheels start to spin. I then took up the challenge and went. Mud went everywhere, particularly all over her windscreen. She looked out of the driver's window as I pulled her round in an arc and we stopped facing back to where we had gone in.

The Panda was undamaged but it was covered in mud. She had had her window open and there was mud over her and in the car. With tears, mascara and mud on her face she put her head on my arm and said, 'What a mess, what are we going to do?'

'You are going to Ladywood to change, then you are going to deal with your prisoners. I'll get the car washed and nothing more will be said. How does that sound?' That was agreed and I later returned her car to her washed and clean. I'll bet she never follows a Land Rover across country again.

There was a chronic shortage of sergeants throughout the new Force. Other posts had been filled and only the new sergeants were to be appointed and posted. The other promotions had sent men and women in all directions and almost all had been moved out of their last Force area. I was to be one of the new sergeants and I would be promoted with the Force just twenty eight days old. Prior to the amalgamation rumour, I had been keen to advance but now I did not have a current Promotion Board assessment and in

Birmingham I would not have been considered. Now there was no option. Paper qualification was all that was required. I was right. Amalgamation did mean a lowering of standards.

I breathed a huge sigh of relief as Sir Derrick read out the posting. I would stay with traffic. That was his decision, under which traffic rested with the division. Fifty-six men were promoted that day. There was much swearing and cursing when many found out that their journey to work had just been increased by dozens of miles. Some had no transport. They cycled to work, or went on the bus whilst their wives used the cars. One man from Coventry wore his old Coventry City uniform. He had not had it changed in the eight years with his last Force. He was a coroner's officer: a uniformed post, but undertaken in plain clothes. He had got three years to serve. He was going back to his old job, in charge. He reckoned he would hand that one in then.

I went straight from the Chief's office to traffic HQ. Chief Superintendent would see me straight away. He welcomed me, warmly. I had never met him before. He was from the old West Mids. I would remain at Duke Street, change shifts, and run a bike shift.

'I am not a police motor cyclist, Sir. I can only ride lightweights.'

'You will up-grade. You start your course on Monday week.'

Jesus, they are moving quickly, I thought, new job Monday, course Monday week. News was rife that the stores on the Western side had tons of motorcycle kit in stock and that was my next port of call. Brand new boots, suits, mitts, gloves and a crash helmet were all mine for the asking. I was well satisfied. I suspect that their stores buyer had a surplus of cash towards the end of his year and had blown the lot on some decent kit, knowing that amalgamation would put demands on his cache.

There were not huge numbers of women sergeants in Birmingham but most of the more recent ones were from a new generation spawned to some extent by the expansion of the Cadet system. Of the fifty-six of us promoted on the day four were lads whose wives were already sergeants.

The recruiting department decided that the publicity was too good to lose and promptly got us all together for a media photo-call. Our pictures soon found their way into the paper.

Pugh was still persisting in his task and seemed now to be on to something different. All the car crews were questioned about one specific date. Where were we? Who did we work with? Who did we deal with? Simple interview. For my part I was on the 'E' division early on then at Court for the rest of the day. I dealt with one offender whose name was in my book. I know I was on my own because it was raining and I dealt with him in the car. He sat in the passenger seat. I was asked had I worked with

The husbands catch up. L-R: Sergeants Geoff Longmore, Dennis Dixon, Ralph Pettitt, Clive Mole, Barbara Mole née Bleasdale, June Pettitt née Robinson, Carol Dixon née Peach, Janet Longmore née Reeves. (With credit to the Birmingham Post & Mail Ltd.)

Bill Glastonbury on that day and I truthfully answered that I had not. No other days were discussed and I was sent on my way. The interview had been a totally informal affair. It did seem though that Bill's name might be in the frame for something. Bill and I had worked on the same shift but we rarely worked closer together than that.

The motorcycle course was in fact two. For fifteen years I had ridden a motorcycle nearly every day. I had been tested to ride small machines for the police in 1963, and now I was about to spend three weeks with learner motorcyclists whilst they got a D of T pass. On satisfactory completion of the first course I would then do a second, to familiarise myself with the bigger machines. There would then follow a test, and that test would determine what category authority I would have. I did not have six weeks to spare. I was going to the Isle of Man for the TT races at the end of May and would barely have time to complete the first. This was a long-standing arrangement and was paid for. It was agreed that the second part of the course would fit in on return from the Island.

By the third day of the course, and the second on the road, it was obvious that I was of the required standard for phase two. It was then decided that I would return to Duke Street and present myself for the second part on return from holiday. Fate then showed its hand. On the Friday morning a rider on the second phase came off heavily and was unable to continue. That course had room for me if I felt that I could cope with being a week behind. I took the place.

The next two weeks were fun, pure fun. Wally Paton, the instructor, was a former Birmingham traffic motorcyclist. He knew my capabilities and he gave me my head of steam. Go for gold. Enjoy it. No risks. That was my instruction. The rest was sheer motorcycling, one of my hobbies was being paid for and I was getting paid to do it. There was a variety of BSA, Triumph and Norton bikes at our disposal, all identical to those used operationally. At the end of the course I was top student, both with theory and the ride. I was given an unrestricted Grade 3. Any motorcycle, anywhere. That was the same as off the advanced course. Thus I was ineligible for the advanced. Shame, that would have been serious fun!

It did also mean that standards were being lowered. I was to take charge of a unit of men who were on paper better qualified than me. The standard for the car crews had also been lowered. A grade 2 advanced driver could now use a traffic car solo. The reason was simply that the constituent Forces had not worked to such a high standard as Birmingham City and now there had to be a compromise. At that point the Force failed itself. Warwickshire let a man drive a traffic car for two years to make sure he was suitable for the job, before they spent money on the course.

There were occasions when our 3rd sergeant would have a day out on the bikes. The late Albert Poolton had the nickname of Mighty Atom because of his small stature. Albert had been on the bikes for years before he went to the Driving School on the cars. When the school upped sticks and went out into them Albert had opted to come back to traffic. Albert had difficulty with the Nortons. The old BSA Flashes that he had been used to were a lot lower in the saddle than the Norton and Albert had a problem in both kicking them into life and holding them up at the same time. One morning he had borrowed the bike to go somewhere and as he came back in along Hagley Road he stopped an M&B brewery lorry for tanking on a bit to get back home.

So far so good. Albert dealt with our man and went back to his bike. Albert changed his mind about the paperwork after the drayman picked him up from under the Norton. He had lost his footing as he tried to start the bike!

The driving school had been moved out of Duke Street and transferred to

Halesowen. The old garage had no more room. Halesowen was a brand new station, abandoned by the fleeing West Mercians. It had the room for the school. It also had bedrooms so that courses could be residential. There were no garages. The entire driving school fleet was reduced to standing out in all weathers. The motorcycles had the benefit of a carport. Eighteen years on, nothing had changed. In the winter the bills for de-icer must be huge.

The stable block remained. On paper the Duke Street stables were the HQ of the Mounted Branch. Horses were dispersed throughout the City at Thornhill Road, Kings Heath and Tally Ho! but Duke Street was home to them and the horseboxes. It was also our home and we had to share it, sensibly.

One Sunday during the first summer of amalgamation there was a parade or march in the City. The bottom line was that the Donkey Wallopers had to come in on a Sunday other than to clean up muck. Traffic had some disruption as well because I was working a 2 to 10 car shift using a bike. I posted the car crews and nipped out locally and came back for 3 pm to see the 7 to 3 bikes off. Everything seemed perfectly OK.

What I didn't know was that there had been some pranking during the morning. The lads' bikes that were wanted for the parade were spruced up and the lads went for breakfast. During their breakfast the Mounties had put horse muck in the spare pannier on those bikes. One pannier took official kit; the second was for your leggings, a clipboard and probably a flask of coffee in the winter. They had then gone off to do their thing. The motor cyclists found the muck and sorted the bikes out and then went to join the marchers.

It then seems that the rest of the bike shift sought revenge and barrowed around four tons of horse muck from the 'stink store' as it was known back into the stables. They then chained and locked the two wheelbarrows together and left them on the far side of the muck they'd shifted into the stable. For good measure they then hid all the muck forks.

As I came back through the gate, I was ambushed by a flour bomb. Somewhat surprised I stopped and was greeted by a grinning thirty-five year old child who promptly made dough on the front of my Belstaff with a pump action water pistol!

That routine greeted the next four bikes in before one of them grabbed a fire extinguisher from the bike bay and shot the man with the water pistol. Bedlam and chaos followed. Buckets came out, the hosepipe came out and then Hell's Bells, the Superintendent, Ron Cato, came home with Mrs C on board. Ron lived in the flat above the garage and his sense of humour was measured in minus numbers. Most of the revellers vanished. Ron took Mrs C home, she'd actually seem quite amused, and then came back to see me. He'd obviously had a bit of a fresh lemon to chew since he'd come back home.

To my immense relief he took it in good part. He asked what happened to cause the party and I honestly didn't know. He had a quick look round, tutted, shook his head, and then almost as an afterthought said, 'Serge, make sure the extinguisher gets filled before you go, won't you!'

Question or order, I didn't know. But I'd see to it. Ron was a bit funny about fires. His son, Ian, was a fireman.

I came from the 'A' division and the Central Fire Station was three minutes walk away. They popped out in a car and did the business.

Ron had been at the Birmingham City driving school, latterly as Chief Instructor, and had fought hard to maintain the high standards which he felt the service should project to its public. His belief was, 'The higher the training standard, the fewer serious or blameworthy accidents we had.' Ron Cato gave me my Grade 2 after the traffic attachment. He also gave me my Grade 1 off the refresher. He died shortly after retirement.

My personal survey that I mentioned earlier about the big Triumph cars being safe was based on the experiences of the fact that we ran, in effect, three pools of cars within the Duke Street fleet. There were five big Triumphs, both 2000 and 2500. The Austin 1800 S accounted for another six and their big brothers the 2200s gave us another six. Over two years, with all the cars doing roughly the same distance, and driven by the same drivers, it became very clear that the Triumph was the safest. The 1800 S and 2200 had an average of three bumps each. Only one Triumph was ever damaged. That hit a dog at about 80 mph and reduced the front spoiler to scrap. The dog didn't run off.

Stray dogs accounted for a number of dubious shunts over the years and the telex message which followed that accident said, 'It is with great pleasure that I have to report that the stray black dog which for years has run in front of police cars has tonight been killed by a traffic car.' I'll bet that caused a wry smile in HQ!

My bike shift consisted of twelve men. They were a mixed bunch from all over the Country. All were ex-Birmingham City men and varied in service between about six years and twenty-eight. They had been grouped previously in pairs and they remained together whilst I worked with them. They spent a month on each division 'A' to 'F'. The role of the motorcyclists was similar to that of the car crews, but they did not work nights, then. They had a responsibility to traffic law enforcement but had other functions as well. The escorting of abnormal loads, ambulances and HM Judges was a major responsibility for them.

Sergeant Ralph Pettitt astride Norton 750cc Commando Interpol, June 1974.

I had done the duties with a car and was anxious to learn the technique with a bike. I normally used a Norton 750cc Commando Interpol, a machine designed for police work. First gear was very low and acceleration was phenomenal; even then 0-60 mph could be done in 4.2 seconds, with perhaps one gear change. Wheelies were easy, and not recommended. The strain on the rear spokes could easily cause the wheel to collapse.

Within a few days I had undertaken my first high speed ambulance escort across the City and found it very exhilarating. I was sure that it was probably quite addictive and thus had hidden dangers, not the least of which was a disregard for one's own safety, tending to rely on the noise created by up to a dozen sets of two-tone horns in unison, to say nothing of the screaming, powerful engines. The 750s were extremely noisy at the top end of the revs.

By their nature high-speed ambulances normally carried critically ill people. The very future existence of patients is dependent on urgent treatment. They fell really into two categories: transfers from one hospital to another, and those starting at the scene of an accident, or similar locality, such as a serious assault or a shooting. Over the months there were many but the most memorable was one from Burton General Hospital to the Burns Unit at Birmingham Accident Hospital.

A young boy had suffered serious burns in a fire at home and had been taken to Burton. They decided that he must be transferred to the Burns Unit if he was to have any chance of survival. By some wonderful twist of fate one of the brewery company ambulances was at Burton, and also a Staffordshire Traffic car. The brewery ambulance, based on a Ford Zodiac, was offered. Whilst not ideally suited it was fast and it was used, driven by one of the traffic car crew. His mate would lead in the police car. The lad was loaded up and rolling when we organised our end of the run. The time of day was not in our favour. It was Birmingham evening rush hour, the City Centre was packed and we had to go through there. There was no time to loop round the motorway.

The 'A' Division organised the City Centre and with a little help on some major junctions the rest was left to Traffic. On that day there were probably about twenty bikes available and they were all to assist. The change over to put local vehicles in the front was done on the Sutton by-pass at over 100 mph. There were six bikes and two cars, including the one from Burton, then the ambulance. We later tucked another car in behind the ambulance as a reserve in case of mishap or failure. The run was to go A38, A38(M), Lancaster Flyover, Queensway Tunnels, and right at Holloway Head. The pedestrians on Tyburn Road must have been horrified at this lot, plus a few more bikes to do the junctions, howling down at break-neck speed. The din was beyond belief. It is also the only time I have done the ton on the Tyburn. I don't recommend it; it is very, very hairy, if not dangerous.

The 'A' division did us proud; we screamed through the Queensway tunnels to find Holloway Head deserted, the rest was easy. The lad was still alive when we got him there, less than 26 minutes and 32 miles after leaving Burton. We were chuffed; it hurts when you fail after trying so hard. The Staffordshire officer had been brilliant in the ambulance. He had never driven a Zodiac before; what a time to learn a car.

Ivan Heath was on the front bike from change-over to the end and he had worn some of his fairing away on the islands, and his brakes got so hot they were fading dangerously at the end. Good team work all round. The Air Ambulance now makes these sprees just a page in history. It's less fun but much safer. That's good progress.

Despite our own department being happy, we had seen very few changes; there was a degree of gloom over the Force and June and I decided that if the opportunity arose we would move on. Such was the desire that we were both prepared to forgo our rank to transfer. The pension was the only bar to leaving the service entirely, as it could not then be transferred. That legal loophole to blackmail has now been changed.

It was not unusual for drivers to complain about the police officer after they had received a summons. This happened to me as a result of a very routine speeding offence. I had checked a car over Hockley Flyover at a speed fast enough for prosecution. The driver was stopped and reported for it and the papers submitted. When the summons was served the driver wrote in and complained that I had been rude in my dealings with him.

Because it was an official complaint about my conduct it had to be investigated by a Superintendent, or above. I was duly sent for by Gerry Finch. He was not a man I either liked or trusted. I had met him when he was a sergeant in 1963. Then, although posted to the 'C' division he was seconded to the 'A' division, to supervise the newly formed Corps of Traffic Wardens. I had gone with Ray Blake into the boiler room of the Eye Hospital to get a warm. Finch had almost followed us in and very rudely told us to leave.

Ray was quite abusive to him and Finch threatened him with a discipline charge. Ray wasn't bothered. He was due to resign in two days so it would make no difference. Finch might well not have remembered that incident, but I did, well. I wasn't looking forward to meeting him again.

He read me the allegation and I acknowledged that I understood it.

'I want you to make a statement.'

No please. No thank you. Just a demand. I had a right to be advised that I need not make a statement. I had not been so advised and I refused to make a statement.

'You will make a statement. It will be your opportunity to tell me your side of the story.'

'My side of the story is in the prosecution papers. That's what happened.'

'This is an allegation that you were rude to this man.'

'I understand the allegation.'

'Then tell me your side of the story.'

I was entitled to be cautioned, and I was entitled to a copy of the allegation. I had had neither. A lot of demanding went on. In the end I said, 'Very well, I will write my own statement.'

That agreed, I wrote, 'I understand the allegation made against me. I have been instructed that I must make a statement. This is that statement.' I then signed it and gave it to Finch.

'That is no good,' he told me.

I shrugged my shoulders. I said nothing. Nothing more was ever done about the complaint. The defendant went to Court and pleaded 'Guilty' in person.

After Court I asked him about the complaint and he said, 'I told somebody about it and they said to complain. That way, the police drop the charge.'

Charming! So we are faced with that sort of advice going out to a perfectly ordinary speeder, which in turn ensured that a Superintendent was wasting his valuable time and getting all hot under the collar about an incident which had not even occurred. It is now an offence for such false claims to be made, and legal action has been taken by officers in similar situations

At about the same time there was a complaint about a Superintendent who was doing a complaint enquiry. The situation was that two Bobbies from the Black Country had gone out with their wives for a meal. When it was served it was apparently not up to scratch and they had rejected it. Words had been exchanged at the restaurant and both couples had left. They had not touched the meal. Everything would probably have rested there but one of the punters knew one of the Bobbies and gave the restaurant owner enough ammunition to fire in a complaint.

They were both seen about all sorts of wrongdoing. Obviously they denied any. What they had done was legal and they had left with dignity. They thought that the matter rested there. One of the wives was a former WPC so was well switched on about procedures. One afternoon, unannounced, the Superintendent had gone to their house to see her, knowing hubby was at work. He then started a line of questioning which suggested that hubby was in deep shit and she had better make a statement to help him, or he might find himself out of work. She asked to be excused for the toilet and phoned hubby at work from the bedroom phone.

He phoned the Police Federation for advice and they phoned the Superintendent direct at her house asking why, if her husband was in the mire to that extent, hadn't he been told when he had been seen earlier? That's what Regulations demanded, unless he was working to a different set. They then made a formal complaint about his conduct in the investigation of a complaint. No wrong doing by PCs, but Superintendent seen by the Chief and advised. Nice one!

I never ceased to be amazed at the number of drivers who were unable to comply with the minimum eyesight requirements. Two sets of circumstances in particular emphasise this.

The first was during my first attachment to Traffic when I was with Ron Cornwell in a Cooper approaching the M5 junction at the A456, a fast dual carriageway, on a long sweeping, downhill, right-hand bend. It afforded a super view of the road.

I was driving and coming towards me I was aware of a car apparently on my carriageway. I slowed down drastically and then saw the car veer off to its left and onto the into city lane. We were able to get a part of the number and noted that the car was a Rover 2000.

Using the island under the motorway bridge I went after the car and we finally stopped it in Hagley Road West. The driver was all of seventy-five and almost senile. He was unable to read the names over the shops across the road, let alone a number plate. Such was his eyesight problem that we drove his car to his house with him in it. He died before his case came to court.

The second incident was less frightening but really just as potentially serious. I was driving out along the A441, Redditch Road, one Sunday afternoon when I was surprised to see a car being driven at about 25 mph, virtually along the crown of the road. The speed limit on this stretch was 60 and that was quite often exceeded, hence my presence.

When I approached the car I called the driver to stop by using my loudspeaker and then my headlights, both to no avail. I then overtook it and slowed right down, and signaled the driver to pull in and stop. He didn't. He just drove slowly on. When I finally managed to stop the car it was obvious that the driver had a serious eyesight defect. He was unable to read the traffic car number plate at eight yards. The man was eighty-two. He had been a fighter pilot in the First World War and a pilot in the second. He had retired with the rank of Wing Commander.

He was a pleasure to deal with and I was a little sad at the action I was forced to take. His reply to me was, 'For many years I have done my duty to the best of my ability. I now accept that you are doing that self same thing.' He never drove again and handed his driving licence into the Court, in person. He was given an absolute discharge and required to take another driving test.

The Inspector with overall charge of both my shift and the cars on the same unit was Harold Smith. Harold had been at traffic for years, and had been a sergeant there before promotion. He was well into his fifties and really past his sell-by date for the job he was doing. He had the rather unkind nickname of Apple, for Granny Smith. I remember having him as a passenger one afternoon when no motorcycle was available for me. He was very unimpressed with an urgent fast drive I did across the City to a serious accident. He really was not a good passenger.

He stayed on after his retirement and became the process clerk at the garage. He had to devise a system to prevent a recurrence of the Pugh problem. Whether he made a good job of it or not is beside the point but certainly there was never another problem along those lines.

Birmingham City's motto is 'Forward'. The City Force used that as well. It seemed very appropriate. The new Force adopted the motto 'Forward in Unity'. At this point that was a joke. The Force was in chaos and disarray and the motto 'Backwards in Chaos' would have been appropriate.

The IRA terrorist campaign was in full swing and in November 1974 they killed twenty-one people in two bomb blasts in pubs in the City Centre. Those bombs went off on the very day that the remains of James McDaid were flown out of Birmingham. McDaid had blown himself apart whilst planting a bomb in Coventry. He also holds the record for the fastest cortege between Coventry and Birmingham. He had a police escort into the back of the airport and straight to the plane. The next few days after the bombing were very sombre, but everybody concerned just got down and did what had to be done. I didn't see June, except on the TV news, for three days. She was at the Accident Hospital, running the police post there. There were armed officers guarding the injured in case of a further attack. I spent many miles on the roads of the country collecting plasma and blood.

The arrest of the men thought responsible presented another security headache. They had to be conveyed between the prison and the Court on a regular basis. The route had to be changed every time and was known only seconds before the convoy, with armed escorts, moved in either direction. I was on that escort many times.

Probably the long hours and cold weather combined to wear me down but early in December I crashed my own bike on the way home from work. It was the first time I had ever hit anything other than the road with a bike. A car driver 'U' turned from my left on a dual carriageway and then stopped in my path. I hit it broadside on and took to the air. My life did go before me, as they say it does. I thought I was dead.

To my amazement I remained conscious, rolled over as I landed and got up running. As I rolled I saw lots of lights and I feared that I was amongst traffic, but they were only streetlights. There was nothing broken but I had eight weeks off work with multiple bruises. Very sadly the lovely bike I had from Eddie was written off. It was repairable but the insurers couldn't get the parts because Triumph had just gone belly up. It was replaced with an almost identical one before I returned to work. There was physiotherapy every day. I was collected from home and returned afterwards by one of my colleagues.

Whilst I was off, my good friend Colin Nichols was killed in an accident far less spectacular than mine, riding our police bike. I broke the rules for Colin. I went to his funeral in uniform despite being on sick leave. I owed him that!

In January 1975, June was assaulted in Belgrave Road nick and suffered a serious shoulder injury, or rather an aggravation to an earlier one. The hospital dictated total rest so we both had two weeks of convalescence. It did neither of us any harm.

When I returned to work there was a new 850 Norton waiting for me. I much preferred the 750 but that was written off. The 850 tried to finish me as well, but that was an engineering problem. One Thursday morning, there was an armed robbery at Dudley Road hospital. There had been a spate of Thursday jobs in the region and a plan was in place for such an event. The gang escaped in a car and the number was circulated. Within minutes it had been spotted in Perry Barr and was being chased by a traffic car. The traffic car was rammed by the robbers and the crew were then taken hostage at gun point. They were then robbed of their car and set free, unhurt.

I found a radar crew in Perry Barr and I went through the radar at about 80 mph. I braked hard, stopped and told them what had happened. Their personal radios could be useful. I then roared off towards the scene of the hijack. As I approached the traffic lights at College Road and Kingstanding Road they showed red. I braked but nothing of consequence happened. There were two cars side by side at the lights and there was probably enough room to get between them. I was going too fast to go left so it was through on red and pray! I went between the cars with only inches to spare; I was slowing down but not enough. I looked left: there was a 32 ton artic bearing down on me with smoke off his tyres. I kicked 2nd and yanked the throttle wide open. There was no way either of us was going to stop, so I had one chance, speed. It worked.

I rolled to a stop just clear of the junction and was violently sick on the grass. When I felt better I said aloud, 'Shit. That was close.'

When I climbed off the bike and put it on the stand I was shaking like a leaf. Both car drivers had already stopped behind me. I hadn't seen them until one said, 'It was, wasn't it? I thought you were dead, what happened?'

'I lost the brakes.'

He was obviously visibly shaken; the other one never even got out of his car.

The problem with the brakes was simple. The wrong pads had been fitted. The 850 and 750 had a single disc on the front. They were on different sides of the wheel. They were also made of different metals, thus they required different pads. Mine had got the wrong pads (750s) on it. Somewhere, somebody had dropped a clanger. I had been very fortunate!

The Pugh enquiry was ongoing and it was apparent that Bill was the target of the current enquiry. One afternoon I spoke to him about it and realised that there was common ground between us. Pugh had asked me about a specific date. Bill mentioned the basis of the allegation and I realised that I was the officer that Pugh was trying to find. The event Bill described to me happened the day afterwards.

On the day in question, a Saturday, I had worked early shift and should have finished at 2 pm. However, there was a football match on at Villa Park and an extra traffic car was required to have the keys in case any vehicles had to be moved. I agreed to work until 6 pm. Bill partnered me. That fact was in my pocket book. Whilst the match was on we did a couple of enquiries and went into Queens Road for petrol. Bill wanted to see an officer there and I dealt with the fuel. When Bill came out he said the man he wanted to see was in a nearby street. I drove there and Bill spoke to the officer. It now seemed that the policeman made an allegation that Bill offered him a bribe. In his interview the officer had described a two man car crew. He had also obviously got his days and dates mixed up, hence Pugh was asking everyone about a wrong date and getting nowhere.

The officer in question had also been in the corridor and canteen at Duke Street in an effort to identify the car driver. I had seen him but not recognised him. I let the matter rest.

The shambles of the amalgamation was beginning to get to me a little. The quality of unit inspectors and sergeants on divisions was terrible. Virtually all the promotions into the City were from outsiders. They were not all good policemen, in the main. Some were products from the Special Course, a sort of accelerated promotion scheme, and were not around long enough to leave any continuity, and they were being joined by the 'butterflies'.

'Butterflies' is a term used to describe potential high fliers who are short on experience. They come in all shapes but all have the uncontrollable desire to get to the top. They answer advertisements for promotion to other forces, get the promotion, a bit of experience, leave their mark, usually a bad one, answer another advert and flutter on. Prior to the amalgamation the old force had men of sufficient quality to fill posts without advertising, now it hadn't. Yet again standards were falling.

I was asked to substantiate my theory and I quoted a true example. One of the lads I had been with in the Air Cadets wanted to be a policeman. Birmingham rejected him. He failed the entrance exam. Chief Inspector Mervyn Morton was in charge of recruiting and I had worked with him when he was an Inspector. We respected each other's views and I asked him if he would give my friend another chance. He said he couldn't, and wouldn't, but he did. He failed a second time but this time Mervyn referred him to Warwickshire and they accepted him. In 1974 he was at Solihull and is now part of the West Midlands Force. A man who was not good enough, twice, had now joined us. My case rested.

Many years ago the City had a very effective Road Safety Section.

Visit to school media studies project, Stockland Green Comprehensive School, 2 May 1975. Entire event committed to video by school who also took this photograph.

Primarily it was child orientated and promoted such things as safe cycling. We now had an all-embracing department called Public Liaison, which covered Road Safety and Public Relations.

Occasionally Traffic sent teams to various places at the request of the PLD. One of the best projects I went to was a school media studies day at Stockland Green Comprehensive. We took a couple of bikes, the dog section gave a display and the Mounted Branch also put in an attendance. The Fire Brigade brought in a water squirter.

The kids recorded the whole thing on video and took hoards of photographs which were all developed in-house as part of the process. A super day out, but a shame about the school dinner; it took me back twenty years.

Bad news travels fast, they say, and the news that Bill Glastonbury and Derek Jennings had been suspended from duty and served with summonses, together with garage owner Don Parsons, moved at the speed of light. It was a very sad day all round.

June was having a recurrence of previous sinus problems, together with ongoing problems from the shoulder and later in the summer she spent some more time at the Convalescent facility at Hove. Whilst she was away I fended for myself. I spent many leisure hours riding my own motorcycle. One morning after Court I met one of our friends in the canteen at the Lane.

Gillian was a little older than us and had been a policewoman all her working life. I had known her about ten years and she had worked with June so she was a well-established friend. She had divorced and seemed well happy with her lot. We talked wind, weather and motorcycles. She mentioned that she had never ridden on the back of a big bike, although I knew she had a scooter which she took all over the country.

With the evening spare we agreed that we would have a ride out that very evening. The weather forecast was OK so the roads would be good. I collected her from her flat and when I got there she was in a one-piece leather suit and leather boots. Her white helmet made up the outfit. I was surprised that she had leathers and said so.

'I bought them when I had the scooter. They are hopeless for local rides but when I go away they are ideal.'

I couldn't argue with that, leather is the best protection for a motorcyclist's body.

We set off and had a steady ride out into Worcestershire. Once I was happy that she was settled I went very quickly on the open roads and, admittedly, really hurtled along in places, but traffic was light. We stopped in Kinver for a glass of pop and then zoomed off in a big loop to get back to her flat. In all we did eighty-five miles.

As she got off she said, 'That was wonderful, absolutely wonderful, I have never experienced anything like that. It was so exciting. Thank you, can I offer you a coffee?'

A coffee sounded great, I accepted. She switched the kettle on and I hung my jacket over the door. She put the helmets in the hall. Then she unzipped her suit to the waist. She was wearing a white top and I took no further notice. As I sipped my coffee, still standing in the kitchen, she peeled off the top of her suit and let it hang from her waist like men would with a boiler suit. This revealed, fully, her figure. She was wearing a Lycra leotard and nothing else. I know I stared at her breasts. I couldn't help it. She had a full figure and was a lovely shape. There were constant, neat curves. Gillian had obviously enjoyed her ride very much and as she cooled off her nipples swelled under her top. Shit. Her body was sending very positive signals, she was becoming highly aroused, such signals are contagious and my body was starting to respond very powerfully indeed.

We didn't speak. I think we were both a bit surprised but we both now knew that the other knew. Her nipples distorted the leotard and pointed upwards. She walked into the hall and kicked her boots off. I stayed where I was. I had been faithful to June since we became an item, and as Gillian was a mutual friend a wrong move was not in our best interests. When she came back in things were less prominent and I thought that her urge had died. I hoped so. Then she said, 'I didn't know what to expect, but I didn't expect that.'

'Expect what?' I asked her, not quite knowing whether she meant her boob show.

'The effect was amazing; when we stopped I was like a jelly.' Her nipples started to grow again as she spoke. Eighty-five miles, lots of it flat out, with a Triumph Bonneville between her thighs had excited her sexual quarters. I had heard of it happening but had not seen it.

She walked towards me, put her arms round my neck and kissed me. Her tongue hit the back of my mouth and she rubbed her right thigh against my tackle. I pushed her away a bit awkwardly but she hung on. I was now reaching point alpha. She then came up for air, unzipped my fly, dropped to her knees, and took me. I was stuck with my back against the units. Her arms were round my hips, for what seemed ages. As she stood up my hands were inside her leathers. Nothing was said. We went to her bedroom.

I stayed late into the night, we had got to talk. Gillian had sexually saturated on the bike, couldn't control it and was full of apologies for what followed. Neither of us had planned it, neither of us had expected it and in the end neither of us could do anything about it. It had happened. Such was the power of our silent signals. Purists would say that I could still have said 'no'. We were both past that stage once she pulled the zip.

Oddly, whilst in the Isle of Man the year before I had bought a sticker which was now on my locker at work. It said simply, 'Put something exciting between your legs . . . ride a motor cycle.' Total innuendo but it came straight back home.

I went home to digest the last few hours. I lay awake for ages. What had started as a normal day had ended so bizarrely. I questioned the fact that we had been together at all, but why not? We'd known each other for years. We had been friends a long time, but what we had just done had broken aside the barriers of friendship. We hadn't talked sex and we hadn't even held hands. So why? What had gone wrong? Why did it turn out like that?

I thought back to Izzy. She'd taken the lead, when she needed urgent relief. Had Gillian done the same? She was never short of escorts, so why choose me, and why then? I found no answers. The thrill from the bike was the most likely though. That was the only factor which had been new to her. If I had been asked to make a list of people likely to get in that situation she wouldn't have been near the bottom; she would have been left off! She had always come across as very prim and proper, then that. We'd even been together at Bob Osborne's funeral. Bob had re-kindled her flame immediately after her divorce, before moving on. We had erred seriously and I knew not why. I made no plans to see her again and became quite philosophical about that night.

I was quite upset when Gillian suggested we meet again and continue a clandestine affair. That would not be a good idea. Our paths crossed regularly at work and that didn't help. When she talked plans for the future I knew something final had to be done. We made strenuous efforts not to see each other again, even at work. That night now had the danger of becoming public and it had to be mentioned to June before then.

June was quite sensible about it. It had happened, that was a pity. It was, in the circumstances, understandable. It was not likely to be repeated so it did not present a problem. It was consigned to history. Sadly, Gillian died within weeks of retiring.

Within days of that encounter a sombre hush fell across the Force, but the City in particular. PC Dave Green had been stabbed to death on the 'A' division. I had met Dave when I was on the 'A' but I never knew him well. He was the first bobby I could recall who had been murdered in Birmingham. Gordon Law had come close in 1966. He had been stabbed in the back whilst on foot patrol alone, in Balsall Heath. He lived, but was permanently disabled.

Before Bill and Derek went to Court, I had been approached by Bill's solicitor, to confirm what I had spoken to Bill about. I was duly interviewed and made a statement. I was to give evidence at the trial, should the case get beyond the Committal. It did, and I did.

The trial in August 1975 had started with the words, 'Members of the jury, the case before you is but the tip of an iceberg of corruption within the traffic division of Birmingham City Police.' With those words the prosecution damned us all. If we were corrupt why had we been allowed to remain in office, doing the job we were supposed to be corrupting? That was a wicked statement indeed. That prosecutor was not an impartial agent to the Court. He had apparently pre-judged the issue and given his verdict. Defending the men in the dock was now impossible.

Towards the end of the trial I was called and took the Oath. I was asked by the defence to describe my duties on the day in question. I did. I was then cross examined and told I was a liar. The prosecutor read out an extract from Pugh's evidence in which he described his interview with me when I had been asked about what was now accepted as the wrong date. Pugh had told the Court that he had not only asked me about the date but also about the whole week. In those circumstances I should have told him about the Saturday.

That extract was *untrue*. I explained that I had not been asked about the whole week. Indeed Pugh had inspected my pocket book for the whole month and the information he had required was in there then and was in there now. He had single-mindedly only asked about one date.

I was warned that I was under Oath and asked, 'Are you telling the Court that Mr Pugh has not told the truth?'

I replied, 'If Mr Pugh has said what you have just read out then either he is mistaken or untruthful.'

'You are saying then that Mr Pugh is a liar.'

'Either he is mistaken or he is a liar, yes.'

'Which?'

'That is not for me to decide. I answered his questions truthfully.'

After I left the Court I knew that I had been wholly honest. I had told the truth. I had been in a casual interview with Pugh. I had told him the truth then and because he had been unsure of his facts he had failed to elicit the information he required. My conscience was clear then and is today.

All the men were convicted and went to prison. Bill and Derek were dismissed from the service. I, and eleven of my colleagues from Duke Street, were returned, overnight, to the divisions we had come from originally.

I was absolutely shattered when I was told by the Chief Superintendent that I was to be kicked off Traffic for misconduct. The man who, in April the year before, had told me that I was too good a traffic officer to move off the division on promotion was now, sixteen months later, branding me a liar and effectively destroying my future as a policeman.

The other movers were all men who had a high work record. They were also men who had gaps in the old dispatch ledger.

I had one chance left to keep my good name. Bill Donaldson. He was now Assistant Chief Constable, Traffic, the ultimate Boss. Donaldson and I had never seen eye to eye but the man wasn't stupid. June had applied to Cheshire for a post there; if accepted they would take me as a constable and offer promotion, on merit, in the future. In those circumstances it would be pointless to move me to a division, only for me to transfer to Cheshire within weeks. Could my transfer be postponed?

'No, and neither you nor your wife are available for transfer. This Force is only transferring in.' He was adamant. He would allow me to resign if I wished.

If I was going to resign it would be when I was good and ready and not before. I suspected that, in fact, it might not be that long before I did.

After Bill and Derek had served their sentences their case finally went to Appeal. The convictions were quashed and they were reinstated into the Service. Both later retired on full pensions. My decision to give evidence at the trial had been vindicated.

I had told the truth at Court. For my efforts I had been taken from the one job I had loved and had my career prospects ruined. Pugh was promoted. No other officers from Duke Street were ever prosecuted. None, including all who left at the same time as me, were ever disciplined for any breach of Regulations or instructions. The iceberg did not exist. Pugh was biased from the start. Both Pugh and the prosecutor had apparently pre-judged a non-existent situation. Pugh had sought a result. He had not sought evidence. The evidence proved Pugh's result to be wrong.

I was transferred back to the 'A' division, this time to Digbeth. Such was the hurry to move me that I made the division top-heavy. There was no vacancy for me.

CHAPTER 12

Policewomen

IT IS PROBABLY NOW APPROPRIATE to make some mention of the women officers in the City, their role in the early days and the impact they had on the male officers.

In 1963 Birmingham had a department staffed solely by women officers, with special responsibilities for dealing with offences committed on or by women or children. It was a relic of a bygone age: The Children and Young Persons Act 1933. In one way it still was but it provided a vital backbone of support service and the contribution of its staff should not be overlooked or glossed over as ineffective.

The department was headed by Superintendent Norah Grey. She was a lifelong career policewoman. Its headquarters was in Steelhouse Lane, adjoining the police station. The HQ undertook the local specialist training of all newly recruited women. The small nucleus of experienced staff remained for that purpose. The rest of the policewomen were posted to divisional departments.

A Chief Inspector was posted to the 'A' division, Inspectors to the remainder. We liked to think that the 'A' had the Chief Inspector because we were the most important division. That may have been true but the official reason was that she would be on hand as deputy. Each sub-division was also entitled to a sergeant and the constables were allocated as required.

There was a high quality of girl cadets in the system. They were also loosely under the umbrella of the department. Many former Birmingham cadets and departmental officers hold high rank in the service, around the country; these include Alice Harding, Erica Norton and Trish Anthony, Ann Alden and Rhona Cross, MBE who has now retired.

Norah Grey, was, in herself, a gem, but she did not like her girls being dated by those 'nasty single men' from next door. There were nearly fifty living in at the Lane, so I can understand some of her concern. Neither did she approve of them kissing their boy friends good night outside their hostel. Where possible she had the housekeeper, Miss Fox, take the numbers of all cars from which the girls alighted. Miss Fox lacked subtlety and was easily avoided.

The hostel was a large Victorian house in Anderton Park Road, Moseley, known as Burgess House and nicknamed the 'Virgins' Retreat'. The building was named after the first Commissioner of Birmingham Borough Police, Francis Burgess.

Miss Grey believed the bastion to be impregnable but its defences were breached more than once and not all the occupants were virgins. Many a single man had been summoned to her office to explain why, in x number of weeks, he had dated a resident. I had personal experience of this system, but did catch her off guard a little. The same building also housed T&C, the abbreviation for Traffic and Communications. T&C undertook all urgent office hours motor taxation checks and the requests were kept in a large ledger. You put the number on the ledger and they got you the result. I put a number in, and a few above it I saw Miss Grey had requested details of my own car. That figured. A couple of nights before, I had taken a girl home to The Retreat. I spoke to the office man and he said to go and see her and he wrote down my name and address on a piece of paper. I took this in to Miss Grey and she said thank you or something and I said, 'That's me, I understand you want to see me.'

"Um well, eh, yes.' I had wrong footed her.

The lads were well used to her routine so I was fully aware of what she wanted to know. So I said something like, 'I am single. I am dating Ann Russell who is also single. I don't think I will cause her any difficulty.'

With that Norah seemed relieved and she sent me on my way. She would now go and assure Miss Russell that I was a suitable beau.

When Ann got to hear that our dating had become public she promptly called it off!

The proximity of the department HQ to the 'A' division meant that those men posted there had a preview of all the girls prior to their transfers to the suburbs. It also meant that the 'A' division always had a reserve of women officers to call upon in emergency.

One of the reasons the department existed at all was because of the conditions of service imposed on the women officers. They received only 90 per cent of the salary of their male counterparts and should only have worked 7½ hour shifts instead of 8. The duty was still 8 hours though; they were not paid for the refreshment period. The men were. That anomaly prevented total integration. For example the women did not work nights on a regular basis. Two were posted to the department HQ from 10 pm onwards, one from a division and the other from the department. They were then available to be called out as required. Not a satisfactory system if they were needed at two places at once, as they often were.

Regional Specialist Course for Policewomen, Tally Ho!, 1967.

The HQ department closed within about eighteen months of my joining the City.

With the facility of Tally Ho! at its disposal the force hosted Specialist Courses for Policewomen on a Regional basis. These courses were so sought after that they were almost a growth industry. The speakers included many of our own staff but also high profile outsiders from many walks of life.

The divisional departments were arguably some of the most useful. They had established over many years a local index of all 'at risk' families. They had friends in the public who made sure that all children were cared for properly. They also had excellent relationships with the schools and care agencies. They had the powers to act in the best interest of the child and no doubt saved the Social Services many of the mishandlings which they were to suffer in later years.

The Police view was that an ill-treated child should have its future decided by the Juvenile Court, not by a care worker, whose opinion would always be to keep family unity. The incidence of care cases dropped dramatically with the abolition of the divisional departments. They have now been reformed, under the guise of child liaison, or family protection, following lots of criticism.

The arrival of the Sex Discrimination Act, which exempted the police from some sections, caused panic within the Service and an intense recruiting drive brought in vast numbers of women officers. These by-passed, completely, the departments and were deployed onto shifts, to work with, and alongside, their male colleagues. The divisional departments disappeared, together with their records and indices and many combined years of experience. I am sure we failed the City children that day. The departments may have belonged to another age but the work they did was current and vital to the community.

Many of the older women were not what could be described as fashion conscious and were treated with scorn by some of the men, particularly those with whom they had worked for many years. Some were, without doubt, lesbians. The new generation were indeed different.

Many of the department girls were trained drivers. They were initially the only women officers to be given driving courses. Gradually more women were trained and then some were trained to advanced standards. In 1974 there were two at Duke Street. They were both were Graded 1. They were Annette Hubbleday, and Gaynor Rourke and at the time they were our own celebrities, appearing on the TV and in the papers. There was also Christine Read who was a traffic motorcyclist. She was Dave Northam's sister. I would later work with him.

It is difficult to pinpoint individual women officers in a chronological sequence because, unlike the men, they were not around for too long. The average length of service tended to be about five years, then babies arrived and they left. Some in later years had their children and came straight back to work. It was cheaper to pay a nanny than it was to be out of work. Such were the changes.

I never really worked closely with any women until I was posted to Digbeth.

One exception was Sylvia Draper, who I had worked with during my CID attachment and who June had worked very closely with whilst on the 'C' division. Sylvia was a native of Birmingham and very proud of the fact. She had been brought up in the Winson Green district. She was an excellent policewoman, one of the few engaged at that time on detective duties. In 1972, for the Force magazine, *Forward* she wrote a poem, which she called, 'My Brummagem'. It probably summed up the population of the City, not just its police.

My Brummagem

Our city holds so many tales,
The inhabitants are proud,
We have a place in history books,
Our praises shouted loud.

In industry we're world renowned,
The City of a Thousand Trades.
Our machinery rolls, and side by side
Work study men and maids.

Personalities in politics,
In Theatre and Art too.
I cannot name them all right now
But we have our own *Who's Who*.

A big Town Hall and stately homes,
Yes, we're got the lot!
There's a clock to honour Chamberlain
And a statue of James Watt.

Brummies are held in high repute
And we jealously guard the breed.
If you're accepted as one of us,
You're a lucky man indeed!

But once you are within our ring,
Our loyalty holds no bars
But reciprocation we'll expect
and you'd better buy our cars.

We have a language all our own,
To strangers it's frustrating.
We never mean just what we say,
It certainly needs translating.

The sing-song tone the locals have
When speaking in the vernacular
Is abhorrent to some folk
But to others it's spectacular.

Everyone is 'Skip' or 'Kid'
And now, to test your brain,
When, 'It's black over Bill's mother's'
Would you guess it's going to rain?

'Our mom' gives the kids a 'tank'
When they get her 'on a line'
For playing in the 'horse road'
When it's way past their bedtime.

We 'knock off weark' and 'ketch the buzz'
We'em 'gooin 'um' you see,
To our house which is a 'back to back'
In Nechells or Hockley.

And as I walk along the 'cut',
Through factory smoke and stench.
I know that this is my sweet home,
For I'm a Brummagem wench!

CHAPTER 13

Digbeth

I REPORTED BACK TO THE OLD Division. I was very dejected when I saw the Superintendent at Digbeth, John Tonkinson. Tonky, as he was affectionately known, been a traffic motorcyclist himself and he was well aware of the crazy system that had caused all the troubles. He was the first man to show any degree of sympathy but his operational requirements were such that I had to be posted to 'D' unit. That was the first problem. I had come from 'A' which was what June was now on. Before promotion I had been on 'B'. That meant three unit changes in sixteen months.

June was unable to change her unit and therefore for the foreseeable future we would be on different shifts. That was another punishment for us. I suspect that Tonky had been told to give me an unfavourable posting, because he also told me that for the first few months I would work indoors and not have contact with the public. Presumably I was now 'unclean' and should not be seen.

For just over twelve years I had, except for a brief period, been at the pointed end of front line policing. I had received fifteen commendations in that time. Not a bad record when the average was about six in thirty years. Now, I was going to have to sit on my arse in an office and watch a TV screen, and answer the telephone. I was not impressed!

The Unit Inspector was Ron Longstaff. He was a gent. I had known him for many years. He had briefly left the police for a career in the Fire Service. He was top student on both his police and fire initial courses. That is as far as I know a record in itself. Ron explained who everyone was. Most I knew but there were some new faces. There were some very good policemen on the unit and Ron ran a happy shift. That was a plus. He wanted me to be the unit controller, the radio and computer operator. One snag: I was not trained to use the computer. In those circumstances I would start being awkward. Messing people about can work from both ends. It was now my turn.

The problem would have been resolved if I could have had a course. The system was shortly to be phased out and a new one implemented, therefore no further training was possible. I knew the answer and I had the cheek to suggest it. The Information Room had a number of consoles. I knew the City and I knew the radio. They could teach me the computer. I also knew that there was a spare seat on one unit owing to long-term sickness. I found out that they would have me before I made the suggestion to Ron.

He warmed to the idea, spoke to Tonky, and he agreed. There was never a mention on paper and I went back to my old traffic shift for two weeks. Two weeks on the other end of the radio. I knew the basics of the Command and Control computer system before but the two weeks using it in anger was far more beneficial than a week in the classroom and I quickly became quite competent. I was sorry when the two weeks were up. I would have liked to have stayed for two years.

Since I had worked the 'A' division it had grown. Stuck on the side was a great big carbuncle called Nechells. Nechells had been very similar to Newtown prior to redevelopment but was now a mixture of industrial and residential properties, many of which were fairly new. I afforded myself a day working there to familiarise myself with the new territory. I urgently needed a little local knowledge if I was to send resources there. There was also a police station there, a newly built satellite with a couple of cells and a few offices. There were four beat officers there. None of them had ever worked the 'A' division. They had a free transfer in 1974 when the 'D' division lost Nechells and gained Sutton.

I settled down to my new job but I found it very mundane. I had never before worked fully indoors and that combined with the anger I still felt towards Pugh made me quite morose at times. The unit deserved better of me. They were a good team, and a good mix. Some well experienced, a lot with around five years service and more than our fair share of probationers. Something had got to be done and I had a long chat with Ron.

As I saw it there were two options. Either resign, get away from the job altogether, or bite the bullet and suffer for a couple of years in the hope that I would then be able to return to traffic. Ron advised against leaving. He had been along that road himself, and come back. I might not be so lucky. He had no complaint with my work. As he said, I knew the City Centre better than him. There were now two types of sergeant: the sergeant who was there simply because he had to be one to go higher, and the one who would remain a backbone of the shifts for the rest of his service. It was an important rank and there was great potential for variety. He saw me in that role.

There was also the financial side to consider. Two sergeants on top rate pay drew a salary equal to that of one Assistant Chief Constable. On top of that there was a rent allowance, but more importantly there was ample scope for paid overtime. The Income Tax situation was different then and there was little financial advantage in further promotion in our circumstances. The only long-term advantage was in the pension, and that was sixteen or more years away and therefore quite uncertain.

On the promotion side the service was starting to look towards men and women with higher education and I had not sought that. There was little chance of Force sponsorship for a degree but I gave serious consideration to an Open University course, but shelved that idea. I had good library at home, the new *Encyclopaedia Britannica* had been published in 1974 and I had bought one. I had, at my fingertips, most of the knowledge I would ever require and decided that I did not need a degree to enjoy that knowledge, or indeed to be a policeman. I had managed well up to then. I would remain a career sergeant, as would June.

Obviously a holiday was a good idea now and we went to Gibraltar, very British but with sunshine. The laws there are in essence those of the United Kingdom and the policemen wear a helmet similar to those worn here, only white, in the summer. I was to see during that visit a piece of policing which would not have been out of place anywhere at home.

By the strangest of coincidence we had a drink in a bar and I thought I recognised the barmaid. I had no idea where from; she was a native of Gibraltar, I was told. Her father kept the pub. A few nights later I met her boyfriend and it all fitted into place. His father ran a pub on the doorstep of Digbeth. She had been to England to visit him and I had seen her in the pub. He had been in the Navy and had met her whilst ashore in Gibraltar.

He had remained in touch with some of his former shipmates and a few of them, together with June and I, stayed behind for a drink. The sailors got a bit tight but refused a taxi. We were in a hotel about a hundred yards away from the pub and were happy to walk.

The sailors left about five minutes ahead of us. We saw them throw a number of road works barriers into the road works hole. It was a typical act of drunken stupidity. As they did so a policeman appeared out of the shadows and spoke to them. He didn't arrest them. They looked resplendent in their white uniforms so he gave them the ultimatum. Put the barriers back or get locked up and miss the ship. The brown mud of the hole soiled their lovely uniforms, punishment enough. Message received and understood. It was a wonderful example of a man knowing his job, and his customers.

With the future more clearly mapped out I settled down to do what had got to be done. Digbeth was a very busy station, probably the busiest in the City at that time. The building was unfortunately totally unsuited to its task and its Grade II listing meant that very little could be done with it. Therefore, in the true traditions, we muddled on. The front office and public enquiry counter was moved around three times in the next six years.

There were also single quarters for about fifteen men and these rooms were very noisy, but the lads in them liked them so they were kept allocated. There were no social facilities. It was expedient for all staff to be members of the Midland Red Social Club, opposite the back door. The beer was cheap and the food was good. There was also an excellent snooker table. Things did improve over the years but not to any great degree. It is still too small for the job it has to do. Parking was desperate. There were six Pandas, a CID car, a minibus, half a dozen spaces for single men in the tiny yard. If all vehicles were there at once they could not all be used.

Digbeth was the first time I had worked with policewomen on the shifts and Ruth Bryan was very sensible to work with. She was married, she could drive and she didn't mind getting stuck into the work. She later worked in plain clothes with much success. Eventually, like most before her, she left to have a family. When I last saw her she was driving a black taxi.

The other sergeants on the shift were both likely to move up the ladder. They both had quiet social lives and tended not to mix with the shift socially. I was different. With June and me both in the Service I found it easy to spend spare time, particularly after a shift, with the other members of the unit and I got to know them very well. That helped to build a bond between us and I was viewed as a friend. Socially, I was 'one of the lads' and June was readily accepted.

At the Christmas 1975 party I had the first opportunity to meet wives and girlfriends and it was there that June had her first brush with snobbery from the wife of a promotion-seeking sergeant who had been invited as a guest.

She approached June and said, 'I don't think we've met. I'm Sergeant Smith's wife.'

June's quick reply was, 'Good, I'm Sergeant Pettitt.'

The lady was obviously confused, 'I thought Sergeant Pettitt was a man.'

'Oh he is; I'm Sergeant Pettitt's wife as well.'

That really killed any more conversation with her. June intensely dislikes any form of snobbery and didn't take too well to Mrs Smith. The evening though was a great success. It was something the unit had not done before. I brought the idea from traffic. There we often had a unit party or night out. The following year we booked the restaurant fully on the night it was usually closed, and combined with the unit from the Lane.

At around the following Easter, 1976, I dusted my helmet off and went walkabout. My isolation was over. I could try and be a policeman again. It didn't take long. Within three days I had found another car thief. I was walking out with Clive Green. Clive had transferred from Lancashire where he had been a traffic man and we had a lot in common. He had moved to enhance his promotion chances, an ambition he was to achieve within months.

We were walking along Lawley Street when a Rover 2000 drove slowly past us and then stopped. The driver nipped into a pub. I looked at the number of the car and it was an invalid combination. I told Clive and he went to the side door of the pub and I went into the bar.

In order not to embarrass the man in the pub I complained to him about his manner of parking. As soon as we were outside I arrested him. Clive was about to call on the radio for a car to take us back into Digbeth when I said, 'We've got one. We can't leave this here.' To Clive's surprise I drove us all in. It seemed logical. The car was evidence and had got to be removed anyway, why not all at once?

The enquiry which followed was quite interesting. The driver was disqualified. From the chassis number we found the car had been reported stolen for over three years, but the current driver, who admitted to being the thief, insisted that he had only had the car for about a week. He had repainted it and changed the number plates. He had dumped the original number plates on wasteland. We went there but couldn't find them.

We went back to the start and found exactly where the car had originally been taken from. Once I had that sorted out I discovered that the theft had been reported to Stechford. Records there gave me the number that was on the car when it was taken by our man, here, and also of the man claiming that it was his car. The vehicle records were checked and they disclosed that the number plate which had been on the car when it was recently stolen had been allocated to the current keeper since before the car was first stolen. That suggested that the man who had reported the recent theft was probably the original thief.

He had to be seen next. I told him on the phone that his car had been recovered and was at Digbeth. Yes, he knew where that was. Give him twenty minutes. That was easier than going to his house to arrest him. He identified the car as being the one he had reported stolen. He was able to tell from the interior; amongst other things the driver's seat had been replaced. He had used the car as a taxi and the seat had collapsed with use. That seemed positive enough. He had at my request brought with him the Logbook. The details in that did not agree with the car. The car was about a year newer than the one in the Logbook.

He accepted that. Yes the car was 'ringed'. His original car had broken down and was beyond repair. He had found this car with keys in and had taken it home. He had substituted the number plates from his original car, which he had then scrapped, and had used this car for about three years as a taxi. It transpired that he actually worked from the Digbeth area and both he and the car were well known to the police. He had driven it round for three years under our noses and had never been detected.

He was charged with the theft of the car. On legal advice the driver was charged with theft also. Although the car was already stolen his actions had amounted to theft. He had intended to prevent its use by anyone else. He agreed with that and pleaded guilty.

It was a nice little starter, I'd got back into the swing of things, but how many had got away through my incarceration? I had a flair for things like that.

Midway into 1976 I was called for audience with the Chief Superintendent. Unworried, I sat in comfort, with coffee and biscuits. 'Serge, you know this division as well as any man on it. You will remember when we had a traffic squad. God knows why, but the idea seems out of fashion. So much out of fashion that the whole bloody City ground to a halt twice in the run-up to Christmas. The Chief has had flak from everywhere, Chamber of Trade, the Press, the AA and the Fire Service. If there had been a fire in the town that day, they would not have been able to get there. Something has got to be done. You know where the black spots are, have a few days out and about, speak to Tottle, speak to Traffic Wardens and the car parks. Sort out a viable plan, put it on paper and send it up to me, direct, don't bother the Inspector. The bottom line is *you* have got to make it work.'

'That could be an interesting job. I take it that it covers both sub-divisions?'

'It must do, yes.'

That was a nice project to be given. Quite how I went about it I didn't really know. The City was different now. There were underpasses, fast roads and flyovers, all carrying an increasing number of vehicles. Some traffic was local. Much would go straight through. The biggest single problem was parking. Not lack of spaces, but lack of organisation.

I found out that on the occasions when the City had clogged up, most of the car parks had spaces available. The prime sites were full, as always, but those on the fringe had hundreds of spaces. We had to educate the motorists. The City Council did a map of their sites. NCP did a map of theirs. Nobody did a map that covered all of them. That had to be looked at. Possibly put one in the paper.

Full, must mean Full. There was a tendency for drivers to wait in anticipation. That had got to stop. They were the culprits. It was they who were causing the congestion. Manpower was the only way to move them on.

Since the Land Rover had been given to traffic the division had lost its exclusive use of it. However, Barry Tottle was now a sergeant in charge of three Land Rovers. All were now based at Bridge, but had a citywide responsibility. I had to redress that and have one posted permanently on the division during whatever operation I mounted. Barry was supportive but he would have to put it to his boss. I disagreed. Once Chief Superintendent 'A' division had decided what he wanted any negotiations on deployment would be in very high places indeed. I argued that if Barry was happy, in principle, with the idea I would suggest that it be implemented.

Next stop was Mervyn Morton, now retired, and head of Traffic Warden operations. He had served on the 'A' division and he knew the problems facing me. His problem was results. If I reduced his available numbers of staff, his figures for enforcement would fall. Questions would be asked and he would have to explain. What I had proposed was within the jurisdiction of Traffic Wardens, but it was not an accepted function in its true sense. Within the Parking Meter Zone (and most of the area I was concerned with was), the Wardens had ultimate power. For example only a Traffic Warden could seek removal of a vehicle from a parking meter. The police had powers to enforce all the other relevant legislation.

I suggested for that reason, that all traffic squad personnel, police officers or traffic wardens, drew their supply of Fixed Penalty Tickets from his office, direct. The completed ones would then go back through his system, thus boosting his numbers. At the same time I would have the benefit of his staff to deal with my traffic.

I had known Mervyn a long time and his grin said it all, but he added, 'You knew I'd say "yes" didn't you?'

I thanked him and promised him a preview of the end product, at least as far as it affected his department.

The manager of National Car Parks agreed to run a sort of 'early warning' system between his car parks. Officers on duty near to them would be in radio contact and as a site filled up a diversion route to the next could be set up. The corporation were unable to offer such a facility and that would have to be done by the men on the spot.

Staff wise I decided that I needed around twenty in total. That would mean twelve traffic wardens and eight constables. The eight constables would come from each sub-division at a rate of only one from each unit. That way nobody was denuded of strength, and over the duration of the squad each shift would benefit by having an extra six men on the ground.

I made noises for a motorcycle for myself, but that was not on. I wasn't a traffic man! I settled instead for two traffic motorcyclists working close to the division to monitor traffic flow and potential congestion.

I committed the plan to paper and sent it up. Virtually untouched, it was implemented the following Christmas. It worked, well. I was pleased.

Having got the bones of the job together, and the principle approved, the PR attack was the next step. The Chamber of Trade, NCP car-parks, the Public Works, our Press Office and the *Evening Mail* got their heads together and there was a huge publicity campaign before we actually got the thing working on the ground. We also had a Press Conference at the Lane and this was attended by many from the retail industry.

It was a good exchange of ideas and the ground rules were laid out. We would give them all the help we could and in turn required their co-operation. Without that there could be friction. I would not tolerate unlawful parking, but would assist deliveries in every way I could. I had a huge pound at my disposal and had the staff and skills to use it to great effect. I hoped impoundings would be rare.

When the squad had been live for about a week the *Evening Mail* wanted the story which had been promised in return for the initial publicity for the car park maps. Thus I spent a whole day with a very patient and leg-weary Maureen Messant, who although a busy journalist wasn't used to walking about all day. She was, to use her phrase to me as we parted, 'bloody knackered'.

The publicity did the squad a lot of good and it remained a regular feature of Christmas for the next decade.

It was with some amusement one of the first mornings that we found a brand new Renault on NCP in Snow Hill in a very sorry state. It was covered, inside and out, in NCP yellow paint. It was wrecked. The owner thought he knew who was responsible. He had spent the night in the Grand Hotel with the man's wife. That was an expensive night out.

Digbeth was host to many nightclubs and was then probably the entertainment capital of the City. They did bring prosperity to the area but they also brought a degree of trouble, particularly at weekends. It was normal to operate a van patrol in order to have a mobile team to give support to Unit personnel on Friday and Saturday. For the most part the duty was out to overtime and there was never a shortage of volunteers. Often a show of strength was enough and the crew very rarely had to be deployed as a group. When I worked the van I preferred to leave perhaps three on the van and have the others on foot, nearby.

The duty was not without its lighter moments and I have a vivid recollection of a young, rather mouthy, officer getting himself cut down to size by one of his older and wiser colleagues. I was in the front seat and there were about five officers in the back. One had been on foot patrol and was

1976 Christmas traffic squad. (With credit to the Birmingham Post & Mail Ltd.)

about to join the van by the back doors when the van moved forward. The lad fell headlong on the road behind the van and his helmet rolled away. The sight of the policeman on the floor was a great source of amusement to one or two revellers. It was a foolish thing to do but I understood the sentiment and let it pass without comment. When we returned to Digbeth the vanquished and the victor discussed the matter in the yard, but the result did not change. The young officer got wiser.

The vision of Pete on the floor took me back many years to when I walked out of a shop doorway one Sunday evening, slipped on the glass insets above a cellar, and fell over, in full uniform, in front of a crowded bus queue. No one said a word until a little boy said, 'Daddy, the policeman fell over.' That caused a few laughs and I ambled away, unruffled but very embarrassed.

The van was sent out one evening before the usual time. The incident we went to was in itself very unusual. One of the older pubs was built on three levels. The two lower bars were always staffed, the third rarely was. That upper room was rented out on every second Saturday to a group of girls. They provided their own record player and came to the lower floor for their drinks. They had never knowingly been any problem. On this particular night the regular licensee was on holiday and a relief manager was in charge. He was a miserable old sod by any standards and he had complained about the noise from the records. The girls decided to annoy him and made the music louder.

Having had no success with his request he went to the room to order the music to be turned down. When he got there he was not prepared for what he saw. The girls were lesbians and were dancing with each other. There were also a couple of vibrators about. He panicked, and phoned the police. I went with the van and he told me what had happened. The inside of a pub is the responsibility of the licensee and if any requests were made for people to leave they were going to be made by him. I went up to the top floor with him and took a constable with me.

The scene was more or less as he had described, but with the progress of time some dancing had reverted to necking and kissing. The manager was not the most tactful when he told them to leave the pub and take their clockwork cocks with them. From then on things could only get worse. The girls refused to leave. Not one, but all twenty-five plus of them. The difficulty I was in then was that it is an offence to refuse to leave licensed premises and I had all these refusals. At any request of the manager from now on I was obliged to do something about the refusal. I did not relish the task.

Sure enough, he requested action. That was what we had. The request to leave had now become a demand and we were now faced with the total removal of the girls from the pub. My first concern was that these were regular customers; by their very nature they would have difficulty in getting similar facilities elsewhere, and Barry, the licensee, would be unhappy with trouble in his pub. I put it to the girls that the initial problem had been the increase in volume of the music. There was nothing at this stage on paper so a sensible and peaceful solution was still an option open to us all. Some agreed. Could they have their money back from the rent? I would find out, and sent my mate to speak to the manager.

No, they'd used the room, they had to pay was the verdict. Dammit! The cost of the room was a fiver. I had that if I needed it. What I had hoped was that if they got their money back they would drink up and go. I could see Barry when he came back from holiday and square it with him for the arrangement to continue. I wasn't really happy with the way the manager had dealt with them so far and a lot of the problem was him.

I said, 'If I can guarantee the money back, how many of you would leave?' About half nodded or put their hands up. 'You others?' They all shook their heads.

I made my decision, 'I will give five minutes to drink up and leave the pub. If you don't we will have to take action. If we take action the brewery will know and they may well decide to stop you booking the room.' I went downstairs, spoke to the manager and phoned in for some more help. Even with eight of us I didn't fancy tipping a couple of dozen pint-swilling butches out of a crowded pub, made worse with two flights of stairs. The manager was useless. He didn't want to know. A fiver would reduce the problem by 50 per cent or more. In the end he relented. I took the fiver to the girls.

'He's given me the money back,' I showed them the money.

The organiser took it and about ten girls got their things together and left. Some had already gone. We were left with a hard core of eight. A second van arrived and we started to try and get names and addresses but that idea was abandoned when one girl poured a pint of what looked like urine over the policewoman. They were all about to be arrested and removed from the pub. What a scrap! A pub full of men would have been easier. It took us nearly twenty minutes to get the last one down the stairs. They fought, kicked, struggled, swore, bit and spat every inch of the way. When we got them to Digbeth we had the same fighting, screaming and kicking to get them into the cells.

Digbeth was not short of cells, but Saturday nights could be busy and eight females at once was unheard of. Ideally they should have had single cells, two in a cell works well, but I was reluctant to let them start performing with each other so they were bedded down as two threes and a two.

I spoke to Barry on his return and he agreed to give the girls another chance. That was my part of the bargain done. The brewery was advised that the relief manager was not suited to his task and he never worked a City Centre pub again. The girls were all bailed to Court and pleaded guilty. The silly Saturday night got lost in history.

Ron Longstaff moved on and Bob Millner joined us. Bob was an old time City man with about twenty-two years service. He was newly promoted and had not been on the streets for about five years. I knew him from the old area car days. He was well established then. He had the nickname 'Curly', probably because he was as bald as a billiard ball. He and I got on well. He decided that I would show him round the sub-division, and we had a lot of fun as well as a lot of work. Bob had worked a lot with the Irish community and he knew a lot of people from all walks of life. He also made an effort to visit every pub once during the month of a shift cycle and made a point of speaking to everybody. He was, in every way, a community policeman.

He was also a policemen's policeman as I found out one evening. We had taken a Panda up into the town and parked it near the Futurist cinema. The only reason we had used it was that he needed to go to Nechells to sign the books and would go straight from his walk. Within seconds of parking there was a call on the radio to say that a man had been glassed in the Glue Pot pub. We were probably fifty yards away. The man was seriously wounded; he had had both cheeks slashed with a glass and then that had been thrust into his chin. The man responsible had a badly cut hand but he had gone.

Urgent First Aid was vital so the search for the attacker had got to wait. We used up our ambulance pouches and a great deal of a tablecloth from the pub. The ambulance arrived very quickly and we left the chap with them.

The assailant had bled badly and we were able to follow a trail of blood to the Shakespeare in Lower Temple Street. The gaffer there nodded towards the toilet at the back. I went in the gents and found our man bathing his hand under the tap. The palm was well split. I arrested him and put him in a car which had come to back us up. He was taken, first to hospital, then to the station. The gaffer suggested that I spoke to a bloke in the bar who probably knew the man I had just arrested. They had spoken when he had come in. That was when the hand was noticed.

I spoke to the man in the bar, and he came into the street to talk. He explained that he didn't know the chap at all but when he had come in he had said, 'I've been here all night.' I thanked him for his help. As I did so I was pushed over. When I stood up, I was confronted by a very drunk Irishman who made it clear that I was not going to arrest his friend. His friend was the man I had just thanked. I made it clear, however, that I was going to arrest him. He went berserk. Another Panda had arrived and the driver got out. The driver was immediately hit in the face by the man I had got some sort of hold of, and went out like a light. It was one hell of a punch. That officer was Glen White. He said afterwards that he knew nothing of what had happened until he woke up in the ambulance. Fortunately, there was no lasting injury.

Two beat men arrived as well and we bundled this drunken oaf into the back of the Panda; with them holding him down, I drove the car. Bob had by this time gone off to sign his books at Nechells. The journey back to Digbeth was hideous. The prisoner overpowered the officers in the back of the car and was pulling me out of the driving seat. At one stage he banged my head on the roof. Things were now pretty serious and needed drastic action. One of the two Bobbies in the back was dazed from a punch and the other one was putting up a good fight to restrain the prisoner, all in an Allegro.

I drove onto the car park off Edgbaston Street, right out of view. The fewer people who saw what was about to happen the better. I stopped and said, 'Right. A deal. You and me now, man to man. If I lose I shan't come looking for you. If I win you stay nicked. Deal?'

His reply was, 'Deal.'

He was a fit, powerful, steel erector. He was well pissed and I was stone cold sober and very angry. I fancied my chance. As he got out of the car he had both fists, locked like a hammer, straight across his nose. It slowed him a little but not enough. I took policing back fifteen years or more that night. This scene belonged to another age. We were there, bare knuckled, battling out a principle. If he wanted it rough, so be it. In the end I put in a good head butt and he gave up. He then puked about five pints of Guinness over the car. I had won. He stayed locked up. I had two black eyes and a very sore wrist. He had a broken nose, a black eye, and vile hangover.

We were now well overdue at Digbeth and there was some genuine concern for our welfare. The prisoner was now quite peaceful. I searched him, listed his property and put him in the cell. As I did so he held out his hand. 'You're a fair man, Sir. I had my chance, you are the first copper ever to get me in a nick; you beat me fair, there's no hard feelings.'

I took his hand, 'No hard feelings.'

Bob came back in, heard the end of our conversation and saw me looking a bit battered. 'You had a problem?' he asked with innocence.

'Yes. After you went, I had a chat with the bloke at the bar, outside, and his mate set about us. Glen's gone to hospital. He smacked Dickie and Pete and then he wanted me in the back with him. Anyhow, I took him round the back of S & U and taught him some manners. I did him a deal.'

'What was that?'

'Like we used to: if he won, he walked, if he lost, he rode.'

'You can't bloody do that nowadays.'

'He knew no other way. He's never been locked up before. He'll be OK now.'

Bob sent for the Police Surgeon to examine the prisoner and the three of us from the car. The prisoner was fit to be detained. We were fit to continue duty, but he strapped my wrist up for a few days. The prisoner was more than happy with his treatment. He had been dealt with fairly, in his view. There was never a complaint.

We looked a sorry bunch when we went to Court on the Monday morning. I by now had my arm in a sling and my black eyes looked far worse than they really were. For his part, our fighting oaf was now sober and a rational and nice bloke! His nose was twisted but his eyes were fine. Drink had sent him silly. He had been working on a contract which had finished early and he had had a good bonus. The simple problem was that he had tried to drink it all in the same day.

He pleaded guilty to four charges of police assault and of being drunk and disorderly. The prosecutor outlined the circumstances and the Magistrates sought a brief adjournment to consider imprisonment. In the end, because of his previous good character, and that reason only, he was fined, £150 for each assault, £50 for being drunk and a further £50 costs. He was very relieved. Afterwards he insisted I went to the Crown, across the road, and had a drink with him. I accepted. He had expected to go down the steps and was very happy indeed with the case I had presented. We parted on good terms.

I remember assisting two officers from Digbeth when I was off duty in the City with June. We were going to a birthday party at a pub, and then on for a curry. As we made our way to the pub I saw Steve Harrison and a police woman on the floor with a crowd of yobjects stamping all over them. They were in real trouble. I'd been there twice, down, alone, and a crowd wanting blood, it's frightening; I knew how they felt. I went straight in with fists and feet flailing, June followed and dragged out a woman who was kicking everybody.

Before the Bobbies went down they had managed to get in a call for help and I heard the two-tone horns of the help coming. We were by now all taking a bit of a battering. I had the advantage of not being in uniform and was known only to Steve. When the vans arrived there were good pickings. I had downed two and June still had hold of the girl, by the hair. The girl had bitten me as I dealt with her boyfriend. In all about eight found their way to Digbeth. There was some amusement there when those locked up wanted to know who the 'great bear' was who had come out of the crowd and got stuck in. I was passed off as 'a passer by'.

I was a little unhappy the next day when I had a phone call at home telling me the glad tidings that the girl who had bitten me was receiving treatment for syphilis. I had better have a jab. I did not relish a visit to the Pox Doctor but it was sensible as syphilis can be passed by body fluids.

The Special Clinic in Birmingham was a revelation in itself. Everybody is dealt with as a number. Although names are recorded these are never spoken, except in private. The chances of me having any disease from the girl were remote. She was known to the clinic and was in the final stages of her treatment. As a precaution I was given an injection and I had no further problems. As I was about to leave I met a man I knew.

He asked, 'You as well?'

'No I got bitten in a scrap, dirty cow had a dose.'

'Unlucky. I paid £50 for mine in the Albany.'

That summed up the clinic. There were all kinds of patients there.

With the policy of Inspectors always attending a fatal accident, Bob was a bit concerned one afternoon when I asked him to join me at the scene of an accident on New Street at Corporation Street. A truck had swayed a little as it negotiated the junction and had glanced a traffic light set. The head had dropped onto a woman waiting to cross the road.

I did not like what I saw when I got there! The lady was obviously very seriously hurt and I thought it probably wise that we treat this as a fatal from the start. Bob trusted me and came out, despite being very busy with other urgent things. Things were critical for a few weeks but happily the good lady made a reasonable recovery. What we did was easier done then than a few months on if she hadn't recovered.

As I got round the area with the lads on the beat I was able to guide them towards enquiries which they could generate themselves. One Sunday afternoon I was out at Nechells with Geoff Kedney. Geoff was very street-wise. He had been brought up in Aston and had spent nine years in the Navy. He had been round the world twice and had set foot in fifty-four countries. As he said, 'not bad for a kid with nothing'. He was modest. He had a lot to offer the service and the public. As we went to a block of maisonettes we read the graffiti. In letters nine inches high were the words, 'Tracey Jones is a super slag.'

'Like to meet her,' chuckled Geoff, rubbing his hands.

'Might be a good idea.'

'Why?'

'If the kids have written that it's probably true. If it's true, I'll bet she's under sixteen,' I reasoned.

'That means the boys who've been there can be nicked.'

It was decided that Geoff and his partner, Steve Mabbett, should do their best to investigate. Tracey was found; she was just fifteen. The graffiti was true. She had been having sex with all the local boys, probably a dozen in all; she had lost count. She was put in care. Five lads were traced and they all received official cautions.

The result proved the value of keeping one's eyes open when walking about.

Another Sunday, this time in the morning, I was in at Nechells with Geoff again when he got a call to a tower block to help a caretaker get into a flat. Within minutes we got there and spoke to the caretaker. There was a complete floor of old folk on the 3rd or 4th. This was by design. It was 'sheltered' accommodation without the trimmings. They all kept an eye on each other and for security reasons the flats had been fitted with special front doors. Instead of a Yale or Chubb or both, they had got a locking door handle, which in turn had a mechanism whereby, when it was locked, the door was secured in three places with much the same effect as internal bolts. The caretaker had a 'master' key in case of emergency. That morning one of them couldn't be roused so they had gone for the caretaker. He couldn't get in. He unlocked the door OK but it was still fastened.

With an ambulance standing by, the fire service attended. These boys were now high-tech. No axe, but a petrol angle grinder, crossed with a chain saw. This was a new piece of kit from the aircraft fire and rescue camp. It wasn't very healthy, on an enclosed landing in a block of flats, but ruthlessly efficient. In about four seconds flat they had split the door straight down the middle and we went into the flat through an opening reminiscent of a cowboy saloon. The old dear appeared to have died in her sleep.

The 'family' GP gave us the go ahead and we soon had the sons in attendance. I was sickened. These two, both in their mid-fifties, were beyond belief. They were like vultures. I'm having this, she promised me that. I bought her that, I'll have it back. We still had their eighty-four year old mother's body in her bed and these buggers were fighting over her few possessions. I called order and told them to get things sorted out or I would arrange undertakers to remove the body and have the flat secured.

'Oh, and whilst on the subject of security, who is responsible for the extra bolts on the front door?' I asked them.

'I did it,' said one, 'you can't trust people round here.'

'I don't intend to make a scene but you destroyed the whole concept of "help at hand". That's what this scheme is all about. If your mum had been alive we couldn't have got in to give her any help anyway. As it is there's a five hundred quid front door scrapped because you can't trust anybody.' I left Geoff there and I walked back to Digbeth.

I sometimes found that the social lives and late nights of some of the single men caused them to oversleep, sometimes because their mates had let them down, forgotten to call them, or even overslept themselves. One morning I was an unusual member of the unit short. The rest had come downstairs and had not realised that Chris was adrift. Whilst Bob took the parade I went upstairs to wake him. I went to his room, flicked the light on, peeled the covers back and shouted, 'Hands off cocks, on with socks.' As I said it I looked down and realised that the sole occupant of the bed was a naked female. She snatched the covers over herself and looked, not surprisingly, quite shocked. I apologised and said, 'I was looking for Chris.'

Rather sheepishly she said, 'Eh. He's in Pete's room. He said he needed some sleep.'

Pete was on holiday so that was reasonable. I went to the room and woke Chris, with a little more subtlety this time. To my considerable surprise he had a woman in bed with him. Fine.

'Chris, you're in my time now. I'll see you downstairs in five minutes.'

Chris joined the parade and I took him on one side, 'Get those women out of this building before there's a bloody war. Run two if you like but keep them apart.'

'Serge, to be honest, the other one is Pete's. She lost her handbag and stayed the night 'cos she couldn't get home.'

I had to smile. My rules had always been to keep away from other coppers' birds and here was Chris, giving her one in her boyfriend's bed.

The rules about women in bedrooms were simple. They were not allowed! I took the view that the room was the lad's home. They were all grown-up and they were all reasonably healthy young men with active sex drives. They were holding down responsible jobs. If they were sensible there were very few problems. I just didn't like the idea of unattended women being in the station, mainly because of the confidential information which surrounded us. Chris became quickly aware of my feelings.

The incident brought back to mind something I had done there many years before. A lad living in there then had a 500cc AJS motorbike, the single cylinder job. He had come back to the station to find the gates locked so he left the bike outside, and went to bed. I dropped a pal off there on my way home and he had a key for the gates. I pushed the bike into the yard and my pal said, 'Take it in to him.'

'He's in bed.'

'That's OK. Go on. For a laugh.'

I started the bike up and rode round to the front door. The sergeant let me in and I rode the bike up two flights of stairs and parked it outside the bloke's room. Not before I'd woken up half the nick. John Gates, who owned the bike, thought it quite funny at the time. In the morning he hadn't got the bottle to ride the bike down the stairs and he had to manhandle it. That he did not find funny. The Chief Inspector also was not amused! I had to attend and see him personally. He had sent a bobby round to my parents to phone him immediately. We hadn't got a phone at home so I went down to the call box. The late Dolly Grey (he was Norah's brother) demanded to see me immediately. It wasn't a matter of life and death so I saw him in the firm's time.

I had a long lecture about the consequences if anything had gone wrong. There was oil on the floor. Well of course there was, it was a British bike. Dolly couldn't get his head round the fact that it was possible to ride a bike up a flight of stairs. How did I propose it was brought down? He could less cope with the idea of riding it down! That's what I would have done but John had already moved it.

Another tale from quarters which could have had serious consequences was from Bridge. Lou Jones who was married went out to a party and pulled a very smart, tidy girl. He arranged to borrow a room at Bridge in order to bed her before he took her home. By all accounts he did a good job and they saw each other again. Once. He found out to his stark horror that she was only fifteen. She said she wasn't bothered about a date on a calendar, but Lou was. He was very worried for a few weeks, but she was a willing party and was unconcerned. She apparently looked and behaved twenty.

The morning I woke Chris turned out to be a busy one. Just as I was having my breakfast a man decided he wanted to be a bird. He jumped off a tower block at Nechells, hitting the ground hard when his wings failed to open. I put my breakfast between two pieces of bread and attended. I took Chris with me. This exercise would keep him awake. The man lived locally, in another tower. Why he didn't jump from that one became clear later. He had jumped from the flat of his ex-mistress.

They had a big row the night before and ended the affair. When she had gone to work in the morning he went into the flat and wrecked the inside. He really meant it. He tore dresses, opened tins and tipped food all over the place and then shit in the middle of her bed. That done, he opened the window and jumped off the balcony.

Nechells was getting more like Bridge had been. There had been a good domestic in one of the maisonettes one night. It had finished up with a woman getting stabbed. We were on the following morning and were asked to make a few enquiries as to whether anybody had seen or heard anything. I agreed to do the neighbouring block. At the second house I went to the front door, which was slightly open. I tapped on the window and a woman called, 'Come in, it's open.'

I went in and found the woman standing in the lounge putting on her stockings; she was wearing just a bra and suspenders. Well, there was a surprise! She screamed and I walked into the kitchen apologising profusely. She put her dressing gown on and came into the kitchen.

'You did say, "come in",' I reminded her.

'Yes. I've just taken the kids to school. Her from next door was coming round, I thought it was her. Anyway, no harm done, you've seen a bit of leg before.'

She was right, of course, but not in those circumstances. And no she hadn't seen or heard anything in the night. She heard about it this morning, wasn't it terrible?

Bob Millner was a shrewd man and missed very little of what went on around him. I went with him one evening to a wine bar. He had a licensing enquiry to complete. I knew the manageress well. She and I had a fling many years before when I was at Bridge and our paths crossed many times after that. When we left the place Bob looked me straight in the eye and said, 'I reckon you've been there.'

'What makes you think that?' I asked because we had not been involved with each other for about thirteen or fourteen years.

'Her eyes. Eyes tell you a lot. Hers sparkled when she looked at you.'

'You're right up to a point but not recently. I know her from Bridge. Her dad used to keep a pub down there. When he shacked up with one of the punters she and mum moved on. Used to be at Copperfields, and whatever it was called after that.' I was truthful with Bob but I don't think he believed me.

Bob moved back to his old division to run the Admin. That had been his part before his promotion. I missed him.

Our new man was one of the first non-Birmingham officers to be promoted to Digbeth. I don't think John Peake would be offended if I said that he was out of his depth. He had surely never worked anywhere that was so busy. He was thorough with his work but all tasks took him too long and he became bogged down, time and time again, in a sea of paperwork, which was unnecessary. He had not yet amalgamated, but later did very well.

One night when I was the controller there was a fatal car crash at Nechells. The driver had been travelling very fast when he lost control on a tricky bit of camber and smashed into a wall. His passenger died instantly but he was reasonably all right although he had gone to hospital. I had already sent a Panda to assist, but the accident was being dealt with by Geoff Westwood. I had worked with Geoff at traffic and knew he was well able to cope. John went, as duty officer, to see for himself. He was about to start to try and bog himself down again. He wanted all manner of things done at the scene which were unnecessary.

The City divisions had for many years carried a full set of detailed plans of all major road junctions and bridges. Therefore a sketch with accurate measurements, taken at the scene of any accident, could be transposed to one of these at a convenient time. John insisted that Geoff compiled a scale plan at the time. John also wanted a Department of Transport vehicle examiner to the scene to examine the car, again unnecessary. Once removed from the scene it can be examined at will in daylight.

Geoff was becoming frustrated with the situation and had recognised my voice over the radio. He asked John if I could assist at the scene. Geoff knew I had done an accident investigation course and would know what was required of him. To my surprise John agreed and I attended. Geoff and I soon had the loose ends tidied up and I was back at Digbeth within the hour. The driver was prosecuted for causing death by reckless driving and convicted. There was never any criticism of the paperwork, or the manner of investigation of that accident.

That is more than can be said for one incident I dealt with. I was walking with PC John Cook along Smallbrook Queensway one evening when we found a lad beating up his girlfriend. He was giving her a real beating and kicking. We dragged him off and locked him up. The girl went to hospital and stayed a few days. She was covered in bruises, had a head injury and cuts. Although a serious offence, in itself the prosecution file was pretty standard and I dealt with it. The night detective was happy with the action and he left brief details for the morning staff on what was called the 'night note'; it was just that, an update. The case went to Court and the lad was sent to prison.

Some months later he was arrested for another wounding and the officer in that case sought the Crime Report for our case. It could not be found. The Crime Report is a statistical instrument as well as a record of events. It is compiled on a self-carbon, multi-sheet. The reason that the report could not be found was that it had never existed. On paper, at least, the offence had not occurred. I had completed the Court papers, the detective had done a night note and the assault was common knowledge. Ultimately I got a rocket and completed a very belated Crime Report, which the detective had promised me he would submit.

The later 1970s were memorable because of political, economic and industrial unrest. Power workers wanted extra money so we had a spate of rostered electricity cuts. Fuel tanker drivers went on strike again, the Austin workers went on strike, again and again, and then the emergency services got on the bandwagon and the fire service withdrew their labour.

Their dispute, though, came close to us and there were some lighter moments even at fires. The army had dug out the 'mothballed' Green Goddesses. These were essentially early 1950s Bedford RL three tonners built as a fire engine. The logic behind keeping them was sound. By their very nature they had done little work. They had been pooled from the old National Fire Service (which in turn had its origins in World War II), the Civil Defence Corps, the reserve pool and military sources. They would cost tens of millions of pounds to replace, and to sell they were worth sod all, so they were kept. The servicemen drove them and the police, usually traffic bikes, escorted them. Fire Officers were not on strike and attended incidents to supervise any activity.

One winter's morning, it was traffic squad time again, I was in Albert Street when someone told me a caravan appeared to be on fire in the car park under Masshouse Circus. I knew the caravan. It was a store for the workmen who were replacing the surface seals on the road above. It was also full of cans of mastic. I called up on the radio but we already knew and the Cavalry, or was it the Navy, were on the way. I had a quick look. The fire had got a fair hold but I could also see a big propane cylinder in the caravan. Our next task was to clear the area. There could soon be a big bang.

As the fire engines started to arrive, the mastic cans were starting to 'pop'. I told the lads about the propane, as a fair bang took the back out of the caravan. As I spoke to the Fire Officer about the propane some very helpful Joe Public told him that the propane had obviously just gone off as it had blown the caravan 'apart'. I used the escorts from the fire engines to close the street and the Fire Officer decided that the only safe way was to keep the propane cylinder as cool as possible and let the rest take its course. We definitely couldn't hope to save much of what was burning but we could certainly do without a gas 'bomb' going off.

Eventually we 'withdrew' just in time. An enormous explosion tore apart the remains of the caravan, scattered cans of burning mastic and other debris far and wide; split the propane cylinder from alpha to omega, and inside out before leaving it on the bonnet of a car fifty yards away. Joe Public left, very sheepish; he obviously hadn't seen one of those do that before. We had been very lucky. There was still another propane cylinder in the caravan and the lads kept that very cool. There was now bedlam; car alarms were going off, local offices and shops evacuated their staff, drivers were returning to their cars, some of which had been damaged in the blast. I think many thought that the terrorists were back.

The cause of the fire was too silly for words. The mastic men, in their stampede to get back to work after coffee, had left the kettle on the gas. It boiled dry and melted, and hot metal fell off the stove onto the various editions of Page 3 from the *Sun*, which caught light, and the rest, including their caravan, was history.

At another small fire on the edge of the division the Royal Marines forgot they weren't still at sea and pumped so much water into an upstairs maisonette that they flooded most of the rest of the block. It was very much to the annoyance of the housing officer who now had to find temporary accommodation for half a dozen families.

I was heartened one afternoon when a couple of Bobbies came in to see me after playing Rugby. They had had a couple of hours off to play for the force 'B' team at Tally Ho!

Steve Mabbett said, 'Sergie. We have just seen our new policewoman. She is BIG.'

'What do mean BIG? Is she *big*? Or is she tall big?'

'She is BIG *big*. About 5'10" and out here.' He cupped his hands in front of his chest. 'You'll love her. Just your fighting weight.'

They had heard about my liking of large women.

'Mmmm, what's she like to talk to?'

'Great, seems a good sport, just out of Oxford, and talks like it but no side on her. Got a brand new MGB.'

'I suppose everybody will be chasing after her.'

'They just might not. If she said "no" she's big enough to mean it. If she said "yes" she's big enough to make sure you do it. I don't mean just shagging either.' Steve was obviously well impressed with her.

When Jennifer Cook joined the unit she was everything I had been told. She reminded me of Izzy Cox, but she was really a blend between Izzy and Claudine. She had long, dark hair. She looked good. Steve had been right. If I were single I would have made serious moves towards her. Her father was a Worcestershire farmer. She was horse-mad, she had played polo on the best lawns in the country. In the winter she rode to hounds. She skied, played tennis and squash and enjoyed good food. She certainly did not like her allocated room at Bradford Street police station, describing it as a tiny, dank hovel.

I got to know her fairly well whilst she was with the unit. She had her own large circle of friends at home and rarely spent much social time with us. She was dated by a few of the lads, but I think many of them thought she was out of their league. She was never short of money because she had a private income from some she had been left. That degree of independence was a great help to her later.

For reasons I shall never know she teamed up with a detective about ten years her senior, John Davis. John was a good detective, and had a photographic memory. His academic prowess was confined to knowing all first division football results for the past five seasons and the winners of all recent classic horse races. Socially he normally finished his day with a curry or a balti and as much beer as he could swallow within the hours allowed. He had a divorce behind him and rarely bothered with female company. Similarly, very few women could put up with him.

One night Jenny had been to a real filthy hovel of a house at the bottom end of Highgate. I had been there before. It was the sort of place you came out of and wiped your feet before you walked on the nice clean footpaths. The experience had troubled her and she spoke about it in the canteen later.

'How can people be allowed to live in that state?' she asked.

'They used to live in a caravan in the lay-bys of rural England. That was till it caught fire in the City and the Council gave them a house,' said one.

'Don't bother about them, dirty bastards,' said another.

'Jenny, give over, you live on a farm surrounded by cow shit,' was another helpful comment.

Jenny had her reply to that: 'Norman, I may live on a farm and there is cow shit in the fields but we haven't got dog shit in the kitchen and lounge, and rotten bread on the table.'

That really summed Jenny up. She was too nice.

She and John started to drift apart. John became very moody. He obviously knew he had blown it again. Jenny, for her part, did not know how to cope with John as he was and sought my advice.

'Can we have a chat?' she asked, 'Not about work, about me.'

'Sure. Here or socially?'

'Over the road if you like,' suggesting the Midland Red Club.

After work Jenny and I had a long talk about her life with John. They had been happy to start with. He was a rough diamond, but he was honest and kind. She had spent some time living with him but couldn't settle to his habits. When she had suggested a split it had not been well received. John was now very moody and was pestering her, particularly over the phone. What did I think?

'Have you decided to split, completely?'

'Yes.'

'Tell him.'

'Difficult.'

'Why?'

'He's never on his own, I don't like to talk in front of his friends.'

'I can make that bit easy for you. He and I often have a beer together. I'll tell you where we'll be and you can tell him then. Knowing him, he'll want to stay on and get pissed. I can then convince him that you've gone for ever.'

'Would you do that?'

'Yes, for you.'

She thanked me and we set the meeting for a Tuesday evening. I knew John would be in the Malt Shovel, Milk Street, on that evening because there was a 'do' on. He would be there early on so I joined him at about quarter to seven.

'Hi, John.'

'Whato, Ralph, pint?'

John was a man of few words, and in fairness I only nodded acceptance. 'Here for the "do"?' I asked.

'Yes, settle the dust. Get a few under my belt before we start the serious drinking.'

Ten minutes on Jenny came in. 'Sorry, Serge. Is it private, or can I join you?'

'Help yourself, my round, what would you like?'

'Pint of Guinness, please.'

I had forgotten that I had seen Jenny with a pint of Guinness before. She got into our conversation and then said to John, 'I may as well tell you in front of someone, so they can remind you, should you forget. You and me are finished. Dead. Over. I don't want you to keep phoning me. OK?' With that she said, 'Bye Serge,' downed her pint and walked out.

'Bye, Jenny.'

I turned to John and said, 'What's all that about?'

'She lived with me for a bit but I can't settle with women. She was different, somehow. Anyway, what the hell, fuck her.'

'That, I am sure, would be enjoyable, but my missus would not be happy about it.'

'She was good, though, had to cut the piss down a bit to keep up with her.'

Jenny seemed to have solved her problem with John. I had done my bit to make the task easier and John was none the wiser.

A few weeks later she and Steve arrested a bloke for rape of a seven year old. Jenny was very upset by that event. She had gone to the hospital with the mother and had little to do with the man. He had been living with the mother. He had been left as baby-sitter whilst she went shopping. When she returned the child was crying and mother found out what had happened. I was station officer that day and he was in my cells.

Jenny came back from the hospital. 'Is that dirty bastard still locked up?' she asked.

'Yes, and for a few years to come, I should think,' I replied.

'I have just seen that little girl, he has torn her to ribbons. He really ought to have his fucking balls ripped off.'

'Is that with an "F" or a "Ph"?' I asked her, and got back the smile I needed.

'Sorry, but I am so angry, I could do it myself. He's a bastard.'

'I know how you feel, and I've got to be nice to him, and feed him and let him wash.'

'That poor little kid. What she must have gone through.'

Jenny was obviously very upset at what she had seen at the hospital and was probably well cross enough to have carried out her decreed punishment. As it was, due process of law prevailed. Jenny got on with the task and the interview with the offender went well. When she and the detective helping her had finished the interview the offender came back to the cells with her. In a very polite voice she said, 'Sergeant, will you please put this reptile back in his tank. He and I have nothing further to discuss.'

That done I returned to her and asked, 'Why that comment?'

She shook her head, 'He was so honest and candid about what he had done. He considers it to be a perfectly normal way of life. Then he started to chat ME up. Cheek.'

A few days later Jenny and I had another heart to heart. I was beginning to become her guru. She told me that she was seriously considering resignation. The squalor and squalid habits of some of our resident population was too much. Such is sharp end policing.

'Jenny, you have a good career ahead of you. You are good at your job. You are well qualified for the future, and you have common sense well beyond your years. There is more to this job than dealing with the dirty sods round here. The trouble with working Bobbies is that quite often the only nice people they deal with are victims. This lot just happen to be the victims of each other. I personally would like to see you stay, but I can't force you.'

The seed of doubt she had sown was her own. I was only able to delay its propagation. She resigned after three years and joined the Army. When last heard of she was a Captain.

During this period, Tom Sommerville had the doubtful credit of being responsible for an accident involving two traffic motorcyclists. It was reported that there had been an accident in the eastbound Queensway tunnel on the A38 in the City Centre. There was some breakdown in communication and assertions were given that the tunnel had been closed to traffic. Because of the heavy congestion, either from the accident or the closure of the tunnel, or a combination of both, the motor cyclists entered the tunnel from the exit end and approached the accident from the opposite direction to the flow of traffic.

The tunnel has a curve in it at its midway point and to their horror the motorcyclists were confronted with a car coming towards them on the curve. The leading rider was Steve Easthope and he avoided the car and then fell off his bike. Len Knightley was not so lucky. In an effort to fend himself away from the car Len's foot hit the front corner of the car. That impact compressed his thighbone through his pelvis and caused a very serious injury. Len was off work for months and is even now partially disabled. In cold weather he has to work indoors.

It is not for me to make judgments on blame but I know that I would not have done what the motorcyclists did and neither would I have instructed it to take place until I was sure that there was an officer at the scene of the original incident.

Some of the sergeants at Digbeth were well near to retirement when I went there and gradually most of them took their pension and made way for younger men. One particularly miserable individual retired and, to our surprise, had a small party. After the usual presentations another parcel, addressed to him, was found and given to him. When he opened it he found a beautiful rosewood toilet seat, with a brass plate engraved, 'From one shit house to another.' He was not amused. It was, however, very apt indeed.

The routine changed little, characters came and went, and small gems of incidents kept us all amused. I had a spell as station officer. That is public enquiry counter, prisoners and general telephone duties. It can be a monotonous job in some stations but never so in Digbeth. One afternoon I was dealing with two old ladies. Usual thing. Came in to Birmingham on the bus. Walked round the markets. Purse stolen. It was, sadly, a very common event.

Whilst I was dealing with them a fellow came into the public side of the counter, swearing. He was drunk. He banged the counter and demanded immediate attention. He then said, 'How do I get to the fucking Court?'

Without looking up, I hit a release button and I said, 'Go through that door.' He did.

He had just walked into the dock. The door locked shut behind him. I could provide him with a lift to Court in time for tomorrow. Once he realised his mistake he swore even more. He was led away to a cell to sleep it off. I continued dealing with the ladies before dealing with him.

The office was quite busy at night as well. There was an all-night coffee bar two doors away and that generated a fair amount of trade and some of their callers called on us as well. A dosser came in one night to complain that the café had refused to serve him. It was no surprise. He stank. Not just a little either, he was awful. I cleared him off in double quick time. He called in three more times with the same effect. About an hour later he burst through the door, shouting, 'There's a copper being beaten up out here.' We ran outside to assist him, to find nothing. The tramp had conned us. 'That got you off your arse, anyway,' he muttered as my mate chased him up the road.

Another night I was sorting some papers out for the controller when a voice over the radio said, 'Quick, outside.' A policeman in a Panda was stuck at the traffic lights watching helplessly as three drunks urinated up the police station wall. We can't have that sort of thing so the controller and I nipped out and locked them up for a few hours.

The care of persons in custody was of prime importance and was something which could not be over stressed. Whilst working one St Patrick's night there had been a disturbance at a party and there were a lot of very drunk Irishmen being dealt with. I also had a few other people in custody. Mindful that it might be even busier later I put two in a cell where possible.

I took this one big demolition contractor to a cell which was already occupied by a placid West Indian who was fast asleep. My man was best on the floor anyway. He couldn't fall off there and hurt himself. As he went in he looked at the sleeping man, picked him up by his belt and his collar and dropped him on the floor. To much protesting from the West Indian he said, 'Soir, I don't mind sleeping on the floor, but not with a fokking nigger on d' bench.' Point made, change of plan. Fortunately nobody was hurt and the incident was recorded for posterity.

One morning rush hour there was a cry for help from two officers in plain clothes. They were in a car, following a motor caravan through heavy traffic. It was being driven by a disqualified driver, and they wanted help to detain him. I grabbed a helmet and dashed out. Fortunately the vehicle was distinctive and I stopped it. I told the driver he was arrested and why. I was joined by one of the plainclothes men and I drove the van, the driver and his escort straight into the station yard. There wasn't even a delay to the traffic.

One early morning I was enjoying a stroll in the fresh air in New Street. I hadn't got a care in the world until a man jumped out of a doorway in front of me and shouted, 'Boo.' My heart pounded and I nearly left my skin behind.

The culprit was a man called Jimmy Grey. Jimmy had been about the City for years, sometimes, living rough and sometimes in hostels. He had nearly died a few years before when a derelict house had collapsed around him. Jimmy ran off laughing. My heart pounded for some time after that. A few nights later I met him and he reminded me of what he had done. Many years on he spoke about that night with some pride.

In the summer of 1978 the Force advertised internally for sergeant instructors, both police duty instructors and also constable driving instructors. The challenge of a driving instructor's course was very exciting. I had one small reservation. It was over three years since I had had any operational experience of fast driving. True I had been all over Europe in my own car, but that was very different. Neither had I any experience of driving instruction. The course was six weeks, the first two a straight advanced

Instructor Training Course, Pannel Ash, 1978.

refresher and the other four, subject to result of the test drive, instructor training. I liked the idea.

Equally June fancied the other job. That was a ten-week course, resulting in a formal qualification, valid nationally. Her wish was to work locally but the qualification would permit her to work at District Training Centres as well.

We discussed the possibilities at length. Both jobs required a minimum commitment from the officer of at least two years. If we could do the courses more or less together, followed by the two years, that would make a very nice break. It might even open the door for me to return to traffic. We applied, the interviews went well and we were both allocated courses. My course was at the Force driving school and June's at the Central Planning & Instructor Training Unit, near Harrogate. Hers residential, mine live at home. My course fitted in the middle of June's.

My course was excellent. I was surprised that I had retained so much system in my driving and gave a goodish trial run. I wasn't that thrilled with it but it was good enough. There were two crews, each of three plus an instructor. Ron Cornwell was to be mine. I had worked with Ron at traffic and he had done my advanced refresher. The other instructor and I could not work together for long. Whilst on traffic I had reported his son for a very fast speeding offence. The relationship between us could not be over strained. This course could be stressful.

The crews were indeed an unusual combination. There was the head of the driving school. He had been given a post for which he was not qualified, Chief Instructor, and was doing the course. There was more amalgamation efficiency. There was a motorcycle instructor, two traffic inspectors, a constable and myself.

When we got settled into the course it was very enjoyable. We had a varied selection of vehicles at our disposal and we drove everything that was available, for the first two weeks. These were more enjoyable than some of the earlier courses. On the day runs we also had two crews of Advanced Course bikes running with us. It was very good for them to actually have very fast traffic to overtake. It was especially good for us to have eight very fast over-takers to watch out for. These boys were on really quick bikes!

We then settled to driving round in the Allegros, which were used on the basic courses. To give us some total novices to test our skills on, the cadet office was asked to nominate a dozen cadets over seventeen who did not hold any form of driving licence. They had to be total novices. We finished up with half that number. Such is progress.

I was given Julie Appleton. At the end of the day Julie could move off, change up and down the gears, steer and stop. Not once did she stall the car. The private site we used was not ideal for six cars, all driven by novices, to parade around but there were no touches at all. Julie and I had given each other a vast amount of confidence. She got a provisional licence immediately. She now wanted to drive. I wanted to teach. I worked with Julie many times in the future. She is now a very competent detective sergeant.

There was a final Advanced Test at the end and I had really decent drive. I passed the course and was 3rd, but I drew satisfaction from the fact that I had been beaten only by driving school personnel. Ken Walker, the motorcycle instructor, was easily top student.

With the course behind me I waited for June's results. She passed, too. We both now had the certificates to go into training. Despite June wanting to remain local she was asked to take up a post at Ryton, not really what she wanted, with a husband on shifts. In the short term she declined the post. A decision would depend on my interview. I was accepted, subject to a satisfactory attachment of four months. I would then be expected to do a further two years at least.

The driving school had, for years, been run as a section of traffic. Since amalgamation it had been part of training. That's the same depart-ment responsible for June. In the circumstances June was seen again and accepted the Ryton post. Her condition was, as it was a favour for the force, that I went to the driving school. Chief Superintendent McDowell gave us the necessary undertakings and we both commenced new jobs within weeks.

My first crew consisted of two novices and a mature driver. At the end I had one with a Grade 4, one with a Dept. of Transport pass and one unmitigated failure.

Next I was to have two crews of non-police drivers to upgrade to 4. No problem, five out of six. I then had a couple of crews of Grade 4s to upgrade to 3s. Very enjoyable. It would take more experience before I was allowed to train advanced drivers. The nice Mr McDowell broke his promise. After four months of satisfactory instruction I was being returned to Digbeth. The reason? Money. The driving school was up to strength on sergeants. I was doing the job of a constable at the pay of a top rate sergeant. The constable who had been on my course, and got a lower mark, would have my place. I protested at the promise I had been given and was told simply: 'It is impossible to make long term promises of that nature.'

I was not very pleased with McDowell. He obviously did not have the honour of a Birmingham City policeman and I'm sorry to say I told him so. He seemed quite shocked.

I went back to Digbeth just in time for Christmas, but not the traffic squad. That had been allocated to a colleague. He made a right pig's ear of things, much to the chagrin of the Chief Super. Before New Year I was back on the job and I did it afterwards for the next six or seven years. There was by now a lightweight motorcycle on the division and I made good use of it. I hoped that we did not repeat the Len Knightley exercise.

A year or so on, one of the butterfly superintendents who passed through Digbeth was frightened of his own shadow and terrified of the traffic squad. The very nature of what we were doing was not popular with motorists. Generally they are creatures of habit. Same route in, park in the same place, the same route out. Suddenly they were being shepherded to where we wanted them, moving them on and keeping things moving. One or two whinged, because they couldn't have it all their own way. I told one bloke off about parking outside his shop on a bus stop. The message didn't sink in so I put a ticket on his car. He went into Digbeth, saw the superintendent and had the ticket revoked.

A few days later he was there again and got another ticket. Same thing followed but he didn't see the superintendent. The office man filled in the appropriate form (yes, we now had forms for everything) but the ticket stood.

By now the driver has got a message that he has paid for the space outside his shop and is going to be there all day. Wrong. Another ticket, followed by a visit to the pound. This time, he has written a letter to the Superintendent. This time he wants to see me. It was one of those very pleasant December mornings when the sun had gone on strike and the rain had come in on overtime. I'd got a full motorcycle wet suit on but I was still a bit damp round the gills. I was dripping on his carpet. I am hounding this man. It must stop. He has a business to run. So had I.

'He thinks he owns the street. I don't mind him unloading stuff, that's got to be done. I cannot, and will not let him park there all day, every day just because he runs a shop. Everybody in that road runs a shop and most come by car. No others park there. Put it this way, would you let me park on Digbeth front all day on double yellow lines?'

'Of course not. It's far too busy and it's a bus route.'

'Quite, so why should I allow him to park on double yellow lines on a busy road and on a bus stop?'

'I'm having a lot of these ticket complaint forms come through.'

'Sir, We're moving about 650 tickets a week between us. There are bound to be a few who feel aggrieved. This time of the year is different; we are near to a zero tolerance situation on bus routes and main thoroughfares, and those are instructions from Chief Superintendent. This isn't just a Digbeth thing, it's divisional and what we do in town has a knock-on effect on all main routes back to the suburbs. If the town clogs up, the buses can't get in; if they can't get in, they can't get back out and so it goes on.'

'Sergeant you have lost me. You seem to know what you are doing and why, but I'm lost. 650 Fixed Penalty Tickets is an awful lot, and I don't really like impounding vehicles. Are there any guidelines on what you do?'

I went back to my work folder. In there I had a copy of the original draft plan for the squad and copies of the comments from HQ when it was originally set up. There were also copies of the previous two years of Christmas Traffic, plus loads of statistics, which had filtered back to me. I gave them to him and asked for them back when he had read them. An hour on I was back in his office.

He seemed surprised at what he had read. 'You, as a sergeant, do all this?'

'Except the stats. They're done at Lloyd House.'

'Aren't you answerable to someone?'

'Yes, I have direct access to Superintendent Owen, divisional deputy on all matters relating to this operation on an annual basis. It is a divisional responsibility.'

Gulp. 'I see, then I have probably taken up enough of your time. Thank-you for that file, very interesting.'

I went back to the rain-drenched streets a lot warmer than before. I think the butterfly had just had a surprise on how a big city copes with traffic at Christmas.

I had to go back on Christmas Eve. Father Christmas had been seen in the City riding a Police BMW, accompanied by Rudolph on another, and half a bike shift with two-tones sounding. The Brums had loved it. Cheers and clapping and a good laugh. Did I know anything about it? No, but it's happened before. Well done to the lads. Apparently the Press had got wind of it and wanted confirmation. It took me back ten years or more when a crowd of us had mistletoe behind our helmet plates. Two got their picture in the paper, for kissing old ladies in New Street! That's proper Cop-munity policing!

On the Unit we now had another inspector, Bill Smith. Bill was around Bob Millner's age and prior to 1966 had been a policeman in rural Staffordshire. Two amalgamations had given him two promotions. He bemoaned the distance he had to travel, but he enjoyed himself and was a good bloke to work with. He considered that at his age he had done well to get further promotion and obviously wanted to create the right atmosphere. We had a couple of younger sergeants on the shift and I spent increasingly more time as station officer or controller. That now suited me and working the City Centre streets would do them good.

I also enjoyed my enforced bachelor existence. June came home most weekends and on Wednesday evenings, her half day. The arrangement actually suited better than we had ever imagined. I had a great crowd of lads to work with and it was even better to socialise with them properly. Dickie Dormer had got himself a decent motorcycle and we did a few miles together on our days off. A quick zip to Aberystwith or Rhyl was a nice way to spend a summer's day off. I was also able to spend social time with June at Ryton. The centre held regular dining-in nights, with dinner jacket and bow tie, of course and social evenings in the instructors' mess. They normally involved an unofficial overnight. No problem, unless the fire drill revealed too many heads.

I came close to getting my fingers rapped for a bit of devious policing during this time. As station officer, I had dealt with a man for a breath test. He knew, and I knew, that he had given me false details, but I couldn't prove it. His address checked out. Summonses were issued but never served. Eventually I found out his correct identity, and, lo and behold, he was disqualified. There were also two other sets of summonses for the same thing outstanding. At this time the law was such that the offenders could not be charged and kept in overnight for this. They had to be summoned, and that gave them chance to disappear, something he had effectively done by using an alias.

One night I had an hour out of the station and I set a trap. The following night I checked the computer, and our friend's car had been reported stolen. I arranged for one of the unit members to look for it and he found it, neatly parked at the kerb, locked. He radioed in and I phoned the owner. My message was brief, 'We've found your car, call at Digbeth for the rotor arm.'

Within the hour he had been in, and collected three sets of summonses. He didn't check them. I told him where his car was, and he left to collect it. He forgot all about the rotor arm. He got himself arrested at his car for attempting to drive whilst disqualified. It wouldn't start. He was brought back in and stayed in my cells to go to Court in the morning. He could be charged with that and some others which were outstanding. The summonses could also be dealt with next morning. The next night he was in Winson Green Prison. His car was removed to the pound for safekeeping. I was a trained car thief and it took a long time for the full circumstances of those two nights to become known.

It is often said that women who get raped deserve it. I would put that into a kinder concept and say that women who deserve it don't get raped. It is those who are totally innocent victims who seem to have the problems.

I remember walking through a car park near to Digbeth one night when I saw a couple having a real serious kiss and cuddle in the shadows in the corner. They were really getting each other worked up. Her skirt was nearly over her shoulders and she was rubbing herself into his thighs. As I walked past I said, 'Goodnight, be careful.' I carried on and received a 'goodnight' back.

A little later I was in the office when the girl came in and complained that she had been raped. She may well have had sex but she was not going to convince a Court that she had been raped.

I said, 'Why didn't you tell the policemen when he said, "goodnight"?'

'What do you mean?'

'Not half an hour ago I saw you and your bloke almost at it, yet you say you were raped by him. You were certainly making no efforts to stem his advances when I saw you.'

She persisted in her story and she was interviewed by a policewoman and made no further allegation. The basic problem was that she was late and her clothing had got soiled.

A week or so later I didn't need to ask what had happened when a rape victim came to the counter. She was in a hell of a state and had obviously had a very bad time. Her complaint was genuine and some weeks later a man was arrested for the offence.

Back out on the Traffic Squad season again we caught for a particularly snowy winter and the Council had done pretty well with the snow ploughs, but the stuff they had left in the gutters reduced the width of the road, and consequently the width of the loading bays.

One morning in New Street there was chaos. A coach was picking up passengers from the hotel over the Big Top site. This place had no loading facilities for passengers so the coach was parked against the snow. It would have been OK but the passengers, a pop group and their road crew, were still at breakfast and kept telling the driver to wait. I was telling him to load or leave. In the end, with traffic flow at a total standstill, and getting worse, I ordered him to move the coach or I would have it impounded and arrest him for the wilful obstruction he was causing.

He dashed into the hotel in panic but the group couldn't care less. One shouted, 'Tell him bollocks, we're having breakfast.'

He made his choice, he was staying put. I made mine, he was arrested, and the coach was impounded. There was some delay to the group's departure.

The driver was bailed to court, and didn't attend because the group were away. When they came back to Brum he was arrested, on warrant, and stayed for Court the next morning. This time we did not impound the coach but he had the pleasure of a lock-up breakfast.

Reorganisation was now the key word. Change was again afoot. Nechells station was going back to the 'D' division, together with half the ground. The other half would stay with Digbeth. We were also having a big slice of the 'B' division, Lee Bank and Highgate. The division would also take in the remainder of Highgate, and Sparkbrook from the 'F' division, together with a part of Small Heath from the 'E' Division. Just for good measure we could also have the rest of Newtown from the 'C'. The territorial area was going to be increased about three-fold. To compensate the loss of accommodation at Nechells the station in Bradford Street would come onto the Division and for the first time we would have three sub-divisions. As a final insult we would no longer be called 'A' division. We would be the 'F'.

As one wag put it, 'There's an f in "F" but ain't no f in "A".' Nicely put.

The restructuring was to reduce the old City Force area back to five divisions, as it had been many years before. At that time, probably about 1955, a sixth division was formed because the existing five had been too big. The argument this time was that if the 'A' division extended out of the City Centre, the area of that would increase but the area of the others would lessen. Obviously something that the statisticians had decided upon. I can't imagine that any working policemen or women had been consulted.

I looked at it logically. Since 1960 the City boundary had moved outwards. A number of massive housing developments had been built. There was Druids Heath, Tile Cross and Castle Vale. The entire borough of Sutton Coldfield also been added. With the City now bigger than ever, we apparently needed fewer divisions. I found the logic had left me.

The force HQ had collected the name E.S.S.O. House. That did make sense: every Saturday-Sunday off. It was their idea and working police officers don't get every weekend at home. The HQ division, then the 'R' division, would become the 'A'. The 'R', they said was an illogical choice. How would they know? It dated back to Birmingham City and stood for 'Reserve'. It was collective title given to staff who had no territorial division, but who worked on them all. That reserve had now become 'A' for 'Administration'; it used to mean 'Ambassadorial'.

With the new ideas came an old one: Area Cars. But they couldn't be called that. They would be called Fast Response cars, driven by Fast Action Response Teams. We were to have FART cars. Bog standard Morris Marinas were certainly not my idea of a Fast Response car. Anyway, Area Car sounds better. Any response for help from a member of the public should be fast, particularly if urgent. In the end Zulu stuck, after the call-signs.

Unfortunately the Command and Control computer was suggesting that response times were not good. That gem came about because the man who interpreted the information failed to understand the system used to record them. The system allowed an arrival time to be included in the information field on the screen by the controller. That had to be put in manually. As the screen often contained information useful to the officers attending the incident, and was constantly being used for other incidents as well, the arrival time shown was the time that it was put onto the screen by the controller. A false picture. Once that loophole had been pointed out vast sums of money were spent to install equipment in the area cars to record arrival times by radio. This was not extended to Pandas which only used UHF radio.

Not long after this sort out I was working overtime on the overtime van. Unusually there were no volunteers from 2-10 sergeants to do it so I'd gone in on a leave day. As the lads had all done eight hours I offered to do a stint driving the van. We were parked up near the top end of Broad Street, near Five Ways Island and I was chatting to a Traffic Officer. On his radio I heard a call for 'policeman in trouble', got the location and jumped back in the van. The crew had no idea what was up as I shouted for them hold on. The call was for assistance in Sparkhill, three miles away. There was a policeman 'down' outside a nightclub on Stratford Road at Showell Green Lane. I knew this was a dodgy spot (a few years before there had been a shooting there) and from where we were it was easy to get at. To me these were really urgent calls and got the full treatment. Horns, blue lights, the lot.

Straight down the Middleway, under the Bristol and Pershore Roads and through the lights at Walford Road. It was the number 8 bus route with short cuts. The 3 litre Transits went like stink and we even beat the Divisional Fast Response car to the incident. The Bobby had had a good hiding and was not well, and he went off to hospital. My haste had been justified.

A quick roundup gave us six of those responsible, with apparently one more to come. The divisional cavalry finally got there and wondered how we knew about the call, when they didn't. That showed again the benefits of force-wide communications.

I'd got the van load into Acocks Green before most of the 'E' Division knew there had been a problem. Amazing! The really annoying thing was that I had ten officers across our division and way onto theirs, locked up six and had an ambulance on the way for the Bobby, to find that they hadn't got that many men out in their own right, and we hadn't even been asked to go!

At the rate things were going we'd get another Dave Green on the route to costing less to run.

All divisional administration offices were the next target to be hit, and they would be staffed by civilian personnel. But, said the unions, these must be new jobs, not retired police officers who knew how the system worked, but civilians who knew nothing of police work beyond what they had seen in 'Z' cars. That should work quite well! The benefits of amalgamation, whatever they were, had now created a vast empire of fresh, new desk jobs.

Dave Cox had been the sub-divisional clerk at Digbeth for a number of years. He made a super job of the task. Everything he did was readily to hand. He was sent out onto the beat. He didn't mind that; what upset him was that three staff were eventually recruited to do what he had done single-handed. He retired in disgust at twenty-five years service to run a post office! A man totally dedicated to the service had been lost. Was that what the new thinking was all about?

One operational snag caused by the introduction of the new area cars was that they could also be used for enforcement of traffic laws, including speeding. That facility was useful, where the crews had been trained to use the vehicle as a tool for a job. Where they had only been trained to drive it they would need that training. That was a nice few days, running a divisional driving school to train up the crews. It was never planned that way, but it worked well. So well in fact that I later made it routine on my own unit so that I knew they were all brought up with the same set of rules.

CHAPTER 14

Bradford Street

JUNE RETURNED FROM HER secondment to Ryton in September 1980 and was immediately posted to the Force Control Room at Bournville. The supervision staff there urgently required a female member to be able to relate to the problems of females working there. June was no stranger to communications She had worked in the two previous Information Room and Control Rooms in Newton Street As luck would have it she was deployed onto the same unit as me. We had the same shifts, same days off, at last. Well, for a bit anyway.

A major change of mind on duty patterns resulted in the Control Room devising a system whereby a supervision team stayed as a unit but moved around the other units on a rotation. In effect they worked a unit for a year, had three months updating records and internal systems and then a year on another unit. It apparently seemed a good idea at the time but it did not take account of the fact that the divisions did not do that and therefore June and I would be on different shifts for years if I was unable to agree a change.

In 1982, when a change of unit became a domestic necessity, it proved difficult for me. Nobody at Digbeth would do a mutual exchange. The units were close teams; moves meant disruption. There was a vacancy at Bradford Street, but as that was a different sub-division it had to be a divisional decision. I went to see Neil Jones, the Chief Superintendent, and told him the problem. He thought the Control Room idea to be 'bloody stupid' but he understood the reason for my request and granted it with the words, 'You've done a good job at Digbeth. Seven years with the same unit. That must be a record, even by Digbeth standards. Go up the road, feel your feet then kick a few arses. They aren't "A" division men up there. Their last inspector was a man you knew well from traffic! Need I say more?'

The new unit could only be described as an ill-disciplined rabble. They had seen no proper leadership for many years. Their old inspector had been of little guidance to them and the sergeants had always worked with the inspector. They now had a new Inspector in Stu Grogan and a wise and devious sergeant who expected them to work as a team, and they were going to have problems with me if they didn't. I had known Stu since his days as a constable on the 'A' division. He had been very much one of the lads until

224

he had to be cut from the wreckage of his car one night, and nearly died. He had now become quite reserved. That was probably because he had spent the last few years as a member of the Commercial Fraud Squad.

To a man, and some of the women, they all drank on duty. In the context in which they were doing it, it had got to stop. In principle I had no objections to any of them having a quick half with a licensee, but going out with the sole intention of doing nothing else was very much not on. Stu's car accident years before had been drink related and he was certainly of the same mind as me.

The Superintendent was Emrys Davies. Emrys had been a very good detective at high rank but was not a uniform man and not really suited for his current post. I found him very hard to work with and difficult to work for. When I went for my pep talk I didn't expect the statement he made, 'Well, Serge, you know why you are here. I hope there will be an improvement in your conduct.'

That made no sense at all. I had come to him with a clean sheet and I was mystified, and I said, 'I don't quite understand that comment, Sir. I have come here merely to change shifts. Not for punishment.'

'That is not what I have just been told.'

Things now fitted together. A sergeant from traffic had been transferred to the 'F' for neglect of duty. He was obviously coming to Bradford Street, as well, and Emrys had got us mixed up. When I explained that to him he apologised fully. The shame was I didn't get the traffic job.

I felt better. He took me to see his deputy, Bob Jones, who was by now a Chief Inspector. We were introduced. I was very touched when Bob said, 'Ralph and I go back a long time, Sir. He taught me to be a policeman.'

That was nice to hear, especially after the reception I had received five minutes before. Introductions over Bob took me to the canteen and we had a chat. He knew the problems I might have with my new unit and he offered his full support. They had indeed got a bad name.

Once I had been able to get amongst them and sorted the wheat from the chaff they were in fact a fine group of men and women. A few had to be found new partners, a couple were moved to other places and one decided to leave. Those few moves had really solved the problem. They had lacked leadership, and purpose. They had therefore elected their own leader, as groups do, and they had drifted from their purpose. Metaphorically speaking, arses had been kicked. Order had returned.

The odd moment of indiscretion still occurred. One night, on a changeover from late shift to early shift, with just a break of eight hours between duties, I had a quick beer with them before going home. I declined the idea of then having a curry. In the morning I was a few short on parade when I had a phone call. It went like this, 'Serge, it's Steve. I'm a bit pushed.'

'Get here as soon as you can.'

'OK. But Dave's with me as well.'

'How come?'

'We went out with Tim.'

'Where's Tim now?'

'Here. His car won't start.'

'Where's here?'

'Barry Island.'

'What the hell are you doing down there?'

'We came down for the ride.'

'Then what?'

'We went to sleep. When we woke up the battery was flat.'

'Right, get back here double quick. You're on the sheet.'

I put the phone down and looked at Stu.

'Do I ask?'

'The prats are in Barry Island.'

'What they doing down there?'

'They went for the ride, would you believe? Idiots.'

When the strays returned to the fold at about 9 am I gave them a severe lashing with my tongue and put everything on paper. The Chief Superintendent saw each one individually and left them in no doubt what he thought about it! There was never a repeat.

The sub-division was a mix of about everything that was wrong with an inner-City area. There were Victorian factories, and all the associated congestion. Men's hostels catering for down and outs. Tower blocks of flats, new Council housing, old Council housing. Victorian houses let as flats, or owned by housing trusts. Together with railway, a canal and a fast road running through the middle of it, and constant redevelopment.

The population made up of native Brums, and Irish and Asian communities, all living in comparative harmony, was the good point.

Once the problems with the shift had been sorted out I used to patrol with each for a day to get to know them better. Helen Myatt, known as 'big 'un' had served for about fifteen years in the Royal Military Police. She was a bright and sensible woman and got on well with just about everybody. She was worldly, having served in Germany, Cyprus, Northern Ireland and Hong Kong. She had also been based in Central London and had met Jenny Cook. Helen had reached the rank of Staff Sergeant before unwarranted lesbian advances and a broken romance directed her towards the police. Unlike

Jenny Cook, Helen was not distressed by squalor. She had transferred her army pension and was content to make her career in her new job.

She offended Emrys one day when she parked a Rolls Royce in her parking space. It belonged to her boy friend, a local metal dealer. Unlike most men in that trade he had no convictions and was of good character to boot. He was also single. Emrys had a thing about scrap metal men, from when he was in the CID, and old habits died hard. Helen lived in single quarters above the station and had a space in the yard to park her car, not his. It had to go. Very petty.

Julie Appleton, my cadet from my Instructors Course, was also with us. She was doing well and showed every promise of being a successful officer.

When June had settled in her new post she realised that in the two years she had been absent from the Force, things had changed, dramatically and not really for the better. In order to have her say, and also to be heard, she was elected to the Police Federation as representative of the female sergeants in the Force.

She kept this position very actively until her retirement.

With the move up to Bradford Street I had lost some of the routine of the City Centre but I was still asked to run the Traffic Squad.

1983 Christmas traffic squad. (With credit to the Birmingham Post & Mail Ltd.)

For 1983 we had to revise the plan a little because in the past it had been overtime orientated but this time, because of economies, we had to operate a flexi-time scheme. It had always run from 8 am and 6 pm which meant there was a share of overtime for everyone who wanted it. This time it was run between those hours and the overtime was very little. I was OK but the troops on the ground only got about four hours a week. Very useful, but peanuts compared with other times. As always we managed, even if the operation wasn't as slick as in the past.

At my request the Press Office got us some more publicity on what the ground rules would be for the duration, and the usual request for a story followed. It was in many ways a high profile posting so a few pictures in the paper often worked well.

When economies were ordered, yet again, the first thing that affected us was a fuel restriction. Impossible mileage limits were placed on all vehicles. The ten miles per shift limit on the Metro Pandas wouldn't even get them to the garage and back, having taken on fuel. I got round that by simply allowing the vehicles to be re-fuelled as a separate entry in the driver's Logbook, and not during the shift mileage. Emrys didn't like that. I had to attend. My suggestion to let them then run out of petrol and then be towed in by Land Rover was thought to be insolent.

In the end I decided to go back to basics. The Pandas would be taken out onto the areas and parked up. The officer would then patrol on foot. That had, after all, been the original concept of Unit Beat Policing. Over the years the public had been told that all calls would get an immediate response. If we had to save petrol, and the cars could not be used without it, then the public would have to come back down to earth. This was after all the same public who wanted to see their policeman on the beat. A few complaints about arrival times again, soon relaxed the restrictions on the Pandas but caused other vehicles to be restricted more severely, including the lightweight motorcycle.

The division had two Kawasaki 200cc runabouts. They were worth their weight in gold. There had been no restriction on their use but suddenly the Bradford Street one was limited to 100 miles per calendar month. That's about six litres of petrol. That would cost less to buy than it would to allow one policeman have his breakfast. Remember we all got paid for a forty-five minute break in every shift. The restriction was stupid and I made my feelings known.

On 31st May I re-fuelled the machine and used it in June until it ran into reserve at 127 miles. I then parked it up until 1st July, when I refueled it.

When the fuel returns were done for the month Emrys sent for me. 'You have broken my rules over the motor cycle mileage. My restriction is 100 miles. You alone have ridden that bike for 127 miles. That is a 27 per cent excess. I take a serious view of that.'

I could not believe what I was hearing. We were talking about 2½ quid's worth of petrol. He would earn more than that whilst chiding me.

I said, 'Look, sir. The object of your exercise is to save money. You budget monthly. All 127 miles on that bike were paid for in May. I gave you 127 free miles in June. I filled that bike up again in July. You have a nil petrol bill for that bike despite the miles it has saved the cars. I reckon that is good management, not wilful wrong doing.'

'That is not the point. It is still restricted to 100 miles a month.'

'Why?'

'To save money, of course.'

'Precisely, exactly what I did. I saved you 7 litres of petrol. About 50 bob in old money. It's peanuts. That bike does about 90 to the gallon. It restricts itself anyway. Only a handful of us can use it. By using that we leave a car for some one else.'

He was not convinced, but the restriction was lifted and sanity returned.

Stu Grogan left and went back into the CID. We had a new man. A butterfly. Alan Jones had got about eight years service, almost four of those as an Inspector. He would not be with us long. He expected to be a Chief Inspector, within a year. I have never known one man to demoralise a shift so quickly as he did. The first time I heard him address the shift I knew we would have problems.

'Right, ladies and gentleman. I'm Alan Jones. I'm not newly promoted. I've been in the rank for four years. I know what the job's about. I don't expect find any of you drinking on duty. The sergeant will now take the parade and I'll speak to you later in my office. Serge, carry on.' With that he walked off.

'Mister bleedin' nice guy he is. Stuff him.' said one of the men.

I needed to say nothing. Alan Jones had said it all; in less then a minute he had undone most of what Stu and I had achieved with them in thirteen months. Management is the art of using resources to the best advantage; he would never hope to do that with them.

Fortunately, I didn't have to spend too long with him. I was shortly to move around again. June had her date for moving shifts.

The remaining time with that shift was enjoyable. I tried my best to tame Alan down a little. He had an unfortunate manner. He was a product of Warwickshire thinking and had only policed the old county area. Out there the Inspector had been looked on as a demigod. In the City he was merely a team leader, no more important than the members of the team. He just carried the can. He was so conscious of his need to succeed that he was frightened to death to put a foot wrong, in case his promotion chances subsided. It was a very sad approach to the job and one which has marked many men over the years. I had found a chink or two in his armour and I was confident that he would cause me no harm.

The Inspector who followed Alan Jones to that shift had all the problems with them that had been possible. The worst problem was that one of the lads who persisted in drinking on duty was dismissed the service for driving the area car with excess alcohol. I can offer that man no sympathy at all. He deserved what he got.

The time came to move and I was delighted to work again with Bob Millner. His Admin. job had melted away under him, the civilian army was building its empire and Bob had been put out to grass. I would see him retire before I left his shift. Bob was conscious of the fact that I had been a great help to him in his early months at Digbeth and he sought to redress the balance. This was his old pitch. He knew it like the back of his hand and most of the people on it. He introduced me to many of his friends as a friend. I appreciated that very much.

The previous unit had been drinkers. This lot, with few exceptions, liked a drink but much preferred women. They were a young shift and mainly single. In many ways the area we worked was good for contacts. We had two Irish Community clubs, many Irish landlords and a large, happy Irish community. Bob knew these places well and had introduced some of the unit to them therefore the single men got round these pubs and clubs and thus met some very nice women. One lad got himself the sack because of one but that was only part of the story.

Maxie Boyle had for many months been seeing a separated lady who lived way off the division. She worked as a bar maid at a pub in Digbeth and was well known to us all. One quiet night Maxie collected her from the pub and took her home, in a Panda. Whilst he was in the house the car got run into and was damaged. There was no sign of what had been involved so Maxie collected up the debris and took it with him. He then came back onto the division and parked up. He radioed in to patrol on foot. He then called up to say that his car had been hit whilst parked. No problem with that, if it had been true.

The report was dealt with and the car was taken to the garage for repair. After we had gone home the driver of the car involved in the bump got cold feet and reported the accident to Sheldon. There was no record of a Panda being damaged out there so they phoned the garage. Yes, one was damaged.

Been hit whilst parked on the 'F' division. No, the driver was insistent. His bump was in Sheldon, and it was a marked Panda. It had to be that one. Samples of paint were taken from the two cars and they matched. Maxie had a problem!

He was interviewed and stuck by his story. The driver went back with the police to where he said the accident had taken place, and, sure enough, there was still some debris from the impact. This was collected and came from both vehicles. Maxie was proved to have been there. Had the matter been taken further Maxie would have lost his job. As it was he resigned, and it ended there. The P.R.B. syndrome had another victim. The thing between his legs had ruled the thing on top of his shoulders.

One of the people Bob introduced me to was Patrick Maguire. He kept a pub called the Horse and Jockey, in Miles Street. It is long since demolished. At that time it was the headquarters of the 'Cycle Tramps' motorcycle club. They were little short of a full Hell's Angels Chapter. If you didn't know, you wouldn't know. They had been attacked previously at a pub and really had a friend in Paddy, because most pubs wouldn't touch them. They certainly didn't want trouble and went to great pains not have bother near the pub.

One night I was walking along the Small Heath by-pass when one of them rode towards me, pretty fast. That didn't bother me but the girl pillion rider without a helmet did. I signalled for him to stop, and he did, probably because he was so near to the pub. I read him the riot act about the helmet, or lack of it. He wasn't anti about it but felt I knew very little about bikes. I had his helmet off him, gave the girl mine, sat him on the back without one and then gunned 900cc of Kawasaki up and down the by-pass. I rode back to the girl, told her to walk back to the pub, and drove him back on the bike. I caused a degree of consternation when I pulled up.

The lad was shocked. He had not met a human copper before. From then on I was 'their copper'. I was going to use their pub in my time and occasionally it would be on their night. We had got to get on from the beginning so it might as well start from then. It worked very well. I caused them no trouble and they saved me lots. They called me 'Boss': a respectful term a lot of criminals use when they are locked up.

Paddy had a CB meeting there one night and it was attended by a disabled lad. He left his 'rig' in his little van. When he went back the 'rig' had gone. Paddy called the police and I went to see him. The lad was very upset; it was more important to him than almost anything else because it gave him contact with the outside world. Paddy and I had a good idea who had pinched it. A local toe-rag was a CB freak and he stood a good chance of being the culprit. When I called to see him, he denied all knowledge but he failed to convince me. He showed me his own 'rig' but that wasn't what I was looking for.

The next night, when I went in with June, I mentioned the theft to one of the 'Tramps'.

'That's bad. Kid disabled an' all. Where's this bastard live?'

I felt problems if they decided to take their own action. I said, 'Paddy'll tell you. He knows.'

Once armed with that information two of the 'Tramps' left the pub and walked away. When they came back after about twenty minutes the one I had spoken to, said, 'The kid's CB will be back here tonight. If it ain't, tell me.'

I thanked him. It hadn't come back when Paddy closed but while we were having our supper with him there was a knock on the door. When Paddy answered it there was no one about but the CB was on the doorstep. Something had worked.

I went to Paddy's one night, after work. The bar was packed with a darts match so I went into the corridor, which was fairly quiet. I had noticed a bike outside but it wasn't a 'club' night. I didn't take much notice until I heard a familiar sound. I looked into the back room to find the biker, trousers round his ankles, trying to pump up his girl friend across the pool table. At least that what it looked like, he really was going at her. Neither of them noticed me and carried on for some time. I took no further interest. June had joined me from work when they emerged, and I was well into my second pint.

The 'Tramps' accepted June as well, and she had sufficient contacts to direct a couple of their girls towards the abortion clinics. The girls could confide in her and they trusted her with their innermost secrets, something they couldn't do with Paddy's wife, who would get embarrassed.

I recall two incidents involving the 'Tramps', which were quite helpful to the community in general, if not to the miscreants involved. In the first Mary, Paddy's wife, was running the pub on her own when she had a lot of trouble from a very drunk Asian. He had the problem of going from sober to crazy in about five minutes, and he could be a handful. Paddy was wary of giving him his ticket because of fears of being called racist. Mary called the police, but before they arrived, two or three 'Tramps' had rolled up for their night. They saw what was happening and put him outside very quickly. Once that was done they took him up the road and showed him a railway engine on a nearby bridge. They promised him that if he ever went in the pub again he would be on the front of the next train, going to London. He never came back. One of the 'Tramps' finished his beer for him. When the police arrived there was nothing to report.

It has to be accepted that in a general sense most of the 'Tramps' were from a criminal background and they had many brushes with the law. Indeed there was a feud with a rival gang for most of the time I had any contact with them, and Bruno Tessaro, their president, was shot dead during this time. In consequence I never considered them as my friends but they could be useful, as they had proved. I even met their solicitor and was introduced to him. That was trust, indeed.

A local girl had run away from home and was thought to be living with Asians, and working as a prostitute. Her father had relented, when he heard that and wanted her back home. The father spoke about it, and before I got involved I directed him to Paddy, who in turn put him in touch with a 'Tramp'. Dad was well pleased to get the girl back and bought a fair sup of beer for the lads. News drifted back later that the Asians had been very frightened when the 'Tramps' rode into their house on bikes and made serious threats about their future welfare. There was never a formal complaint, and I had made sure not to know the address the girl was supposed to have been at.

One of the problems from Bridge and Nechells also plagued Bradford Street, wife beating. One poor woman named Ann Battersby said that her name arose from the fact that 'my husband batters me.' At least she could laugh about it, sometimes. The first time I met her she had taken refuge in a pub and the landlord had called the police. She had received a good smack but declined to make the matter official. She vowed to see her four children through school and then leave home, but not before. She had already had her share of bad luck when she lost one child through meningitis.

I saw her at a hospital one night. Her daughter Dawn had been a passenger in a car, which had overturned. Dawn was also a cleaner at police headquarters. When I found out who the girl was I arranged for Ann to be brought to the hospital by the police. She looked very well; for some reason the beatings had stopped. The children were growing up and he might have got wind of her intentions. She went home with her daughter. Ann was so pleased with the kindness various police officers had shown her over the years that the station was on her Christmas card list. Six weeks after her youngest son left school Ann left the family home to live with her sister in Cornwall. She had done what she had threatened to do many years before. I liked her, and I admired her courage. Lesser women would have left years before.

I went to a domestic in one of the new houses one Saturday afternoon. Birmingham City were playing at home and I had been out with a van patrol until kick off. We were just on our way back to the station when we had the call. A mini bus-load of Bobbies to a domestic is a little over the top so just the driver and I went in. The woman kept the house immaculate. She and her two early teenage daughters had been on their own for nearly three months whilst hubby had bummed around from one lodging pad to another. There was a Matrimonial Injunction in existence but it had never been served on him.

This afternoon he had returned unexpectedly to the house, had a shouting match with his wife and smashed some of her possessions. She believed that the Injunction would protect her from such visits, and told me so. He demanded to see a copy. I hadn't got one, but was assured that there was one at the station. However, she had her copy. I read it to him and served it on him, there and then. To say that made the situation a little volatile was an understatement. He went ballistic. In a single movement he took everything off the kitchen table and knocked it onto the floor. He lunged at his wife with a saucepan. In an effort to defend her, I punched him in the face.

I must have been getting older because it wasn't fully effective. The Matrimonial Injunction gave us a power of arrest and that was the next obstacle to overcome. He didn't want to be arrested, certainly not in front of his wife and kids. I had all the help I would ever need sitting in a van outside but to call them in would have provoked the situation more, and I had no wish to wreck the woman's home, solely to arrest her husband. In the end we bundled him out of the house and into the front garden. He could now be arrested from there by the van crew. They saw him tumble out of the house and thought that that was probably the end of the matter. When he kicked the glass panel out of the front door he got himself arrested.

When I got back into the van he was quite proud of himself, and boasted that he must have been a hard man if the police had been forced to send a riot van to his house to get him out. He then became a real handful. I was glad we had taken the van.

We kept him in over the weekend and he saw the Judge on the following Monday morning about the Injunction. Although the police had made the arrest the Injunction was dealt with by the wife's solicitors. Their interpretation was that having been served with the Injunction and ejected from the house, his kicking the door in had been an attempt to get back in the house and amounted to a breach of the Injunction. The Judge agreed with them, and sent him to prison. I wish criminal law was that easy.

A few weeks later I went to a house a couple of doors away. Again the couple were separated, but there was no real history of violence. There was a Court Order granting him access to the child on a Sunday. It was now about quarter past midnight on Sunday morning. He wanted to see the child. Not unreasonably the wife told him to go away and come back in daylight. He persisted. The matter was resolved very amicably when I suggested to him that I could smell drink on his breath, and could imagine therefore that he was drunk enough to be locked up. If that happened he wouldn't get to see the child at all that day because he would be in the police station. He decided to leave.

One night I was using the motorcycle at Bradford Street when I received a report of a gunshot having been heard from a pub. By then it was ages past closing time. When I got there I found the lights on and there were voices coming from the bar. I was alone and I rang the doorbell with a little trepidation. I had no idea what to expect.

Fortunately I knew the licensee. He was a big jovial Cork man, and proud of it. He opened the door and I could see that his clothes were covered in blood but he seemed reasonably well. Before I could say anything he said, 'Come in. I've had some trouble, but it's not what you think.'

He let me in and there were half a dozen people in the bar, some family, the rest I thought were staff.

'What's happened? Somebody has heard a shot, is that right?'

'Yes. I've shot the dog.'

'Why?'

'Savaged me, so it's gone.' He showed me his arms. In the light I could see that there were teeth marks and bruising.

'How did that happen?'

'I took his bone off him. He's always let me before. This time the bastard bit me and held on. As soon as I was free I kicked it to fuck in the yard and then got me 12 bore and shot it.'

'Where's the dog now?'

'Still in the yard.'

We went into the courtyard at the back of the pub and sure enough there was the Alsatian, shot dead. The shotgun was licensed. The dog was his. I saw no further need for police attention. I advised hospital treatment, and left. I had feared the worst when I went in, I breathed a sigh of relief when I came out.

During my stay at Bradford Street I worked alongside Tony Onions. I had known him since very early days. I liked his positive approach to his work. He had always been very conscious of his name and had once called himself O'Nions but the Chief Superintendent of the day had said to him, 'I do not plant O'Nions in my garden. When I do you can call yourself that. Until then you will remain Mr Onions.'

Tony dealt with a brawl involving Irish travelling people single-handed one night. The travellers had arrived for a big funeral at St Anne's and had taken residence in the local pubs until they had finally been turned out well after the proper closing time. For whatever reason a fight had started and Tony was in the middle of it before he realised what was happening. He called up for help but that took a little time to arrive.

The travellers were setting about each other with all manner of weapons and fortunately Tony was not being set on. At some stage during the fracas Tony found a pickaxe handle and made an ultimatum to the revellers. 'I will count to ten. After that I use this,' he told them.

'One, two, three, ten.'

Wallop! He brought the handle down against a large dustbin. The noise prompted a pause in the proceeding. Realising that Tony meant business most of the fighting stopped. The people wanted to go to a funeral in the morning, not a Court. Those who persisted in fighting were arrested when Tony's help arrived. In all four men were arrested; between them they had £4,200 in their pockets. They went to Court the next morning, were fined and arrived back in time for the funeral. That went off without incident.

The funeral was not a local one. It was for the young son of a traveller from the London area. He was of hierarchy and huge numbers of mourners were expected. For some reason his local priest feared their church was not big enough so it had come up to St Anne's. There had obviously been huge amounts of co-operation all round because it was specifically 'no caravans'.

I was out in the Transit when they gathered for the Mass. They came in all sizes. One old lady made hard work of parking her Fiesta and a huge bloke, the biggest man I'd seen out of captivity (I'd met wrestlers Big Daddy and Giant Haystacks) literally lifted it into the parking space with the rear wheel arch.

I called him over and said, 'Nice touch. If you don't mind me asking, how tall are you?'

'Seven foot two, Sir.'

'What do you weigh?'

'About 30 stone, Sir.'

'Take care, won't you?'

'Yessir.'

When he was gone the policewoman with us said, 'What would you hit a man that big with, Serge?'

'Nothing less than a Transit.'

Everyone laughed.

Tony finally changed his name, He is now known as Frazer. At least, to most.

Bob did most of the licensing enquiries on the sub-division for two reasons. He knew from his admin. days the procedures and requirements, and he knew the people. They couldn't pull the wool over his eyes. One night we went to see a woman named Julie McCann. Julie was not Irish herself, but had married into an Irish family. She had been a very bright girl at school and had been a pupil at King Edward's High School. She passed her 'A' levels and was hoping to go to Cambridge. On a night out to celebrate the end of the exams she met Peter McCann, fell for his charms and got pregnant. Her family offered her no support at all and she and Peter had married. They now had two children.

Peter was in the plant hire business and had offended the VAT man to the tune of eighteen months imprisonment. That was now behind him and they were seeking to take on a pub as well. On paper she was suitable to hold a Justices' Licence.

Bob knew them both well and he had his doubts. When Peter had gone to prison the couple had owned a large house in Hall Green; they were now living in a small rented one. Bob was not happy that there was now a sound financial background on which to hold a licence. Julie had worked to support the children whilst Peter had been away and she had spent most of her time working in bars.

She had also had a serious affair with a policeman. So serious that marriage had been discussed. Bob did know his people. Knowing that much background Bob had his doubts. Whatever Bob decided became irrelevant in the end because the brewery withdrew the pub from offer.

Julie was still working in a bar a few months later when I saw her having a dispute outside the pub where she worked. She had apparently stayed behind for a staff drink, had ordered a taxi and was in dispute with the driver. I was with Roger Clarke.

'What's up, Julie?' I asked.

'They've ordered me a taxi but I don't want this one. I won't get in a taxi with a Paki. No offence meant, but I won't.'

'That's up to you.'

'He won't call another on the radio and he wants a quid for coming this far.'

'You still at the same house?'

'Yes.'

'How'd you like Roger to walk you home?'

'Fine, It's not the walk, it's the time of night.'

With that I sent the taxi on its way and sauntered off towards the station, to relieve the office. Roger had got about a five-minute walk with Julie. I would see him later.

When he came in nearly an hour later, there was mud on his mac and a smile on his face.

'How well do you know her?' he asked me.

'I've spoken to her a few times, otherwise not very well, why?'

'She's just given it me on a plate. We got to Farm Park and she wanted a wee. When she came out of the bushes she'd got her tights in one hand. She lifted her skirt up and stuck her fanny in my hand and said, "get on that," or something like that. Bloody hell, what was I supposed to do?'

'Roger, when they ask you that nicely you do as they ask, and wash the mud off your mac before you go back out.'

'It was a hell of a surprise I tell you. That was why she didn't want to go home in that taxi. She needed a man, but she wanted a white one.'

Bob had been right all along. Finances were tight. She was keeping her taxi fare and paying the driver with her body. Sad, very sad.

The slower pace of life at Bradford Street allowed the units to have more time than most to deal with unusual things, which would normally be dealt with by specialists. Two were in themselves very interesting. The first involved a burnt-out car.

The car had been driven into a narrow cul-de-sac at about 1 am and deliberately torched. The fire brigade had been, put the fire out and left. The police on nights had been and gone. The car was of no value now. I decided that I would at least have a look. It was probably an insurance fiddle at least. It was Sunday afternoon and there was not much happening. I took a young policewoman with me, Nicki White. The car was an Allegro. My first impression was that it had not been stolen. The spare wheel was missing, as were the jack and wheel brace: not the sort of things a car thief is going to remove before firing a car. All the wheels, yes, but not just the spare.

We managed to find the chassis number, the number plates had been burnt in the fire, and played with the computer at the station. The stolen vehicle index had recently been uprated to take chassis numbers at the time of reporting a theft. There had previously been a delay of about two weeks. The computer showed nothing for that car. By now we had what was called the Police National Computer, PNC for short. It used to be available from dedicated terminals only, but our engineers had now interfaced the whole thing onto the command and control system. It was a read only facility so it could not be updated locally, but you could get at all the information without having to phone a dedicated terminal. It had not yet been reported.

The command and control system had a facility to send miscellaneous messages to other terminals (something akin to what we now call e-mail) and we sent details of our car to all terminals in Birmingham. To our immense surprise we had a response within the hour. Our car had just been reported at Belgrave Road as having been stolen within the past hour. That could not be. I retrieved the necessary reports and waited.

The PNC was based at Hendon and the vehicle side was updated daily with data from the DVLC at Swansea. It carried basic information from their records, such as make, model, colour, engine and chassis numbers, age and current known keeper. There was provision for 'interest' reports of various categories to be tagged on by the police. A 'stolen' report would in fact make the engine and chassis numbers 'live' for a separate search using other codes. It was a very useful update to an excellent piece of technology.

The next morning we collected the owner from home. The spare wheel for an Allegro was in his hall. We've found your car, bring the Logbook, identify it and we'll get it moved, was what he was told. At this point he hadn't really committed any offences, so he wasn't told when we had found the car. We identified the shell from the Logbook and took the owner back home. I got from him his insurance details and told Commercial Union the situation. If they received a claim they would phone us. On the Friday they did. A claim had been made for the car, the theft allegedly having occurred fourteen hours after the car had been burnt out.

The insurers were very helpful. They would not honour the claim, and the bogus claim now amounted to an attempt at deception. The owner had to be seen again. This time he would be arrested and charged.

A second rare enquiry for beat officers concerned the issue of fraudulent MOT Test Certificates. One of the girls on the shift found a lady driver with a broken down Mini. Neither of them had much idea about cars, and they sent for a man. The area car was sent and the crew asked for a vehicle examiner. I was nearest so I went.

The girl had bought the car two days before from an advert in the paper. It was supposed to have a new MOT for a year. It would never have passed the test. The brakes were duff, before looking any further. The girl had not seen the MOT certificate. It was promised through the post. When it arrived she brought it in. It had been issued at a garage in Hertfordshire. She had bought the car in Nuneaton and the mileage recorded on the ticket was so close to the current speedo reading that it could not possibly have been correct. In forty-five miles the car could not have gone from Hertfordshire to Birmingham, via Nuneaton.

The Ministry had to be our next port of call. They were superbly helpful.

They arranged for the vehicle to be examined and all the faults recorded, whether a test requirement or not. At their request the girl kept phoning up the man demanding the MOT certificate. After about a week of pestering she received another one through the post, this time one issued in Birmingham, a day later than the first, and posted to her from Nuneaton. The Ministry confirmed that both certificates were genuine. Genuine in that they were the proper thing, not forgeries, and had been issued by official testing stations. In forty-five miles the Mini had now been in Hertfordshire, Birmingham, Nuneaton and Birmingham.

The Mini was then submitted for a test at the Birmingham location. It failed, on many points. The engineer agreed that many of the faults were long standing. The man from the Ministry then questioned why the car had passed previously. The engineer was adamant that he had never seen the vehicle before. He was shown the certificate issued at his garage. He remembered that vehicle. It was not the same one that he had just seen. Somebody appeared to have substituted a vehicle to cover the test by using false number plates, or he was not telling the truth. We didn't know which. What was certain was that a man in Nuneaton was selling un-roadworthy vehicles and had a source of test certificates.

Back to the girl. The phone number she had used was a Birmingham one. The man had met her and taken her to Nuneaton. We would go to Nuneaton. The girl hadn't got an address and she couldn't direct us. In the end she rode out with us and pointed the house out. The electoral register at the police station gave the name of the occupier and the collator gave us some background. He was a general dealer. He had a few minor traffic convictions and been done in the past for fraud. I went to see him. I took an instant dislike to him but I didn't know why.

Yes he had sold the Mini. Yes it had a full MOT. Yes it was tested in Hertfordshire. No it hadn't been tested in Birmingham on the day after. He was sure about that.

'Who drove it back from Hertfordshire.'

'I did.'

'Which route did you take?'

'M1, M6, off at junction 3. Easy.'

'Where did you buy the car?'

'At auction.'

'Auction? The last owner sold it to a scrap man, and you bought it at auction.'

'You calling me a liar?'

'No. I am just surprised that you can scrap a car, put it through an auction, get someone to buy it, get an MOT for it and sell it, with no work done to it.'

'Happens.'

'The last owner has been seen. He knew what was wrong with it when he sold it. Those faults still exist. You got a bent MOT for it and you sold it as a good car. I have two MOT certificates for that car, both issued whilst you had it. I have had it MOT'd and it failed. How can you explain that?'

'I had it MOT'd once, not twice.'

'Who got it done the second time then?'

'Not me.'

'The second MOT was done the day after the first and three days before the car was sold. That leaves the car with you during that time. If you didn't get it tested you must know who did.'

The dealer then decided to give his explanation. The car was bought from a scrap yard. He tidied it up and painted it. The MOT from Hertfordshire was done over the phone. When he thought that the car would be sold before that arrived he had arranged for a second one to be done. He had sent the girl the first one but it got lost in the post, so he sent her the second one. He knew there had been a problem coming his way because the lad at the Birmingham testing station had been in touch after the Ministry put the Mini through. That was it.

The Ministry dealt with the testing stations. A few years down the line the full chassis number, the VIN, was a compulsory part of the MOT. The Warwickshire Police decided not to prosecute the trader. There was insufficient evidence! The Birmingham go-between could not be prosecuted because the dealer wasn't. The girl finally got her money back by taking a civil case to the County Court. The car stayed scrapped.

We also used the Ministry to sort out a local problem. We had a difficulty with artic trailers being parked all over the place at night with no lights. Bob went to see the boss at this transport firm and more or less had the door shut in his face. The message was basically go and find something more important to worry about. Bob wasn't amused. I had applied to return to traffic patrol duties but the request had been turned down mainly because I had no recent traffic experience. The answer was to get something on paper that the other applicants hadn't got. The service sponsored a home-study course and I obtained a Certificate of Professional Competence in road haulage operations, a legal requirement in a transport business. Few, if any, traffic sergeants had that, and it was something very useful to an officer dealing with lorry drivers. I also took and passed a HGV Class 1 test. Hopefully, those would make the difference in the future.

It was now certainly going to come into its own. I was fully up to speed on current HGV law. I had done a tachograph course courtesy of Midland Red and was keen to introduce myself to Bob's discourteous haulage operator. I had made a few notes of sightings of his trucks and the drivers were certainly up to something.

We went to see him. This time we didn't talk trailers scattered about, we talked drivers' hours. We had interest in three lorries, four or five sightings of each over about three weeks. Could we see the tachograph charts please? Could we come back later? No. Now. Well it's not convenient. Make it convenient. He went to his filing cabinet and grabbed a handful of charts and thrust them at me. 'Here they are, you sort them out. I haven't got time.'

A quick check at random showed obvious irregularities. The whole thing was a shambles. These were mandatory records, which any decent operator would have carefully filed. These had been chucked into a drawer with the reverence of a second overdue invoice. We seized the lot and took our prize back to Bradford Street. Bob was a little overawed. This was advanced traffic law enforcement, the stuff they had highly trained specialists to deal with, and there it was, on his desk.

I sorted out the discs into truck, date & time and driver order and then spoke to the experts: the Ministry. I arranged an appointment for the next day and took everything with me. Bingo! The Ministry took all the charts from me and had a field day. Shortly afterwards he was out of business.

Bob retired and I ran the unit for a few days until I made a final unit move at Bradford Street.

The new team were quite fun to work with. Most I had worked with before but there were a couple of new faces. The worst factor of all here was the Inspector. I had known him for many years, and was amazed that he had got so far. If there had been a system of reward for results his trophy cupboard would have been bare. It is fair to say he was bone-idle. Steve Johnson was a passenger every inch of the way.

The unit worked better when he was not around which was indeed a sad reflection on a man who should have been their inspiration and leader.

By sheer coincidence, we lived about fifty yards apart. That should have been mutually convenient for travel to and from work, but it wasn't. If I took my car he was first in the queue. When it was his turn it was never straightforward. It wouldn't start; it was low on petrol etc. I also liked to get in early, sort the day out and parade the shift on time. He liked that arrangement, because he could then get in 'just in time'. The two scenarios were not compatible. He had the habit of sometimes being outside my house just as I was backing the car off the drive. He'd then beg a lift. I worked out that he must watch for the kitchen light to go off and then make his move.

One nice summer morning, on earlies, I was crafty. I wheeled the motorbike out of the garage as soon as I was up. I then had breakfast. I switched the light off, locked up and ran to the bike and had it fired up and rolling as he came round the corner. His face was a picture and was he cross when he got in. He'd had to walk to the bus!

One night I was working as station officer when a couple of soldiers came into the enquiry office. They had a problem. They were each driving a lorry from Salisbury to Catterick. The lorries were laden with munitions and one had got a diesel leak. Diesel from a cracked injector pipe was causing a serious fume problem in the cab. They had been in touch with REME and had been told to drive on. The lorry would still run on five cylinders. The motion of the truck should disperse any fumes. Failing that, report to the police somewhere.

They used the phone, and the agreed end result was that I would allow the lorries to remain in the station yard overnight. The soldiers would go to a nearby address of a relative and the lorry would be repaired in the morning and continue to Catterick. Because of the unusual circumstances of the load, and the fact that the yard was by now very full I submitted a detailed report, with all relevant phone numbers and the like included, for the information of the Superintendent.

I was annoyed when the phone rang at home shortly before nine in the morning, 2½ hours into my sleep, with a very irate Chief Inspector on the other end demanding 'what the hell did I know about the army trucks in the yard'. There was a full report on that, I explained. Where is it now? He had not seen it and early shift hadn't seen it. Knowing how keen the Inspector was on night duty paperwork I reasoned that he had locked it in his desk and would destroy it once the lorries had gone. If it was asked for he could say I submitted it late. Fortunately, I knew the new Chief Inspector, George Dunwoody, very well. We had been constables together at the Lane.

He apologised to me and telephoned the Inspector. Initially he denied ever seeing it, but in the end he got dressed and came in to produce it from his locker. I understand he had a real good bollocking over that. He went sick that night suffering from fatigue! We never discussed those lorries again. That incident, combined with others, resulted in a transfer for him to one of the outposts of the empire, Halesowen. Within a year he had left the service. There had been a breach of discipline and rather than defend that he retired.

Miles Cadwallader, then a sergeant, unhappy with the quality of hands-on experience probationer constables were receiving devised a plan for intensive on-street training. They would be given a list of objectives, each a different type of incident, which they would, where possible, deal with from start to finish. This would involve small groups of them working with 'tutor' constables and a sergeant. Once the plan was aired it was put into practice throughout the Force. I ran the second set of courses on the division and I was very pleased with the overall results. In all I did three courses involving thirty-one probationers. Because the sergeant who ran the first courses had been able to select his pupils I had an excess of female officers on the first two of my courses. I resolved that by spreading them all over the whole division and making them available to units on duty. They would send them to jobs. I would monitor the result. When not patrolling with them on foot I would use the motorcycle to get around them.

I was able to select my own tutors and chose Dave Northam who had been a probationer on my unit when I had gone back to Digbeth in 1975, to do all the courses. I had trained him, worked with him and trusted him. Dave was a smashing bloke. He was a veteran of 2nd Battalion, Parachute Regiment. He was tough and he was fit. He was also very wise. He had served in Northern Ireland and had been with the UN in Cyprus. He was a very steady chap and his influence did a lot of good. Martin Richardson was the other. He was young in service but very sound.

The courses all ended on a high note. We went out in posh frocks or suits and dined. On the last course I worked with Chris Collymore. Chris had had a hard time on his own unit. He was of West Indian origin and had been recruited more for his ethnic origins than his academic ability. Not unusually he had some early difficulty with the vast array of forms he had to fill in during the course of his duty. His sergeant, the same one who had carefully selected his guinea pigs, had lost patience. Chris could fall by the wayside. That was not in my thinking and I arranged to take him back to my unit and give him a better crack at his career. I felt he had the ability. He wasn't born a copper, he had got to be taught, just like us all. We had to recruit ethnic minorities. We'd recruited Chris and it was our job to train him for his role. We had no hand in selection so we had to work the raw material we had got. Steve went red with rage. He didn't want another unit's cast-offs. It would also be another report to sign, etc. etc. Chris is now doing very well.

A few sets of nights after the Army lorries I spent the entire night, in pouring rain, with an overturned lorry. It was an artic laden with steel sheets in a container. The driver had got lost, attempted a 'U' turn and the trailer had tipped over. There was little disruption to traffic because of the time of night, but the main Stratford Road was closed and we had to set up a diversion. The recovery of the lorry and load was a major task and there were a number of defects with the vehicle that had to be dealt with. The driver was reported for a string of offences including excess hours. With the road opened again I returned to the station, wet and cold.

The inspector wanted a full breakdown of the events of the night. He then criticised my action, in the crowded office, in creating a diversion. I said, 'If you had bothered to walk 200 yards to the scene you could have taken charge. You left me to it. I did it my way and it worked. If you have any further comments to make, put it on paper and I'll argue with the boss. Don't question my actions in front of the shift. I am wet, I am cold, and I have not had my break. In view of that I am now going home. Good night.' He was utterly speechless. He probably sensed my annoyance at him and his attitude to the job he was paid a lot of money to do. He probably realised also that road closures by the police had to be teleprinted to HQ and that was some more paperwork.

I had ensured that all the necessary documentation was completed as we went along. I would complete the prosecution papers when the outstanding enquiries with the lorry owner had been sorted out. I was fresh from my study course and I quite relished that file. I was complimented on the finished product.

Back on days I was out with a young policewoman, Mair Edwards, when we stopped a motorcycle which had aroused my suspicion. Mair was a motorcyclist herself and she found nothing immediately wrong with the bike. The tank of the bike was not a normal colour and there was a large '2' painted on it. I thought it probably belonged to a fleet.

We checked with the computer and it was reported stolen from North Wales a few days before. There was also brief information on the file about a burglary. The rider was arrested and taken to Bradford Street. I phoned the police in North Wales and found out more about the bike. It had been stolen from a Council owned compound. The bike was used on a STEP (Schools Traffic Education Programme) and was one of two stolen when the store shed was broken into. The other bike had been found on the A5 near Shrewsbury with a puncture.

Things were looking up. We had a burglary, and at least two offenders. The lad was just seventeen and had not been in any sort of trouble before. He was quite honest and straightforward to deal with and we soon had the picture. There were three offenders. They had been to Rhyl, on holiday, and had seen the bikes in use. The compound was not properly secure and the local kids played in it. The shed was locked. They had gone back in the dark, forced the padlocks and taken two of the bikes. The older lad with them had got a car so they could only take two. They slept in the mountains and as soon as the sun was up they headed home. One bike got a puncture so they dumped that. The one we had was the other.

He gave us the names of the other two lads, and they were a bit harder. The lad with the car was banned from driving, so he didn't really want to admit to anything we couldn't prove, and we couldn't prove a lot. Fortunately, whoever dealt with him before had been thorough and details of his car were cross-referenced to his personal stuff. The car was outside his house.

I went back to the original lad and asked him to describe the car. He did so very accurately. The lad who owned it then admitted to taking it to Wales with the other lads. The third one, the unknown motorcyclist, probably hadn't committed any offences in Birmingham so we went to see him with a different line of enquiry. Mair was from Mid-Wales and spoke with a slight Welsh accent, but that was enough. She changed into plain clothes and I stayed in uniform. When we got to his house we saw him with his mother.

Mair was confident when she said, in her lovely Welsh voice, 'I am making enquiries into a burglary at Rhyl, when two motor cycles were stolen. You have been identified as being responsible.'

Before she could say anything else the lad said, 'I wasn't on my own, though.'

Nice one, Mair. He was arrested as well.

Mair didn't say she was from the North Wales Police, but she had set out to create that impression, with good result. The lad thought that we had him bang to rights, hence the police from Rhyl had come straight down for him. Mair had to disappear for the rest of the time he was with us. Once the interviews were completed all the lads were charged and bailed to attend Rhyl Court. They didn't even have a free ride up there escorted, they had to find their own way.

Mair later married a bobby from the unit, Steve Barrel. He was also a keen motorcyclist.

During 1984 Arthur Scargill, and his National Union of Mineworkers tried to topple the Thatcher Government. The mass picket of many collieries around the country caused a massive police operation to deploy officers in vast numbers at these pits. Many officers from the West Midlands were sent away each weekend, in big numbers. I was never sent, because of my age. I could opt out of Public Order training at forty, and had done so. The 'modern' methods were unknown to me. I did, however make large inroads into the overtime budget to take the places, at home, of the men who had been sent away.

The money was not wasted either. From early days together June and I had camped with a small tent. Most weekends off duty we camped in Britain and every year we went somewhere into Europe for two or three weeks. There was one snag. June's shoulder was giving cause for much concern, both socially and within the service. Sleeping on the ground in a small tent, however comfortable we made it, was becoming stressful and job-wise she was now really only fully fit for lighter duties. In other words no physical public contact. The end result was that Arthur's overtime paid for a second-hand Volkswagen campervan. Its first major journey was a six-week trip to Morocco, in late 1985. Yes, we could settle for one of these.

We came back from that trip to the very sad news that Steve Barrel had been killed in a motorcycle accident. Mair, at twenty-three, was a widow, less than a year after her marriage. I was absolutely stunned. I looked at my own motor cycling future. The past had been brilliant. I had ridden almost daily since I was sixteen and I was now forty-two. I had ridden nearly every type of British and European bike made since 1955, and a few modern Nippons as well. I had only been involved in one 'second vehicle' bump and I'd walked away from that. We ran two cars full time. We had just bought a camper and I had the bike purely for me. It would have to go.

I put my kit on and went out on it. No qualms, no fears, no misgivings and I enjoyed every second. Sod it. I'd keep it. It was long paid for. The insurance was 40 pence a day. I did the sums and £3 a week to keep it on the road was worth it, just to go out on high days and holidays. Then fate took a hand. We decided to buy a bungalow beyond Redditch. This would involve a journey to work on unlit lanes. I detest riding bikes on unlit roads. It goes back to when I was in my teens. I went for a very undignified ball of chalk among a flock of sheep. There was sheep shit everywhere and I'd rolled through most of it. Much as I enjoyed bikes, it was too soon to go to the big bike park in the sky. My beautiful BMW would go. I had a ready buyer. After twenty-six years in the saddle the bike was sold before we moved.

Just before Christmas 1985 I was to take charge of the divisional Accident Enquiry Squad. I left Bradford Street, for ever.

CHAPTER 15

Great Changes

THE AES WAS VERY ENJOYABLE. The format followed very closely that of the original squad I had been on all those years before and I got well involved with the team. The skills I had acquired from my practical experience were unknown to the other members and I was glad to pass on that knowledge. The accident investigation course meant more than just accident enquiry.

The most interesting enquiry was actually to become three. All the reports of accidents occurring on the division were logged in the office. (I think back to Norman and the Land Rover all those years before.) One report, a non-stop accident, contained a partial number but a good description of the vehicle. In the same batch was a minor accident report involving a car of identical description and with a full number. It also had the details of the driver recorded. The incidents had occurred within about five minutes of each other and about two miles apart. That was a strange coincidence indeed.

Unfortunately the trail was a little cold. The events had occurred before Christmas and we were now into January. Over Christmas the entire internal post system had ceased to function: yet another hidden benefit of civilian admin. Also, I had only been in the office part-time because of my annual involvement with the traffic squad.

In the first accident, which occurred at about 1 am on Saturday, the witness had seen what he believed to be two cars racing. The leading car had gone out of control on a curve and had hit a parked car and carried on. He had got part of a number. The car was no doubt a Datsun 120 Y, and damaged to the front offside. The damage to the parked Allegro was quite severe and a potential write-off. The girl who owned it was on third party insurance.

The second record was better. A policeman from Digbeth had found the damaged car in the Bull Ring with the driver standing beside it. When he questioned the driver he claimed that he had skidded and hit the Bull Ring wall. The officer recorded the incident because, in his own words, 'he wasn't totally sure that what he had been told was true'. The damage to the right wing was jagged. From a wall he would have expected a smoother dent. He had a good description of the driver, a man of Asian origin.

248

We went to see that driver. The car had been stolen. Most car thieves will not steal a damaged car and the theft of a Datsun is rare. This man was not telling me the truth.

I went back to the computer. Sure enough, reported stolen, a day after the accident. That looked like being our car. What he hadn't told us was that it had also been recovered, damaged, in Dudley Road Hospital grounds, and restored to him. We went to the security staff at the hospital and they were able to tell me where it had been, when they had first known of it being in the grounds and who had removed it. Now there was handy.

Next, we went up to Billy Hall, the Tyseley car dismantler. I had dealt with Billy before, no problems with him. I told him what I was looking for and he pointed to it. Three up, in a stack of five scrap cars. He had bought it from the insurance company as a stolen and recovered damaged write off. I arranged with him to leave it as intact as possible.

We then went back to see the girl who owned the Allegro. She was out but her mother was at home. I updated her on the progress so far and explained that I wanted some paint samples from her daughter's car to compare with the suspect one. As if by magic she said, 'There are some bits from the other car in the boot. We swept up afterwards and it's all in a box.'

She had the keys, good, open the boot. She did and there was a most useful piece of evidence, more than half of the indicator lens. I went back to Billy Hall, took the other bit from the car and we were in business.

The Forensic Laboratory confirmed that the broken piece from the boot of the car matched to remains of what I removed from the scrap yard. We had that car involved in that accident. We had a driver the police could put with the car five minutes later.

He had to be seen again. This time I was a little more persistent with my questions. I had never before mentioned an accident to him. I had only asked him about the car.

'When was the car stolen.'

'The Saturday.'

'When did you report it stolen?'

'The Sunday.'

'Why not the Saturday?'

'I thought my friends might have borrowed it.'

'Had they?'

'No.'

'Was it damaged when it was stolen?'

'Not much, just a few small dents.'

'When did you last use the car?'

'On the Friday.'

'When on the Friday?'

'Afternoon.'

'You used it on Friday afternoon. Who drove it Friday night?'

'Nobody, I was at work.'

'Where do you work?'

'White's taxis.'

'As a driver?'

'Yes. I jockey for my brother.'

'You work nights?'

'Only at weekends.'

'Every weekend?'

'Most.'

'Do you have any other job?'

'No.'

'So you came home on Saturday morning and the car was here?'

'Yes.'

'What time did you get home?'

'About eight.'

'When you got up it wasn't. That right?'

'Yes.'

'Where is the car now?'

'Dudley Road Hospital.'

'What about the Insurance?'

'They are going to pay me.'

'I didn't mean that. Is it comprehensive?'

'No. Third party, fire and theft.'

'So smacking it into a wall would mean you couldn't claim.'

'I haven't hit a wall.'

'You told the policeman you had.'

'What policeman.'

'The one in the Bull Ring.'

'I haven't been in the Bull Ring.'

'I have some papers here which say that your car was in the Bull Ring at five past one on Saturday morning, with the front smashed in. You say that you were at work that night driving a taxi. When you came home your car was here, undamaged. Your car then gets stolen and you report it to the police the next day. You say your insurance is fire and theft. You needed a theft to cover your damage. By the time you reported your car stolen it was safely in the grounds of Dudley Road Hospital. It was in there before seven on Saturday morning. I think you put it there on the way from the Bull Ring to here.'

'That's not right, you can't say that.'

'Just have. If you like I'll send for the policeman who saw you in the Bull Ring. He can recognise the driver. His description fits you. Including the blue anorak with the yellow collar which is hanging up over there.'

'I want a solicitor.'

'You're probably right.'

'Who is he?'

He told me.

'Phone him. Let me speak to him.'

He contacted his solicitor and told him some of what we had said. He then let me speak to him.

I said, 'The situation at the moment is that as far as I am concerned, I have further enquiries to make. I will arrange to speak to your client through you one afternoon next week.'

I left the house with Andy Smart, who had sat through the interview in silence. He said, 'You didn't mention the accident with the Allegro.'

'The reason is I need something for the solicitor. Plus there is a duff insurance claim in the system. We need to speak to Norwich Union. Even if we don't get this home, and I think we will, they won't pay him anything when they know about the Allegro.'

The Norwich Union had accepted the claim form and they were processing it. Because of the value of the Datsun they had treated it as routine. Now they would not act until they had confirmation of the other events. The space we needed.

When the interview started again I was quite confident. I had run through the notes of the previous one with the solicitor and we had common ground.

I started, 'When I told you that a policeman could identify you you wanted a solicitor. He's here, why did you want him?'

'I was worried.'

'What about?'

'The car.'

'What about the car?'

'The damage.'

'What damage?'

'When I hit the wall.'

'What wall?'

'The Bull Ring.'

'So your car was in the Bull Ring that night.'

'Yes.'

'And you were driving it?'

'Yes.'

'And you parked it at Dudley Road on the way home?'

'Yes.'

'Do you use your car as a taxi?'

'No.'

'You did on Friday night.'

'No.'

'Yes. You parked outside Red Star and took a fare.'

'No.'

'Yes. You were seen to poach one. They shouted at you and you drove off. You were chased by one of their number and you hit an Allegro on the way. That wrecked the front of your car. You then stopped in the Bull Ring to check your damage. The policeman had been in the subway underneath and didn't hear any accident, only a tyre rubbing on the wing.'

'I didn't hit any Allegro. I know nothing about it.'

I opened my drawer and took out a piece of the indicator lens. 'That is from your car. I removed it from your car at the scrap yard.' I took out the second piece. 'This the lady found under her car after you hit it.' I then fitted the two pieces together. They fitted perfectly. 'See. Your car wrecked an Allegro.'

I looked at the solicitor and said, 'That's it. I am preparing a prosecution file and it will include everything we have discussed today.'

That enquiry was possible only because an alert police officer was unhappy with a minor situation and made a sensible and proper report of it. He knew in his own mind that all was not well with the car and he recorded the information for his piece of mind. Well done to him. As for the driver, he was found guilty of a string of offences relating to the accident with the Allegro. He was fined for those and attempting to swindle Norwich Union. He was never paid out on his car, and after Billy Hall had put two others on top of it, it was of no further use to anyone else. The witness had in fact been in a car behind the Datsun. He was a taxi driver.

When my year with the AES was over June was still on shifts and I was offered a place at Steelhouse Lane. I had done full circle, but the world was now a far different place. I had about an hour with the Chief Inspector, 'Pip' Postans. Pip had been at the Lane for years; he was almost part of the fittings. He was the man to speak to if you needed to know anything. He had been an excellent detective but his career progress came to an end after he was acquitted of conspiring to pervert the course of justice. The Court decided that there was no case to answer but the Police Service had to shoot itself in the foot and stab Pip in the back to convince people that 'well just in case'.

The Police and Criminal Evidence Act, was shortly to come into force. PACE as it became known was mainly about the care and custody of prisoners detained in police cells prior to a Court appearance. It meant that every station where prisoners were detained had to be approved by the chief officer of police and had to have a sergeant, at least, as a custody officer. Pip would look towards older, mature sergeants for the posts and I fitted his criteria.

In the run up to PACE the procedures were being adopted in order to facilitate a smooth change on the day. The new rules were not going to make much difference to the big forces, like ours, but the smaller ones were likely to have serious manpower shortages. The biggest single problem at the Lane was cells. Or lack of them.

When the station was built in 1933 it was purposely attached to the Central Lock-up. That housed the Lane's cells. The Lane didn't have a custody officer as such. It had an inspector and a constable in the front office, the inspector completed initial papers for each prisoner and he or she was then transferred to the Lock-up cells and detained until required by the officer in the case. That situation was to prevail at the moment but a large section of the Lock-up had got to be partitioned off to give the Lane its own cells.

Pip's offer was simple. I could go in the front office, taking with me the pay of inspector. On the day of PACE I would become a custody officer and adjust myself to sergeant again. He also saw no difficulty in changing units when the need arose, particularly if I could give notice. I gave him the required notice there and then and accepted the job. We had also discussed traffic patrol duties and Pip promised to support my further application to transfer back to traffic. He had first hand experience of how compulsory career breaks tended to be permanent.

When I did the job as inspector my regular office man was Jack Webb. Jack felt very much as I did about the Service. He had gone about his tasks with a great deal of commitment and could see that progress was not going in a way which he would have liked. In his eighteen years of service, all in the City Centre, he had seen the same changes as me. Not all change had been to the benefit of the Service or the public.

Jack was a keen rugby player and also a talented musician and spent much of his time entertaining for various charities. He was also a motorcyclist. We got on well.

Within a short time of losing Steve my good pal Jeff Barnes was killed on a bike in his own time. Jeff and I went back almost to day one. We'd been mates together, we'd got drunk together, we'd fought together and we'd even been in the shit together. In the early 60s Jeff had been off his beat. We were both caught in the Gaiety Cinema, in Coleshill Street, by Dick Walker, a Digbeth sergeant. Fortune was with me. I came out of the gents but Jeff was caught watching the film. Dick put us both on the sheet. I got a divisional ear-bending, Jeff was fined £2 by the Chief. We had been that close for that long.

I was on earlies at the Lane when it happened. We were all having breakfast huddled round a big table playing 'Niggle', a sort of Progressive Whist. Just as we finished Pip Postans came in and made for our table, 'I'll see you before you go back upstairs, Ralph,' he said. 'Coffee, milk no sugar?'

'Please.'

I expected Pip to use a smaller table and as I got up he indicated the quiet one in the far corner. This was by no means unusual; if Pip wanted a chat about something he often got away from the office, secretary and phone.

He brought the coffee over and sat down. He gave me a sheet of paper to read. It was an incident log print out. I scanned through it. Fatal accident... car v motor cycle. A bit further on ... maybe policeman involved ... the bottom line, now identified as PC 2258 Jeff Barnes. Jeff. Gone, I was with him only last week. I looked up at Pip, punched the table, spilling the coffee, uttered some obscenity and walked off to the gents to wash my face. When I came back Pip had mopped up, so had I. 'You OK now?'

I nodded. Pip knew Jeff well and it had also hit him. We both needed to talk and had a long chatter about all sorts of trivia from the past. By any other name this was trauma counselling on the hoof.

Stan Jones was Jeff's work partner and he did a super job on the groundwork for the funeral. In recent years Jeff's private life had got a bit complicated. He had a divorce behind him and a harem round him. I didn't envy Stan his task.

In just a decade I'd lost four close pals and two colleagues to bike crashes, and several others had been seriously hurt on bikes. I came away from Robin Hood Cemetery on low ebb.

With the advent of PACE we had civilian Enquiry Office Assistants. Hilary Crowe was posted to my unit. That suited us all. Hilary had been with us for some years as a computer operator with the divisional controller. She knew her job there and soon mastered the office. She and Jack were a good backup team. Not all the units were so fortunate.

Although only employed as assistants these new office men and women were greatly misused and were later left to run public enquiry offices single-handed. There was no guarantee to the public calling into a station that they would even see a police officer, let alone be dealt with by one. Somehow, it all seemed so wrong.

I got back into my stride quite quickly; the only real drawback was the volume. Steelhouse Lane handles more than twice the number of prisoners of any other station in the City and more than any other in the Force. It could easily be thirty on an afternoon shift, but the day sped by.

I had by now been given the news that I was unlikely to be allowed to return to traffic duties. My age was against me. Bob Hope, the traffic superintendent, had decided that the job should remain with men under forty. Incredible, when more than half the traffic division was made up of men over that age. Bob had been the head of the driving school when I served there. He didn't even remember me.

In 1961 the Birmingham City Police Pipe Band was formed. In 1986, to celebrate their Silver Jubilee they visited West Germany as guests of the Royal Military Police. In order to finance the trip they set up a number of fund raising events. One of these was a 'gentleman's evening' at Tally Ho! Club. It was in effect a cabaret with a number of fairly blue comedians and a couple of bagpipe solos. It was very well attended, and a huge success. As at all these events there was the obligatory raffle. The first prize was a choice of either travelling with the band for the duration of the tour, as their guest, or a bottle of scotch. When my ticket came out first I accepted the trip. I could buy a bottle of scotch on the boat! The second prize also came to our table, so I had the best of both worlds.

When I told June she wasn't overjoyed. We were moving house. Within two days of that we were driving to Spain to open up a friend's apartment for the season. The day after we got back from there I would be off to Germany! I could see her point. She understood my reasons for wanting to go and raised no objections.

That trip was the first I had done with the band. I had known and worked with many of its members for years and I had a really splendid trip. The RMP were excellent hosts and we had a wonderful welcome from them at Helmstedt before they escorted our coach through the old East Germany to West Berlin. We spent the first night in a hotel. I vaguely remember in the haze of the morning having caviar and champagne for breakfast. The next two nights were spent in military accommodation with army food. Lovely meals, nicely prepared and presented.

We were taken into East Berlin, what a contrast. Jesus, it was grim. The clock had turned back forty years as we went through Checkpoint Charlie.

Travelling in reality as military personnel we had uninterrupted right of access to the East and our passports were never stamped with the dreaded East German eagle and hammer. That could be a difficult stamp at some borders, if passports were carefully checked.

Back in the West we visited the USAF base at Templehof for an open day and the band played for them. It went down well with all concerned. The RMP Headquarters was located in the Olympic stadium where Hitler had addressed his admirers, before the war. His deputy, Hess, was still alive then and incarcerated in Spandau. It was a strange sensation to go to the centre of Hitler's orations and to realise that we had been within a hundred yards of Hess himself.

The highlight of the visit for me was the journey back from Berlin to Helmstedt on the Military train. The train was operated by the Royal Corps of Transport, under the charge of the RMP. Breakfast was waiter service. The last day was spent at Helmstedt and a barbecue was laid on. Some bartering had taken place and the US army had delivered some very fine T-bone steaks.

One of the RMP sergeants was a motorcycle fanatic. He allowed me to try his Triumph Saint and the flagship of his fleet of five or six, a Kawasaki GPZ 1000 Turbo. This bike was not available on the UK market. On a straight bit of the Autobahn I shut the throttle off at 200 kph about 125 miles an hour, the fastest I had ever been on a motorcycle. That ride was my last for many years. I had just sold my own bike, and although I didn't know it then, I would never ride another police one either. That really was a climax to finish on.

That trip was a wonderful experience, and I thanked our hosts very warmly indeed. It signalled a pleasurable summer. For most of the summer I worked with the band in my spare time and indeed, on occasions, on duty. The force had a New Standard, like a Regiment would have Colours. I travelled with the band and was Standard Bearer at official functions, the most memorable being the Chichester March, from the RMP depot there. It is a charity event and was a super weekend.

On a Saturday just prior to Christmas 1986 the shift turned up a can of worms that gave us all a great insight into how simple crime can become of international interest. It was, on the face of it, a totally straightforward offence of purchasing goods with a stolen credit card. We had the credit card, the goods and the person using the card. From that point on it started to get complicated.

The card had been reported stolen from a British Army base in Bielefeld, Germany. Since then it had been used in Canada and Denmark.

Standard Bearer at the Chichester March, 1986.

The man we had in custody was a serving soldier, based in Germany, and apparently on leave. As is customary we enquired of the Provost Marshal's office for a contact number for the base in Germany. They did better than that and came back to us with the full background of the original theft. The credit card had been stolen from a changing room in a gymnasium on the base. The theft had been investigated by the RMP and the man we had in custody had been interviewed as a suspect, having been suspected of being involved in a previous and similar offence. In the weeks that followed it was established that the card had been used in Canada. By coincidence our prisoner had been in Canada, with the army, when the card was used. That tended to suggest that the card was being used by a soldier, and probably him.

He had been interviewed again. As no evidence was found no action had been taken.

His explanation to us was that he had found the card just a few hours before using it. He was unaware that we knew much more about the original offence. He was accompanied by a young woman, who had taken no part in the crime for which he had been arrested.

She was interviewed at length. She was the daughter of a senior Army Officer who lived near Broadway. She had met our soldier whilst her father was serving in Germany; they had enjoyed an on-off-on relationship, and there were no long term plans. He had phoned her earlier in the week explaining that he was coming home for Christmas and would like to see her. They had met up at her father's and come into Birmingham for shopping.

Whilst this was going on I had a call from the RMP in Germany that added further problems. Our soldier was absent from his base on a 72-hour local leave. That did not permit return to Britain (except by air) because of the long drives involved to the ferry ports. He had also legitimately borrowed a mate's car. For tax reasons that was not permitted to return to the UK inside two years. It was now probably back ten months early. The RMP were also making arrangements for someone from the RMP in Britain to contact us for access to him for further interview.

The girl told us where the car was and we had the keys for that in his property. That was brought in and was given a thorough search. In it there was the usual Duty Free, a return ferry ticket to Esbjerg, Denmark and not much else.

I duly had my call from the RMP and they could now tell us that the car had been lent out on the understanding that it was going only into Denmark, and then only if weather conditions permitted. Our prisoner had very little money on him when he left his base; he now had several pounds and some Deutchmarks, and had bought a return ferry ticket for the car and himself, and had also spent in the Duty Free. He was not allowed to be in the UK with the car and the military would like to interview him, preferably after Court on Monday. We had not reached the point of discussing bail but I would keep their request in mind. The deception in the City Centre shop was easy to sort. He was then interviewed solely on the basis of that offence. The other matters were really within the jurisdiction of the military.

The officer's daughter was brought up to date and she washed her hands of her boyfriend there and then. That was useful. I spoke to her father and he agreed to collect her. He also agreed to bring with him all the boyfriend's luggage. Our Squaddie was no longer welcome at his home. That also meant I now had good grounds for refusing bail.

I charged the prisoner with deception and on advice, theft of the credit card between the dates of its theft and recovery. That was a precaution in case he was not the original thief. When I refused to grant bail I obviously broke down his defensive barrier. He was due back in Germany on Monday afternoon. 'How come? Your girlfriend told us that you were "home for Christmas", is that true?'

'No.'

'What leave have you got?'

'Seventy-two-hour, Friday to Monday.'

'Then you ain't supposed to be here.'

'Long as I'm back on Monday it's not a problem.'

'You won't be.'

'If I don't get back I'm in the shit.'

'You don't need to be back to have that problem, you've got loads of that following you around.'

'Such as?'

'Such as a tax free car, re-imported into the UK. The Redcaps want to speak to you about that.'

'It's not my car.'

I sent our man to his cell to contemplate his future.

Colonel Thomas duly arrived, burdened down with luggage. His daughter, apparently none the worse for her ordeal, helped him with it. I looked at it in amazement. This bloke was on a 72-hour pass, that's a hold-all trip, not three suitcases. I found a relief Custody Officer and had a chat with the Colonel and his daughter. It was apparent that the Colonel was expecting the boyfriend to be with him for up to three weeks. He wasn't even allowed home on a 72-hour. What could I tell him about the credit card business? What had happened today he would have to glean from his daughter. I could tell him that the credit card was stolen in Bielefeld. I could also tell him that it had been used in Canada, Denmark and Birmingham. I assured him that the Provost Marshal was aware. He seemed pleased with that news.

After the Colonel had left, the RMP sergeant was back on the phone. They definitely needed to speak to their boy on Monday. Could the remand be up early? What were the chances of conditional bail to Military Custody? I assured them that should not be a problem provided escorts were in attendance. It was quite a routine procedure. I mentioned the suitcases and the sergeant asked, 'What's in them?'

'No idea. Colonel Thomas left just as you called me. I haven't had time to book them in.'

'What's his interest?'

'Young son was staying there. His daughter was with him when he got locked up.'

'Are you allowed to go through his cases?'

'I need to list the contents accurately; that could include checking through them.'

'Would you do that for me, and call me back?'

'Am I looking for anything in particular?'

'I'm honestly not sure.'

My runner went through the cases, listing everything. The first was all uniform. The second was all personal clothing, much of it new, and the third was an overgrown overnight bag with 5,000 cigarettes in it. Now there was a surprise. I contacted the RMP again with the news.

'That is wonderful news, sergeant. The NAAFI are short of a carton of 10,000. Can you do two things for me, please. First, don't even mention them. We'll sign for everything on Monday. Two, can this little shit have his best uniform on when he goes before the Bench?'

On the Monday morning I was back on 1st watch, and the soldier was under the care of the Lock-up. I told him that he had got to be in Court in uniform.

'It's at her place.'

'No, her dad's brought it in because the Redcaps want you in uniform.'

'What's he brought?'

'Three bloody great cases. Your uniform's in the issue one.'

He seemed contented so far.

As I was about to go for breakfast the escort arrived, a sergeant and two corporals. They were obviously not from the RMP. These were some evil looking buggers, each about 6'2" with razor like creases, mirrors on their feet and slashed peaks on their caps.

'Where have you come in from?'

'We're from Colchester.'

We breakfasted together then we got the luggage, and sorted out a uniform. As they put together what he needed they all burst out laughing. Somebody had sewn up the sleeves of the jacket and sewn two pairs of trousers together. Either this had happened at the Colonel's house or our man had big time fallen out with someone on the base. There was enough left to make a suit for court but it was a bit scruffy. The kid didn't bat an eyelid when I took him his uniform. He was up by 10.15 and nearly crapped himself when the escort appeared in the dock and followed him down the steps.

The Lock-up staff gave him his property. I got signatures for the suitcases and he went off to Colchester Military Prison for twenty-eight days to await his fate at Birmingham Magistrates Court. The car found its way back to Germany after somebody in high places had spoken to someone equally as high, somewhere else. He came to our courts and got fined £100. He went back under escort for ultimate dismissal from the army. The NAAFI got back half of their 10,000 cigarettes. The credit card use in Canada was down to him, as was the Denmark usage, which was for the ferry crossing. All in all a very complex enquiry, most of which was dealt with by the military.

My final turning point came in January 1987. Since 1975 June had been carrying a shoulder defect as a result of a serious assault at Belgrave Road. She had been the controller there when a prostitute was arrested for wounding her client. A policewoman was dealing with her when she went berserk. June went to help and the woman jumped the dock railings, taking June's left arm with her. The end result of that was a dislocation of the shoulder and major tissue damage to nerves, ligaments and tendons. The damage was repaired to a degree but medical science was unable to make a perfect job. That meant that the shoulder was prone to dislocation without notice, and though it was a very simple process to re-locate the joint, each dislocation weakened it.

During her working day on 1 January, June banged her arm on a locker door and dislocated the shoulder. That did not relocate and gradually fell forward. A hospital visit followed and surgery would have to be undertaken. The shoulder was so weak that no surgery would be possible until all swelling and bruising had gone. That would be at least six weeks. The surgeon was not hopeful. The best result he could see from surgery was a permanent partial disability, probably in the region of 20 per cent loss of mobility, in the joint.

What he proposed was an operation to clean up the socket, which had become distorted over the years with the constant dislocations, shorten all the muscles, tendons, ligaments and nerves and put the whole thing back together. The operation had the fancy name of 'Putti-platt'. He didn't believe that she would ever again do police work.

That seemed to mess up the plans for the future, at least on the domestic scene. I had a 'first possible' retirement date in early 1992, June's was three years after that. I would probably have stayed on until 1994 but if June was in imminent danger of an early and enforced retirement on medical grounds the early 'first possible' date could well be favoured. That meant only five years left and a probable shortfall in our anticipated retirement capital.

We had hoped that in the early years of our retirement we would travel extensively, possibly even selling up in order to be totally free agents.

The service used to run pre-retirement courses and I was due to attend one later that month. The information from that course would surely shape future events. That course dictated that I should retire at the soonest possible time after the date on which I became eligible, in other words the 'first possible'. Decision made!

Whilst I was a cadet there was a major change in police retirement strategy. Any officer joining the Service after August 1961 was affected. Prior to then retirement was possible at any age after 25 years service. That was how Dave Cox was able to retire. Now there are two lines open. The first is 30 years reckonable service and no age restriction. The other is after the age of fifty with over 25 years. One snag though, there are no pay rises until you reach fifty-five. Wise investment is essential. The medical pension is calculated differently so June would not now be bothered by the other factors. She would be out before me. When I left the cadets in 1962 I had been paid back my superannuation. June had done the same. Shortly after we married we had been able to pay back what we had taken, with interest. About £28 bought me 285 days.

During that course my mother passed away and that disrupted normal routine for a few days, whilst I tied up the loose ends. When my father had died the silly things became very time consuming; the old 1*d*. policies that had been taken out by his parents and the like took ages. Learning from that experience made Mum's affairs much more straightforward. She had also made a will, something I wish more people would do. So often when friends and colleagues have died suddenly there has been no will and the matters have hung on for months or even years. Those few days also gave me chance to reflect.

I had to work in close liaison with the Lock-up and a sergeant in there was due to retire in the coming July. They were a good shift. I hadn't got to consider any shift changes in relation to June, certainly not in the foreseeable future. They had abandoned the merry-go-round and the move she had just had would be the last. I had felt that I was probably getting too old to remain at the sharpest end of things for much longer and with only five years now left I could probably manage four of those in the warm and in the dry. In principle the Inspector would have me. The job was to be advertised shortly, apply. I did.

The man in charge, Pete Arnold, held his interviews on a Tuesday afternoon in February 1987. He was totally straight, frank and honest. Duncan MacLachlan, his senior Inspector, had recommended me, Mac wanted me. He trusted Mac's integrity and without further formality he gave me the job, to start when Don Harris retired.

That night Tony Peatman died suddenly. Tony was the Lock-up sergeant on the unit I had recently moved from. Pete Arnold phoned me at home and told me. He also told me that I would be on his staff on the coming Monday.

I would take Tony's place until July and then the promised arrangements would be implemented. That really was dead-man's-shoes. I was in the post before Tony's funeral.

I had one thing left to do. When I had had my dealings with Emrys Davies over fuel economy and kindred matters, I had submitted a lengthy report on the use, or non-use, by the force of small diesel cars. It had done the rounds with various comments attached. The bottom line was that British Leyland did not build a small diesel car and thus they were not an option. Ford and Vauxhall did, but we had to support local industry!

A few years on, there was a paper from the military on their use of diesel vehicles of all sizes, and diesel was to be their way into the future. This, combined with the fact that BL were now producing the Maestro car and van with a Perkins diesel option, prompted me to have a second stab at it. The force was buying huge numbers of Maestros for all small car use. That's Pandas, CID, Driving School, Divisional hacks plus dog and SOCO vans.

These all had petrol engines. Most weren't giving above 30 mpg. The diesel option would offer close to 50 mpg. Diesel was cheaper than petrol and went further, so any extra cost of initial vehicle price would soon be offset with the high mileages that these vehicles would cover in their lifetimes. I also knew that the petrol engines were more or less the same as those that had powered the entire BL range since the early sixties and we had huge experience of what they were like! Put kindly, they were a dated design.

I again suggested the diesel option supported by the fact that West Mercia were using Maestro vans and also that I had run a stunningly reliable diesel Volkswagen Golf for four years. That had done over 80,000 miles at 52.3 mpg overall.

I was thanked for my interest, but other comments suggested that this issue was the subject of a discussion group at a higher academic level than mine and that my opinion was irrelevant. In other words mere policemen were not invited to put their views!

CHAPTER 16

The Last Five Years

BIRMINGHAM'S CENTRAL LOCK-UP is just what its name implies, a cell complex. It is by far the oldest police building in the City and dates back to Victorian times. It is by design, style and character, a miniature prison, a secure, uninviting detention establishment. Its function is to keep in custody those individuals who are lawfully detained by and for due process of law. The impression to most people who have never been inside such a place before, is a scene from *Porridge*, the TV comedy show. That's not far out.

When I first went inside the building in 1963 I was amazed that there was such a place in existence. I had seen inside Winson Green prison as a cadet so I was not surprised by its starkness, just surprised that the police should ever have such a facility. There were around sixty cells on three floors. The landings on the two upper floors were wrought iron grids, designed for easy cleaning. The floor in the basement was sloping from both sides to a central channel, again to facilitate the speedy flow of water from the area. There were washing basins on each level and each cell had a bench and a toilet, flushed from outside by means of a chain. There was a kitchen from where all food consumed by inmates was prepared.

All prisoners were fingerprinted by the staff. The prints were of a high quality and were sent both to the Regional fingerprint bureau and Scotland Yard.

There was more: a tunnel connected the complex to the cells under the Victoria Law Courts. This was yet another secure area of cells. These were only used during the day and aided the smooth running of the Courts of Assize, Quarter Sessions and Petty Sessions or Magistrates Court. The maze of passages and corridors led to the dock areas of the secure Courts. Both the Court cells and the Lock-up were served from a secure van area, within the Court building. The outer gates were a massive wrought iron structure hung into stone blocks from huge hooked hinges. The inner courtyard was foreboding. A solitary gas lamp from the by-gone age hung on the yard wall. Once the outer gates were locked there were two routes, both through heavy, secure doors, one into the Court cells and the other into the Lock-up.

When I went there in 1987, very little had changed. I was to witness the greatest changes the building, or its staff, had ever seen. The only visible

264

change was that the huge iron gates on the van yard had been replaced with a tatty roller shutter, and the gaslight had gone! Fingerprinting was done on Division.

My shift Inspector for the moment was Eric Purkis. I had worked with Eric during the year I had spent on plain clothes on the 'A' division. He had spent much of his early working life in the then Rhodesia. Misfortune had befallen him in recent years; his wife had been killed in an accident and he had suffered a stroke. He was seeing his time out in the warm. So sharp was his wit that he was nicknamed 'The Blade'. The rest of the team was made up of five constables.

Our duties were, in simple terms, defined by Statute, but there was much more to it than that. As well as being a prisoner detention unit the Lock-up had a very efficient administrative function. The Court's list of daily cases was generated from its computer. There was a record of every offender, whether in custody or on bail, who had appeared before the Magistrates. There was a result for the case or a date for future appearance. At night and at weekends we carried the entire City wide fine warrant index.

Force Orders dictated that custody stations would feed their prisoners by way of station canteens or local resources. Obviously, those rules were compiled by E.S.S.O. men. Prisoner care is a 24-hour 365-day function. The men from headquarters had a canteen at work, but they didn't work nights or weekends. In reality the food was supplied from stocks held in a freezer in the Lock-up kitchen. Some five hundred meals a week was average.

All papers for the Court came through the Lock-up, including those for the Court and those for the prosecutor. To get the prisoners into the building there was a twenty-four-hour system of collection from the custody stations in secure cell vans, manned by escorts provided from the shift. That collection van was invaluable as a service to the stations concerned with the constant processing of offenders before Court appearance.

The staff at the Lock-up had the total responsibility to collect, contain, feed and care for every person kept in custody to appear before a Birmingham Court. The chain continued into Court, and out of the building, either as a free man, one on bail or in custody. The task of conveying remanded or convicted prisoners to the custodial establishments nominated by the Court also rested with them. The Lock-up teams also provided a post court collection service throughout the Force, except Coventry, to convey from court stations to establishments, those prisoners so directed by the Court.

It was effectively a logistics centre for prisoners, their distribution, and that of their property and case papers. The building is unique in the United

Kingdom. Only Leeds has anything similar. Birmingham has the largest Magistrates Court complex in Europe, and that has been made possible largely by the facility afforded by the Lock-up. Up to six hundred cases a day were heard in Courts there.

There were few social benefits attached to working in the Lock-up but a staff of seventy did and I was now one of them. My function would be solely that of Custody Officer as defined under PACE. The Inspector took overall charge of the building and was there to offer advice and guidance to any officer seeking it. The constables did the outside duties on the vans and all the donkey work within the building.

The place had seen every villain ever locked up overnight in Birmingham for about ninety years, and a few more besides. If only those walls could talk. Historically it had always been said that the staff at the Lock-up were singularly unhelpful. What that meant was that a lot of officers made enquiries of the Lockup and were not always given the answer they hoped to hear. That was different.

June went into hospital for her operation, almost at the same time that I went to Lock-up, and I was given every facility to visit her as necessary. I was even able to organise a small party for friends to say 'good-bye' to the division of which I had been a part for twenty-two years service, including the last twelve years. Even at Traffic I'd been based on the 'A'. I would, of course, still have contact with many of them as they were still engaged in the business of locking up villains. It was a quiet 'do' with a curry and a beer for all who came. The shift gave me a hip flask, nicely engraved, with an appropriate greeting. They even supplied it full. How thoughtful. That flask has been many miles since then. It's in the emergency cupboard in my motor caravan. June was unable to attend. I found that sad because these people had been her friends as well. I took her many good wishes to the hospital.

The operation was a success in itself but the rest period was difficult. June had her arm strapped to her body and it was totally immobile for six weeks. When she was fit to travel I drove her to Portugal for some sunshine before she took a period of convalescence at the police home.

It was whilst she was here that I had a telephone call that would change our lives completely, at least in the short term. A man asked me whether I was the father of Shirley Helen Pettitt. I confirmed that I was and he said, 'I am her fiancé, it is our wish that you come to the wedding.' I was utterly amazed. The daughter who I had last seen as a little baby twenty years before still wanted to see her father. That was unbelievable. It was something which had seemed less and less likely as the years passed. That was good news.

Eric was good about it. He remembered her being born, and all the trouble that had surrounded my marriage. I arranged to have part of the next Saturday evening off and agreed a meeting. They were now living in Northampton but he and Helen, as she had become known, would make the journey to Birmingham.

Those few hours were the happiest for many years. She had grown up into a pretty, tidy young woman. Helen had her mother's good looks. Regrettably, also one of her habits, she smoked. Her grandparents were still alive. Her mother had re-married, hence her change of name. History had repeated itself. At eighteen, Helen had been evicted from the family home, by her mother. Her mother had divorced again and was now living with another man. Thus at twenty she was finding it expedient to marry. Ian, her fiancé, had used a very simple way to find me. He knew I had been on the bikes. He went to the garage and asked someone who knew me, where to find me. The rest was merely a phone call away.

June was pleased with my news. She had seen Helen. By some quirk of fate she had been the policewoman on duty at the domestic Court on the day Penny and I had one of our battles over money. Children are not allowed in Court and a woman officer was always on hand to hold babies. We went to the wedding, on a beautiful, sunny July afternoon. The bride looked, as every bride does on such occasions, beautiful. She married a Scot. As my surprise for the day I arranged for a friend from the Pipe Band to pipe them out of the Church.

Penny did not attend. The grandparents did. They didn't know I would be there; had they done so, they might not have been. I was not welcomed warmly and was not even recognised. Over the course of twenty years I had put on about four stone, gone bald and grown a beard. When she did find out who I was there was an icy chill on the wind. 'Hello, Rolph [she had never used my proper name] do you remember me?'

My honest reply saved the need for any further conversation, 'Regrettably, I do.' Nothing more was said and she walked away. Years later we have not been in touch.

As with many marriages undertaken for the wrong reasons, history was again to repeat itself and Helen followed her parents through the Divorce Court. Fortune was on her side. The decree was obtained quickly, by mutual consent.

With Helen now homeless she moved in with June and me. June never had any children, but now she had a family.

Don Harris retired on Helen's wedding day and on the following Monday I joined my new unit. Pete Arnold had been true to his word. Duncan MacLachlan was my new Inspector. Like all but two of the staff in the Lock-up he was a former Birmingham City man and I had known him for over twenty years. He knew the Lock-up and Court procedures like the back of his hand. He had been in there for some years as a sergeant before spending a year at Digbeth on my old unit. He had in fact taken my place when I moved to Bradford Street. He told me that the impression my old unit had made on him, convinced him that I had helped to create a team spirit unlike any he had known. He was indeed proud to have worked with them. I was pleased to hear that; they had made me proud too. I knew they were a good team. After the year he was promoted straight back into his current job.

I received my Long Service and Good Conduct medal in 1985. It was a pretty low-key affair at Tally Ho! and it was presented by Edward Shore, the then Chairman of the Police Authority. June came as my guest.

When June received hers in 1988 it was a much more high profile presentation. It was the first time for many years that a husband and wife team had both held the medal and the Force was always on the look-out for good publicity so there were two stories here. The first was the 900+ years of service the recipients had jointly given to their careers and the second was the husband and wife team of June and me.

The Press photograph of us taken that day is probably the nicest picture of us both together that we have. It certainly failed to reveal sign of the shoulder operation which would ultimately shorten her career.

After I had been with Mac for about a year Pete Arnold had a problem. An Inspector from another unit had absented himself from the building, on nights, leaving his unit to fend for itself. He was posted immediately and Mac was put in charge of that unit. I ran Mac's unit until a new man was appointed.

June's shoulder injury had finally dictated that she was no longer fit to serve. She saw the Force surgeon on a Tuesday morning in November 1989. It was the day after her birthday. She had a bad week; her mother died the day before her birthday, she lost her job the day after. A happy birthday it was not. She retired on a medical pension in March the following year, the day she completed twenty-five years service.

It was the custom to have a small party for friends at the end of a career and I urged June to have such an event. It was a wonderful evening. It was hard to believe that we had amassed so many friends during our careers. When I finally left we had another get together and even more attended. Over three hundred guests had a drink with me in the club at Steelhouse Lane that January night, two years later.

Outside the planners were at it again. The old 'A' division was being altered once more. Bridge would go to the 'C' division. The police station at

Presentation day for June's Long Service and Good Conduct Medal, 1988. (With credit to the Birmingham Post & Mail Ltd.)

Bradford Street would be a satellite of Digbeth. Most of the area given in the last change would go back from whence it came and would be policed from Acocks Green. Once again the division would revert to two sub-divisions. The last detail was that in order that the new International Convention Centre could be policed from the City Centre, a lump of the Ladywood area would transfer to the 'F' division, which was of course, the old Birmingham City 'A'.

Because there was to be a new custody suite at Steelhouse Lane, Digbeth would ultimately only take prisoners during the day and almost close down at night with the entire division policed from the Lane.

The 'A' now administrative division would also be split up. They couldn't go back to calling it the 'R' division so they went further down the alphabet and called the reserve staff the 'S' for support division. What was left of the 'A' would still be admin. For good measure civilian detention officers soon would be brought into the Lock-up.

The basic procedures for dealing with any prisoners in police custody are more or less universal. It is the local adaptations which cause problems.

Following the amalgamation some Petty-Sessions areas changed. This meant that some divisions actually sent prisoners to two different Court venues. Documentation was dealt with centrally and quite often the prisoner went to one Court and his papers to another. Surely when mergers are considered all those agencies affected should get their heads together and sort out potential difficulties. It takes more than just planners to plan properly!

The D division use Sutton and Birmingham Courts. Acocks Green send all their cases to Solihull, unless they involve juveniles. That means that a man arrested just two miles from the City Centre could be dealt with by a Court three miles the other side of the City boundary. That's hardly local justice. Chelmsley Wood used to come under Coleshill. That's still in Warwickshire so they have to now go to Solihull as well.

For many years the Prison Officers Association had been in dispute with the Home Office over over-crowding and under manning of the prisons in London and for about eighteen months the Lock-up catered for up to sixteen overspill prisoners from the London area. Other bigger stations also had an allocation. At the same time the normal functions continued. There was no increase in staff. The whole operation was conducted by way of voluntary overtime. That was considered by the staff to be adequate reward. Because the premises were a secure environment Pete Arnold was reluctant to employ officers from the territorial divisions. He felt that could be detrimental to the operational efficiency of both the divisions and us.

When the new Inspector, Phil Saunders, arrived he had a baptism of fire, literally. On the second night that he worked with the unit we had a fire in a cell. It happened during a transfer of prisoners returning to London. The escorts had collected from Coventry and had come to Birmingham to eat. The prisoners in their care were lodged temporarily in a holding cell. Within minutes their cell was ablaze. Very quick thinking by Dave Westlake saved a disaster. He had noticed smoke emitting from the cell hatch and was able to release the occupants from what would have been certain death. Because of the secure environment and the facility of the Court cells the fire procedure was well rehearsed. The main problem we had that night was the lateness of the hour; it was about midnight.

The upper floor housed at the time about ten female prisoners from an industrial dispute at HMP Risley. Their appearance on the staircase in various states of undress, whilst they were evacuated away from the smoke, caused an enormous amount of catcalling and wolf whistling.

The cell itself was gutted. The paint of decades and a non-fireproof mattress had seen to that. There was no other damage and no injuries. The offenders remained with us and appeared in Court in Birmingham. They had secreted some matches about their clothing and had set fire to the mattress as a protest about conditions at Coventry. They had expected a standard prison mattress, which only smoulders, not the cheap disposable ones we had in use. When the fire service inspectors visited later the decision was made to destroy all old mattresses forthwith. It took weeks to get that decision implemented. The cost!

Far more destructive than the fire were the builders. The entire character of the building changed. One and a half landings were partitioned off to afford the Lane their own cells. The capacity of a purposes built cell complex was reduced by almost 20 per cent at the stroke of a pen and £120,000. Not content with that a wooden floor was laid on the landings, now the property of the Lane. This increased the noise in the building immensely. Two reasons were given for the floor. One was that with the slatted floor the prisoners in the Lane could communicate with those in the Lock-up. I noted that they could still communicate by shouting. The second was the fear of female officers working at the Lane showing too much leg to the inmates. Matrons and policewomen had worked in the Lock-up for years and that had never been a problem.

Phil remained with us just over a year. An enjoyable year it was too. Phil had about the same service as me and I had known him for most of it. He had been at the sharp end of the job until he came to us. In reality he had been given a break, time to unwind. His hobby fascinated us all; he travelled to all points of the world to ring church bells. Phil was a campanologist.

When he left us he returned to his old division to take charge of the Admin. Support Unit. The ASU was a giant accident enquiry squad, doing the follow-up work for all outstanding enquiries. Phil would make a good job of that but it posed a question, 'Where were the men on the streets going to get their skills if all their outstanding enquiries were done by someone else?'

The new man was different, very different. He was a former Warwickshire & Coventry man. He had reportedly had a chequered career. He had been moved very hastily into the Force Control Room, from Solihull. He had been the subject of a lengthy enquiry into his conduct; nothing had apparently come of it, but he could not remain in the Control Room. He was far from happy about his transfer to the Lock-up.

He saw it as a serious setback in his quest for promotion. He was a Kenyan Asian and was the highest ranking ethnic minority officer in the Force. He was desperate to continue his progress up the ranks. Personally I was amazed that he had got as far as he had. On ability he should probably never have got beyond the rank of acting sergeant.

The Court took over preparing the daily Court list. That made it very difficult for us to maintain our results lists. Protest was made, the matter looked at and it was decided that the results service should cease. The information was available elsewhere. Scotland Yard, we were told. No, we said, they only get a final result; we can give an interim one. The argument continued; we did not need an interim service. Divisional senior officers like paper. When a man has been to Court, they want to know. The information they want was supplied from the Lock-up computer.

It would have to be obtained from elsewhere. Where else? The Central Information Unit, of course. Great! Their information came from the Lock-up computer; they are connected to it. So it went on. In the end it was decreed that the computer would remain and CIU would update it from information received direct from the Lock-up! Within three months there was a backlog of weeks. Thus an efficient system, which the Lock-up staff had maintained as a sideline, was now in chaotic disarray, solely through lack of manpower to input the data at another place. Next to go would be the warrants index. The information contained therein was apparently no longer relevant to police officers. The enforcement of fine warrants had been given to civilian staff.

We were supposed to be a support service to officers from the sharp end. Support had to mean just that. It was not just black and white. There were important grey areas, which if used with other information could often turn something dull into a positive shade of white or black. That was what enquiry work was all about. Two valuable sources of information were now being cast aside.

The thin end of the wedge was being hammered home. Cracks were appearing. Cracks were also appearing at Strangeways Prison, Manchester. Big ones: the place was wrecked in a riot. Suddenly the Lock-up was important again. Operation Container was launched and the entire population of Strangeways was transferred into police custody. Sixteen came to Birmingham, another forty-four around the Force. Our main co-ordination centre was the Lock-up, run by two constables. Other stations appointed Inspectors or senior civilian staff to run their own operation. Such was the competence of our staff that the whole thing was run again as a sideline to the main function. Paid overtime was the carrot. This operation would still be in place when I retired.

One day there was a joyous shout from our Ops. Office. 'Get Cath, quick.' A fax had just landed on our new 'toy' from a satellite phone in Nepal. Cath's hubby was with a British Police expedition when they had come across a CNN news crew using the machine. CNN had a window of a few minutes left if they would like to use it. There for all to see, in Alan's scruffy scribble, a big 'I love you' which he had just written some 6,500 miles away. She just had time to send back something similar before the station closed down. I stood back in thought. We'd pestered for it for ages, and after much discussion we had been allowed to have it. We had global communication for less than two hundred quid! We could write to people in the middle of nowhere for a few pence.

A few years earlier I had wanted some forms printed, in house, and had to have the permission of a superintendent to use a whole ream of paper on a single project. That same week I had, as a mere sergeant, ordered the takeoff of the £1 million Police Helicopter, to an incident with reference to nobody other than the crew. Thinking was not abreast of technology.

After June retired we bought ourselves a clumber spaniel bitch. These are huge, white dogs with wonderful noses, somewhat of a rare breed but very biddable. One night June was away from home and I brought the dog into work in the car. When the building was quiet I let her wander around. The only difficulty she might encounter was 'Cooking Fat', the station cat! She had a good wander all over the landings and then set out across the steel 'suicide' net, spanned between each side of the middle landing. This was a 4" mesh and she was on her belly as she went across sniffing all the way. We sometimes used to throw a blanket out there for the cat.

I didn't take much notice, but suddenly most of the HMP inmates decided to wake up and there was much frantic activity at their toilets. We had rigged up a system of extensions to the cistern chains so that they could flush the bogs without ringing the bell for us. Something was being urgently disposed of! We weren't sure whether we had a drug problem or not. I suspect a temporary respite was in being.

Nothing was said about that incident for weeks until Pete Arnold's replacement was in post. One afternoon he came to me and suggested that a further visit from my clumber could be beneficial. Word had come back from an outside source that a 'drug dog' had been used in the Lock-up one night.

At headquarters a project was being undertaken to 'evaluate the viability of employing civilian detention officers in the Lock-up'. Was that word evaluation to mean just that or was it a substitute for 'it will happen', then we evaluate?

PACE was quite explicit. Pre-Court had to be police officers. Post-Court could be civilian BUT, and there was one big 'BUT'. The Prison Officers had already been warned of privatisation within their service. They would not allow escorts from civilian contractors into their establishments. The use of civilians was not practicable. The financial benefits would be small and the loss of flexibility in staff posting could be quite serious.

Worse, the matrons who for years had mothered and nurse-maided all the female prisoners were to be offered redundancy. A new breed of younger, and probably less able, women would be employed, one to each unit. Oh, and each unit could have a male one as well. That would release a constable.

The units dealt with PACE prisoners as a 24-hour, pre-Court function. We would have one fewer constable and gain *two* civilian detention officers on each unit. Pete Arnold was violently against the proposals, and he made sure his opposition was heard in high places. His warnings were unheeded and the plan was implemented. Pete decided to retire in protest. Two matrons left. Two became detention officers. The rest stayed. Fourteen civilian detention officers were employed. A handful of constables went back to divisions. These were not Lock-up staff anyway, but from divisions, on loan for experience. It is now done, let us evaluate. No civilian detention officers were used on outside escorts. The collection service from stations was less effective. There are fewer men to do it. Less support.

The Crown Court is now housed in a new building. The actual Courts are now available to Magistrates. More Courts sitting need more constables to sit with arrested persons. Still there was no work for the civilians to do.

As suddenly as he arrived, my inspector left. He would not be replaced. As long as anyone could remember the Lock-up had had five inspectors, one on each unit and one as deputy, working days and running the cells under the Courts. Suddenly there was only establishment for four. One still remained on days. I was paid the salary of an inspector to run our shift. I later learned that our last inspector had been suspended from duty.

I was quite happy one day when I made a routine phone call and had the call answered by a voice from the past. I had known Karen Watts since she was a cadet about twelve years before. It was good to talk to her again. After we had dealt with business I asked after her welfare. We had a long chat. She had married a lad from civvy-street and they lived in police accommodation. Tragically Pawlo had died. He had been in a terrible accident and had remained in hospital for some months afterwards. After she had nursed him back to health he had suddenly suffered a relapse and died. That much I knew.

As if that was not tragedy enough the Service was now about to evict her from the police house. The house was for occupation by married officers, they said. As she was no longer married she would have to vacate the house and live in a single room. She was very upset and rightly so. She had lost enough without the bastards now wanting her last memory of her husband, their home. I was livid when she told me. Ours was supposed to be a caring service. The Police Federation got involved and she stayed put. That was much better!

I had by now become totally frustrated in trying to provide a service. That frustration was not helped when a Superintendent telephoned me and demanded that I did something which I had no power to do. He was the man paid to have the knowledge. He was the graduate. He didn't know his job. He didn't like me knowing mine.

The problem was not resolvable by me, or a Court. When a person has been granted conditional bail he can be arrested if found to be in breach of any of the conditions. The law directs that the person arrested must be dealt with in the area in which he is arrested and no other unless he has less than twenty-four hours before he should appear before the original Court. His problem was that a prisoner originating from his station had been arrested in Cardiff in breach of his bail conditions. He was not due in Court for five days, but had been escorted back to Birmingham to appear before the Magistrates. As the Court had no power to deal with him I refused to accept him for the Court. His detention by me would have been totally unlawful, and I said so. After much reference to the Statutes and Magistrates' Clerks he finally backed down without any apology.

I knew now that the lower ranks of the Force were in a situation which I had feared in 1974. My fears were valid. We were being misled. The quality of leadership was on the wane. We had gone from being the willing, led by the competent, doing the necessary for the grateful to the unwanted, led by the unnecessary, doing everything for the ungrateful.

It was time to go. On Christmas Day 1991 I submitted my request to retire from the service in February 1992. I had had enough. The service to which I had dedicated my working life and which had to me been the most important single factor for over thirty years had finally crushed out of me the last drop of enthusiasm I had for it. As if by way of final insult, whilst I was working my notice I was offered a post as a traffic sergeant. The new Chief Constable, Ron Hadfield, was to implement a policy of tenure of post. Three years in any one post and out. If that came about the entire staff of the Lock-up would have to be moved. Where the Service would find another seventy men and women to take their places nobody knew. It was a job most would wish to avoid.

I never met Mr Hadfield, and neither did I want to be a traffic sergeant. I didn't even want to be a policeman any more. I wanted to be an explorer. Not in the true sense of the word. I just wanted to travel. Travel exudes knowledge and June and I were going to travel, explore. I was sure I would not be seriously missed. I had become a dinosaur, I was from another era, I was a policeman who had learned his job in another age. I reflected on a poem I had read many years before:

> Sometime when you're feeling important
> Sometime when your ego's in bloom,
> Sometime when you've taken for granted
> You're the best-qualified man in the room;
>
> Sometime when you feel that your going,
> Would leave an unfillable hole,
> Just follow these simple instructions
> And see how they humble your soul:
>
> Take a bucket and fill it with water
> Put your hands in it up to your wrists,
> Pull them out; and the hole that remains,
> Is the measure of how you'll be missed.
>
> You may splash all you please when you enter,
> You may stir all the waters galore
> But stop – and you'll find in a minute
> That it looks just the same as before.
>
> The moral of this is quite simple,
> You must do the best that you can
> Be proud of yourself, but remember
> There is no indispensable man . . .

THE LAST FIVE YEARS

That really seems to sum everything up in a few simple words. I had been, I had seen, I had been seen and now I would be seen no more. It had always been busy. Only for about a year was the Force ever up to establishment. A career completed, I left my post and my friends to start a new life in rural Worcestershire. I had not retired from a job, or even a career; what I had left had been a way of life. One around which June and I had woven a fulfilling and rewarding social life as well.

I had been asked why I joined the Police Service. I joined because I wanted a secure and rewarding job. I had joined because I wanted to retire before I was fifty. That was the security. I wanted a reward for my effort and that would be in the form of a pension and a lump sum for investment. That's what I got.

Along the way there had been heartbreaks and setbacks, there had been high points, there had been depressions. I had married twice. The second marriage was very happy. June had helped me achieve a better reward.

I had set about my task with vigour and enthusiasm and had for most of the time enjoyed what I had done. Both inside and outside the Service I had met nice people and nasty people, bad people and good people. I feel that I had done what I had set out to do. The Service had worked for me and I had worked hard for the Service, and in turn the public. I hope my contribution has been enough.

I have written down much of what I remember. Not of the major events, they are well chronicled already, but the little things, warts and all, that have taken place around me, as A Plod around Brum. It is not a full account. Such would be an impossible task.

His Royal Highness Prince Andrew once said in a television interview, 'The Royal Navy is a wonderful career for a single man. It is becoming increasing less so for one who is married.'

That can also be said of the Police Service. I find it very sad indeed that society has now got the Police Service that it doesn't really deserve. The public cannot now have fast response times and a policeman walking around twenty-four hours of a day.

There has to be a compromise. The Police Service, as any other, has limited resources. These are spread about thinly and they are varied and flexible. They used to be quite rigid and stereotyped but things have changed. The old fashioned values of society have gone. So have the old fashioned standards of the Service.

The new generation of police officers are from a new generation of society, a generation born since 1974, the time in my life when I noticed a decline in standards, within the Service. If that decline continues within

West Midlands Police

Chief Constable's Office

Date 5th March 1992

This is to certify that Ralph Alan PETTITT joined the West Midlands Police as a Constable on the 1st day of April 19 74 and left the Force in the rank of Sergeant on the 11th day of February 19 92 having previously served in Birmingham City Police 3rd November 1962 - 31st March 1974

Total Police Service 29 years 101 days
Character Exemplary

Chief Constable

Certificate.

society, the society from which the new generation of Bobbies are being recruited, I fear for the future. If I have a major fault it is probably that I speak my mind and say what I think. Some don't like that but that's how I am. I'll leave the future to the planners, and hope they finally listen to the people who actually do the job at grass roots level. They deserve that much at least.

The long lost daughter went as suddenly as she appeared. She was from a new generation and found my values difficult to cope with.